P9-DNC-620

taste of home
SOUPS

taste of home
BOOKS

taste of home

EDITOR-IN-CHIEF: Catherine Cassidy
VICE PRESIDENT, EXECUTIVE EDITOR/BOOKS: Heidi Reuter Lloyd
CREATIVE DIRECTOR: Howard Greenberg
NORTH AMERICAN CHIEF MARKETING OFFICER: Lisa Karpinski
FOOD DIRECTOR: Diane Werner, RD
SENIOR EDITOR/RETAIL BOOKS: Faithann Stoner
EDITOR: Janet Briggs
ASSOCIATE CREATIVE DIRECTOR: Edwin Robles Jr.
ART DIRECTORS: Jessie Sharon, Rudy Krochalk
CONTENT PRODUCTION MANAGER: Julie Wagner
LAYOUT DESIGNERS: Nancy Novak, Catherine Fletcher
COPY CHIEF: Deb Warlaumont Mulvey
COPY EDITOR: Alysse Gear
PROJECT ASSOCIATE EDITORS: Victoria Soukup Jensen, Julie Schnittka
RECIPE ASSET SYSTEM MANAGER: Coleen Martin
RECIPE TESTING & EDITING: Taste of Home Test Kitchen
FOOD PHOTOGRAPHY: Taste of Home Photo Studio
ADMINISTRATIVE ASSISTANT: Barb Czysz

THE READER'S DIGEST ASSOCIATION, INC.
PRESIDENT AND CHIEF EXECUTIVE OFFICER: Robert E. Guth
EXECUTIVE VICE PRESIDENT, RDA, & PRESIDENT, NORTH AMERICA: Dan Lagani
PRESIDENT/PUBLISHER, TRADE PUBLISHING: Harold Clarke
ASSOCIATE PUBLISHER: Rosanne McManus
VICE PRESIDENT, SALES & MARKETING: Stacey Ashton

FOR OTHER TASTE OF HOME BOOKS AND PRODUCTS, VISIT US AT TASTEOFHOME.COM.

For more Reader's Digest products and information, visit
rd.com (in the United States)
or see rd.ca (in Canada).

INTERNATIONAL STANDARD BOOK NUMBER (10): 0-89821-952-3
INTERNATIONAL STANDARD BOOK NUMBER (13): 978-0-89821-952-4
LIBRARY OF CONGRESS CONTROL NUMBER: 2011933613

COVER PHOTOGRAPHY
Taste of Home Photo Studio

PICTURED ON FRONT COVER:
Hearty Fish Soup, Page 161; Creamy White Chili, Page 351; Zesty Hamburger Soup, Page 44
PICTURED ON BACK COVER:
Chicken Noodle Soup, Page 73; Home-Style Stew, Page 296; Broccoli Potato Soup, Page 260

Printed in China.
1 3 5 7 9 10 8 6 4 2

Enjoy the comfort of delicious soup anytime with this fabulous new recipe collection!

Whether you're looking for an easy and satisfying main dish, a delicious first course for a special dinner or a hot, steaming bowl of soup to brighten up a chilly day, you'll find some great new ideas right here.

This *Taste of Home Soups* cookbook has 429 recipes for every variety of soup. Your family and guests will be delighted with the chicken, turkey, beef and pork versions. And when served in soup, beans, lentils and vegetables are not only wholesome and delicious, they're also an economical way to put a meal on the table.

You'll also want to try the velvety cream soups and chunky chowders. For even heartier fare, tap into the savory lineup of stews and chilis featured in this handy volume. And there's so much more, including insightful cooking tips and hundreds of color photos.

These tried-and-true favorites are from home cooks like you. They're tested in the Test Kitchen of *Taste of Home*, the #1 food and entertaining magazine in the world, so you know they're easy to make and will turn out great every time.

Grab this beautiful, bountiful book and a kettle, and you'll be sipping and savoring a comforting bowl of a new favorite soup in no time!

FLORENTINE CHICKEN SOUP, PG. 69

BASQUE VEGETABLE SOUP, PG. 130

TABLE OF CONTENTS

Start making a broth with cold water. Just cover the bones, meat and/or vegetables with water. Add seasonings but do not add salt. Bring slowly to a boil over low heat. Using a ladle, skim foam from the top of liquid. If water evaporates, add enough additional water to cover the bones, meat and/or vegetables. Strain broth; divide among several containers. Place containers in an ice bath to cool quickly. When chilled, skim fat or remove solidified fat. Refrigerate or freeze.

Add little to no salt or other flavors when making broth, since it concentrates as it simmers and the liquid evaporates. Taste the soup when it is just about ready to be served, and then add enough salt to suit your family's preferences.

Add a pinch of turmeric or simmer an unpeeled whole yellow onion in the cooking liquid for golden homemade chicken and turkey broths.

Store soups in the refrigerator for up to 3 days. If there is rice or pasta in the soup, you may want to cook and store the two parts separately, since those starches may continue to absorb the liquid and become mushy.

Many broth-based soups freeze well for up to 3 months. Thaw in the refrigerator before reheating. It's best not to freeze soups prepared with potatoes, fruit, cheese, sour cream, yogurt, eggs, milk or cream.

1

SKIM THE FOAM

Remove the excess fat from meat. In a kettle or Dutch oven, combine meat, vegetables, cold water and seasonings.

Bring to a boil over low heat. Skim foam as it rises to the top of the water. Reduce heat; cover and simmer until the meat is tender, about 1 hour.

homemade beef broth

YIELD: about 2-1/2 quarts.

Roasting the soup bones brings out delicious beefy flavors for soup base. This broth refrigerates and freezes well to use as needed. taste of home test kitchen

- **4 pounds meaty beef soup bones (beef shanks *or* short ribs)**
- **3 medium carrots, cut into chunks**
- **3 celery ribs, cut into chunks**
- **2 medium onions, quartered**
- **1/2 cup warm water**
- **3 bay leaves**
- **3 garlic cloves**
- **8 to 10 whole peppercorns**
- **3 to 4 sprigs fresh parsley**
- **1 teaspoon *each* dried thyme, marjoram and oregano**
- **3 quarts cold water**

Place soup bones in a large roasting pan. Bake, uncovered, at 450° for 30 minutes. Add the carrots, celery and onions. Bake 30 minutes longer; drain fat.

Using a slotted spoon, transfer bones and vegetables to a large Dutch oven. Add warm water to the roasting pan; stir to loosen browned bits from pan. Transfer the pan juices to kettle. Add seasonings and enough cold water just to cover.

Slowly bring to a boil, about 30 minutes. Reduce heat; simmer, uncovered, for 4-5 hours, skimming the surface as foam rises. If necessary, add hot water during the first 2 hours to keep the ingredients covered.

Remove beef bones and set aside until cool enough to handle. If desired, remove meat from bones; discard bones and save meat for another use. Strain the broth through a cheesecloth-lined colander, discarding the vegetables and seasonings.

2

STRAIN THE BROTH

Remove meat and bones from broth. Line a colander with a double thickness of cheesecloth; place in a large heat-resistant bowl. Pour broth into colander. Discard vegetables, seasonings and cheesecloth. For a clear broth, do not press the liquid from vegetables and seasonings in the colander.

3

REMOVE THE FAT

Let meat and bones stand until cool enough to handle. Remove meat from bones; discard bones. Dice meat; use immediately or cover and refrigerate. Chill broth several hours or overnight; lift fat from surface of broth and discard.

If using immediately, skim the fat or refrigerate for 8 hours or overnight, then remove fat from surface. Broth can be covered and refrigerated for up to 3 days or frozen for 4 to 6 months.

homemade chicken broth

YIELD: about 2 quarts.

Whether you're making a chicken soup or just a broth to use in other dishes, this recipe makes a tasty starter for almost anything. nila grahl // gurnee, illinois

- **1 broiler/fryer chicken (3 to 4 pounds), cut up**
- **10 cups water**
- **1 large carrot, sliced**
- **1 large onion, sliced**
- **1 celery rib, sliced**
- **1 garlic clove, minced**
- **1 bay leaf**
- **1 teaspoon each dried thyme and salt**
- **1/2 cup warm water**
- **1/4 teaspoon pepper**

In a large soup kettle or Dutch oven, combine all the ingredients. Slowly bring to a boil over low heat. Cover and simmer for 45-60 minutes or until the meat is tender, skimming the surface as foam rises.

Remove chicken and set aside until cool enough to handle. Remove and discard skin and bones. Chop chicken; set aside for soup or save for another use.

Strain the broth through a cheesecloth-lined colander, discarding vegetables and bay leaf. If using immediately, skim fat or refrigerate for 8 hours or overnight, then remove fat from surface. Broth can be covered and refrigerated for up to 3 days or frozen for 4 to 6 months.

homemade vegetable broth

YIELD: 5-1/2 cups.

The flavors of celery and mushrooms come through in this homemade vegetable broth. You can use it in place of chicken or beef broth. taste of home test kitchen

- **2 tablespoons olive oil**
- **2 medium onions, cut into wedges**
- **2 celery ribs, cut into 1-inch pieces**
- **1 whole garlic bulb, separated into cloves and peeled**
- **3 medium leeks, white and light green parts only, cleaned and cut into 1-inch pieces**
- **3 medium carrots, cut into 1-inch pieces**
- **8 cups water**
- **1/2 pound fresh mushrooms, quartered**
- **1 cup packed fresh parsley sprigs**
- **4 sprigs fresh thyme**
- **1 teaspoon salt**
- **1/2 teaspoon whole peppercorns**
- **1 bay leaf**

Heat oil in a stockpot over medium heat until hot. Add the onions, celery and garlic. Cook and stir for 5 minutes or until tender. Add leeks and carrots; cook and stir 5 minutes longer. Add the water, mushrooms, parsley, thyme, salt, peppercorns and bay leaf; bring to a boil. Reduce heat; simmer, uncovered, for 1 hour.

Remove from the heat. Strain through a cheesecloth-lined colander; discard vegetables. If using immediately, skim any fat or refrigerate for 8 hours or overnight, then remove fat from surface. Broth can be covered and refrigerated for up to 3 days or frozen for up to 4 to 6 months.

ZESTY HAMBURGER SOUP, PG. 44

SOUPS

beef & ground beef

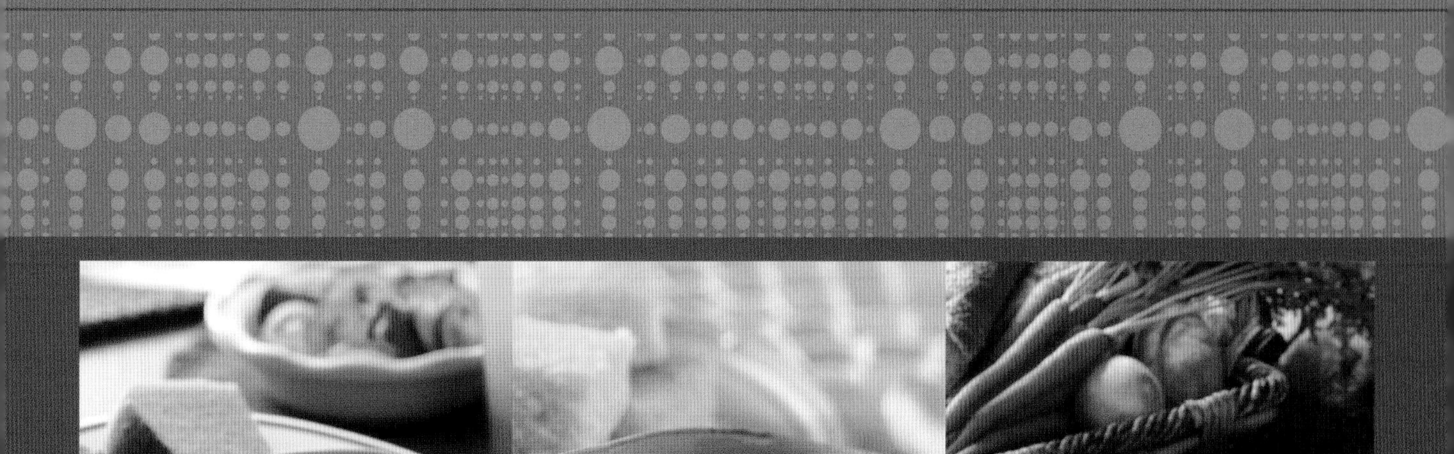

BEEF BARLEY SOUP, PG. 23

ZIPPY SPANISH RICE SOUP, PG. 47

HEARTY BEEF SOUP, PG. 24

beef and barley soup

PREP: 15 min.
COOK: 2 hours 50 min.
YIELD: 10-12 servings (3-1/2 quarts).

I love this delicious yet simple recipe. It comes together easily and simmers on the stovetop, allowing me time to spend time with my children.
phyllis utterback // glendale, california

- **1 tablespoon canola oil**
- **2 pounds beef short ribs**
- **2 medium onions, coarsely chopped**
- **3 large carrots, sliced**
- **3 celery ribs, sliced**
- **1 can (28 ounces) diced tomatoes, undrained**
- **8 cups water**
- **4 teaspoons chicken bouillon granules**
- **1/3 cup medium pearl barley**

In a Dutch oven, heat oil over medium-high heat. Brown ribs. Add the onions, carrots, celery, tomatoes, water and bouillon; bring to a boil. Cover and simmer for 2 hours or until beef is tender. Add barley; cover and simmer 50-60 minutes longer or until the barley is tender.

stroganoff soup

PREP: 15 min. • **COOK:** 40 min. • **YIELD:** 6 servings.

My husband and I share a love for all kinds of soup and came up with this wonderful recipe together. It really does taste like beef Stroganoff. With a crusty roll, it's a satisfying meal in itself. karen shiveley // springfield, minnesota

- **1/2 pound beef top sirloin steak *or* beef tenderloin, cut into thin strips**
- **1/2 cup chopped onion**
- **1 tablespoon butter**
- **2 cups water**
- **1-1/2 cups milk**
- **1/4 cup tomato paste**
- **2 teaspoons beef bouillon granules**
- **1 can (8 ounces) mushroom stems and pieces, drained**
- **1 teaspoon salt**
- **1/8 teaspoon pepper**
- **1 can (12 ounces) evaporated milk**
- **1/3 cup all-purpose flour**
- **2 cups cooked wide egg noodles**
- **1/2 cup sour cream**

In a 3-qt. saucepan, cook beef and onion in butter over medium heat, until meat is browned. Stir in the water, milk, tomato paste and bouillon. Add mushrooms, salt and pepper; bring to a boil. Reduce heat; cover and simmer for 20-30 minutes or until meat is tender.

Combine evaporated milk and flour until smooth. Gradually add to soup. Bring to a boil; cook and stir for 2 minutes until thickened. Add noodles; cook until heated through. Remove from the heat; stir in sour cream.

ONION SUBSTITUTES

When there isn't time to chop onions, onion powder is another option. Substitute 1 tablespoon onion powder for one medium chopped onion. For the best flavor, use frozen chopped onions or dried minced onion (found in the spice aisle). One tablespoon dried minced onion equals 1/4 cup minced raw onion.

unstuffed pepper soup

PREP: 10 min. • **COOK:** 50 min. • **YIELD:** 10 servings.

One of my sisters gave me the recipe for this soup, which tastes just like stuffed green peppers. The thick mixture is chock-full of good stuff. The aroma while it's cooking is delightful. evelyn kara // brownsville, pennsylvania

- **1-1/2 pounds ground beef**
- **3 large green peppers, chopped**
- **1 large onion, chopped**
- **2 cans (14-1/2 ounces *each*) beef broth**
- **2 cans (10-3/4 ounces *each*) condensed tomato soup, undiluted**
- **1 can (28 ounces) crushed tomatoes, undrained**
- **1 can (4 ounces) mushroom stems and pieces, drained**
- **1-1/2 cups cooked rice**

In a Dutch oven or large saucepan, cook the beef, green peppers and onion over medium heat until meat is no longer pink; drain. Stir in the broth, soup, tomatoes and mushrooms. Bring to a boil. Reduce heat; cover and simmer for at least 30 minutes, stirring occasionally. Add rice and heat through.

south-of-the-border soup

PREP: 15 min. • **COOK:** 35 min. • **YIELD:** 8 servings (2 quarts).

Cooking and creating new recipes are favorite pastimes of mine. As a matter of fact, this is an original recipe, which earned me first place in the Wisconsin Beef Cook-Off some years ago. lynn ireland //lebanon, wisconsin

- **1 egg**
- **1/4 cup dry bread crumbs**
- **1/2 teaspoon salt**
- **1/4 teaspoon pepper**
- **1 pound ground beef**
- **1 jar (16 ounces) picante sauce**
- **1 can (15-1/4 ounces) whole kernel corn, drained**
- **1 can (15 ounces) black beans, rinsed and drained**
- **1 can (14-1/2 ounces) diced tomatoes, undrained**
- **1-1/4 cups water**

In a large bowl, combine the first four ingredients. Crumble beef over mixture and mix well. Shape into 1-in. balls.

In a large saucepan, brown meatballs; drain. Add the picante sauce, corn, beans, tomatoes and water; bring to a boil. Reduce heat; cover and simmer for 20 minutes or until the meat is no longer pink.

EDITOR'S NOTE: To make dry bread crumbs, arrange bread slices on a baking sheet. Bake at 300° until completely dry and golden; cool. Place in a resealable plastic bag; crush with a rolling pin. Season with salt, pepper and dried herbs if desired. One slice of bread yields about 1/3 cup dry crumbs.

tortellini vegetable soup

PREP: 15 min. • **COOK:** 65 min. • **YIELD:** 10-12 servings (3-1/4 quarts).

Because of its rich spicy flavor, this soup has been a favorite in our home for years. I think you'll agree the tortellini adds an interesting twist.

tammy nadeau // presque isle, maine

- **1 pound ground beef**
- **7 cups beef broth**
- **2 cans (14-1/2 ounces *each*) stewed tomatoes**
- **3/4 cup ketchup**
- **3/4 cup thinly sliced carrots**
- **3/4 cup thinly sliced celery**
- **3/4 cup finely chopped onion**
- **1 tablespoon dried basil**
- **1-1/2 teaspoons seasoned salt**
- **1 teaspoon sugar**
- **1/4 teaspoon pepper**
- **4 bay leaves**
- **1-1/2 cups frozen cheese tortellini**
- **Grated Parmesan cheese, optional**

In a Dutch oven or soup kettle, brown beef; drain. Add the next 11 ingredients; bring to a boil. Reduce heat; cover and simmer for 30 minutes.

Add tortellini; cook for 20-30 minutes or until tender. Remove bay leaves. Garnish individual servings with Parmesan cheese if desired.

DRAINING BEANS

Canned beans and other canned foods may stick to the bottom and require a spatula or spoon to remove. So open the bottom of the can, where everything has settled. With a little shake, the contents come out quickly and cleanly.

taco soup

PREP/TOTAL TIME: 25 min.
YIELD: 4-6 servings (1-1/2 quarts).

For a meal in a hurry, try this fast recipe. Serving the soup in bread bowls makes for a unique and hearty main dish!

nancy wilkes // preston, idaho

- **1 pound ground beef**
- **1/4 cup chopped onion**
- **2 cups fresh *or* frozen corn**
- **1 can (15-1/2 ounces) kidney beans, rinsed and drained**
- **1 can (14-1/2 ounces) diced tomatoes, drained**
- **1 can (8 ounces) tomato sauce**
- **1 envelope (1-1/4 ounces) taco seasoning**
- **Corn chips, shredded cheddar cheese *and/or* sour cream, optional**

In a large saucepan, brown the ground beef and onion; drain. Add the corn, kidney beans, tomatoes, tomato sauce and taco seasoning. Cover and simmer for 15 minutes, stirring occasionally. Serve with corn chips, cheese and/or sour cream if desired.

hamburger garden soup

PREP: 10 min. • **COOK:** 50 min. • **YIELD:** 5 servings.

We have a large vegetable and herb garden and raise steer on our four acres in the country. The only thing I need to buy for this colorful and tasty soup is the garlic! alma grady // falls creek, pennsylvania

- **1 pound ground beef**
- **1 cup chopped onion**
- **1 garlic clove, minced**
- **1 can (28 ounces) diced tomatoes, undrained**
- **2 cups fresh *or* frozen corn**
- **2 cups water**
- **3 tablespoons minced fresh parsley *or* 1 tablespoon dried parsley flakes**
- **2 tablespoons minced fresh basil *or* 2 teaspoons dried basil**
- **2 tablespoons minced fresh thyme *or* 2 teaspoons dried thyme**
- **1-1/2 teaspoons minced fresh rosemary *or* 1/2 teaspoon dried rosemary, crushed**
- **1 teaspoon salt**
- **1/2 teaspoon pepper**

In a large saucepan, cook the beef, onion and garlic over medium heat until meat is no longer pink; drain. Add the remaining ingredients; bring to a boil. Reduce heat; simmer, uncovered, for 30 minutes or until heated through.

DRIED HERBS

Dried herbs don't spoil, but they do lose flavor and potency over time. For maximum flavor in your cooking, you may want to replace herbs that are over a year old. Store dried herbs in airtight containers and keep them away from heat and light. Don't put them in the cupboard above the stove.

mushroom barley soup

PREP: 25 min. • **COOK:** 1-3/4 hours • **YIELD:** about 11 servings (2-3/4 quarts).

A friend at work shared the recipe for this wonderful soup. With beef, barley and vegetables, it's hearty enough to be a meal. A big steaming bowl is so satisfying on a cold day. lynn thomas // london, ontario

- **1-1/2 pounds boneless beef chuck, cut into 3/4-inch cubes**
- **1 tablespoon canola oil**
- **2 cups finely chopped onions**
- **1 cup diced carrots**
- **1/2 cup sliced celery**
- **1 pound fresh mushrooms, sliced**
- **2 garlic cloves, minced**
- **1/2 teaspoon dried thyme**
- **1 can (14-1/2 ounces) beef broth**
- **1 can (14-1/2 ounces) chicken broth**
- **2 cups water**
- **1/2 cup medium pearl barley**
- **1 teaspoon salt, optional**
- **1/2 teaspoon pepper**
- **3 tablespoons chopped fresh parsley**

In a Dutch oven or soup kettle, cook meat in oil over medium heat until no longer pink. Remove meat with a slotted spoon; keep warm and set aside.

Saute the onions, carrots and celery in drippings over medium heat until tender, about 5 minutes. Add the mushrooms, garlic and thyme; cook and stir for 3 minutes. Stir in the broths, water, barley, salt if desired and pepper.

Return meat to pan; bring to a boil. Reduce heat; cover and simmer for 1-1/2 to 2 hours or until barley and meat are tender. Add parsley.

PREPARING MUSHROOMS

Gently remove dirt by rubbing with a mushroom brush, or wipe mushrooms with a damp paper towel. Or quickly rinse under cold water, drain and pat dry with paper towels. Do not peel mushrooms. Trim stems. For shiitake mushrooms, remove and discard stems. For enoki, trim base and separate stems. Mushrooms can be eaten raw, marinated, sauteed, stir-fried, baked, broiled or grilled.

scotch broth soup

PREP: 3 hours 20 min. + chilling
COOK: 1 hour
YIELD: 6-8 servings (2 quarts).

Early in winter, I make big pots of this hearty soup to freeze in plastic containers. I bring out one or two containers at a time and slowly heat the frozen soup. In a couple hours, it's hot and ready to serve!
ann main // moorefield, ontario

- **2 pounds meaty beef soup bones (beef shanks *or* short ribs)**
- **8 cups water**
- **6 whole peppercorns**
- **1-1/2 teaspoons salt**
- **1 cup chopped carrots**
- **1 cup chopped turnips**
- **1 cup chopped celery**
- **1/2 cup chopped onion**
- **1/4 cup medium pearl barley**

In a large soup kettle, combine soup bones, water, peppercorns and salt. Cover and simmer for 2-1/2 hours or until the meat easily comes off the bones.

Remove bones. Strain broth; cool and chill. Skim off fat. Remove meat from bones; dice and return to broth along with remaining ingredients. Bring to a boil. Reduce heat; cover and simmer about 1 hour or until vegetables and barley are tender.

cabbage zucchini borscht

PREP: 10 min. • **COOK:** 3-1/2 hours • **YIELD:** 12-14 servings (4 quarts).

I know my family will get a hearty, healthy meal when I serve this soup. There are so many good vegetables stirred in! agatha wiebe // winkler, manitoba

- **1 pound meaty beef soup bones (beef shanks *or* short ribs)**
- **8 cups water**
- **4 cups shredded cabbage**
- **2 cups cubed peeled potatoes**
- **2 cups sliced carrots**
- **2 cups diced peeled tomatoes**
- **1 onion, chopped**
- **1/2 cup chopped fresh parsley**
- **2 tablespoons dill weed**
- **1-1/2 teaspoons salt**
- **1/2 teaspoon pepper**
- **1 tablespoon aniseed**
- **3 cups shredded zucchini**
- **2 cups chopped cooked beets**

Place soup bones and water in a stockpot; bring to a boil. Reduce heat and simmer, uncovered, for 40-45 minutes.

Skim off fat. Add the cabbage, potatoes, carrots, tomatoes, onion, parsley, dill, salt and pepper. Place aniseed on a double thickness of cheesecloth; bring up corners of cloth and tie with string to form a bag. Add to stockpot. Simmer, uncovered, for 2-1/2 to 3 hours.

Remove meat from soup bones; discard bones and add meat to soup. Stir in zucchini and beets. Simmer 15-20 minutes longer or until zucchini is tender. Remove spice bag before serving.

CABBAGE TIPS

When buying cabbage, look for those with crisp-looking leaves that are firmly packed. The head should feel heavy for its size. Store cabbage tightly wrapped in a plastic bag in the refrigerator for up to 2 weeks. Remove the core, rinse and blot dry just before using. A 1-1/2-pound cabbage will yield 8 cups shredded.

mixed bean soup

PREP: 30 min. + standing • **COOK:** 2-1/2 hours • **YIELD:** 10 servings (2-1/2 quarts).

Guests and family alike praise this soup and always ask for seconds. The nicest thing about it is that any combination of dry beans can be used. arlene hilman // cawston, british columbia

- **1 package (12 ounces) mixed dried beans**
- **8 cups water**
- **1/2 pound ground beef, cooked and drained**
- **1 can (14-1/2 ounces) diced tomatoes, undrained**
- **1 cup chopped celery**
- **1 tablespoon salt**
- **1 teaspoon dried parsley flakes**
- **2 garlic cloves, minced**
- **1 teaspoon dried thyme**
- **2 bay leaves**
- **Pepper to taste**

Rinse and sort beans. Place beans in a Dutch oven or soup kettle; add water to cover by 2 in. Bring to a boil; boil for 2 minutes. Remove from the heat; cover and let stand for 1 to 4 hours or until beans are softened.

Drain and rinse, discarding liquid. Add water to the beans; bring to a boil. Cover and simmer for 30 minutes. Add remaining ingredients; bring to a boil. Reduce heat; cover and simmer for 1-1/2 to 2 hours or until beans are tender. Discard bay leaves.

hearty vegetable barley soup

PREP: 20 min. • **COOK:** 45 min. • **YIELD:** 5 servings.

My mom picked up this barley soup recipe in her fitness class and passed it to me. It's loaded with goodness! Sometimes, I substitute ground turkey as the meat and use chicken bouillon instead of beef bouillon. emily melton // prophetstown, illinois

- **1/2 pound lean ground beef (90% lean)**
- **5 cups water**
- **1 can (14-1/2 ounces) diced tomatoes, undrained**
- **1 small onion, chopped**
- **1 celery rib, sliced**
- **1 medium carrot, sliced**
- **2 teaspoons reduced-sodium beef bouillon granules**
- **1 bay leaf**
- **1 garlic clove, minced**
- **1/2 teaspoon salt**
- **1/2 teaspoon dried basil**
- **1/4 teaspoon pepper**
- **2 cups frozen mixed vegetables**
- **3/4 cup quick-cooking barley**

In a Dutch oven, cook beef over medium heat until no longer pink; drain. Add the water, tomatoes, onion, celery, carrot, bouillon, bay leaf, garlic, salt, basil and pepper. Bring to a boil. Reduce heat; cover and simmer for 20 minutes.

Stir in mixed vegetables and barley; return to a boil. Reduce heat; cover and simmer 10-15 minutes longer or until vegetables and barley are tender. Discard bay leaf.

BARLEY SOUP LEFTOVERS

Barley and beans absorb a lot of soup broth. If you like these ingredients in your soup but the leftovers are too thick, add extra chicken, beef or vegetable broth to leftovers while reheating to achieve the desired consistency.

shaker herb 'n' meatball soup

PREP: 30 min. • **COOK:** 2 hours
YIELD: 12-14 servings (3-1/2 quarts).

This filling soup is one of my favorite ways to warm up during the cold winter season in New England. The meatballs are fuss-free because they cook in the soup—there's no need to brown them beforehand. carolyn milke // north canton, connecticut

- **8 cups beef broth**
- **2 cans (14-1/2 ounces *each*) diced tomatoes, undrained**
- **3 medium potatoes, peeled and cubed**
- **3 medium carrots, sliced**
- **1 cup shredded cabbage**
- **1 large onion, chopped**
- **1/2 cup chopped fresh parsley**
- **6 whole peppercorns**
- **1/2 teaspoon dried marjoram**
- **1/2 teaspoon celery seed**
- **1/2 teaspoon dried thyme**
- **1/8 teaspoon ground cumin**
- **1 pound lean ground beef (90% lean)**
- **1/2 cup soft bread crumbs**
- **1 egg, beaten**
- **1 teaspoon Worcestershire sauce**
- **1/4 teaspoon salt**
- **1/8 teaspoon pepper**

In a Dutch oven or soup kettle, combine the first 12 ingredients; bring to a boil. Reduce heat; cover and simmer for 1 hour.

In a bowl, combine the beef, bread crumbs, egg, Worcestershire sauce, salt and pepper. Shape into 1-in. balls; drop into soup. Cover and simmer for 2 hours.

savory beef barley soup

PREP: 15 min. • **COOK:** 35 min. • **YIELD:** 8 servings.

A big slice of sourdough bread goes great with a bowl of this heartwarming soup that's brimming with beef and barley.
megan taylor // greenfield, wisconsin

- **1/4 cup all-purpose flour**
- **1 teaspoon salt**
- **1/2 teaspoon pepper, *divided***
- **2 pounds lean beef top sirloin steak, cut into 1/2-inch cubes**
- **2 tablespoons canola oil**
- **4 cups sliced fresh mushrooms**
- **4 cans (14-1/2 ounces *each*) reduced-sodium beef broth**
- **4 medium carrots, sliced**
- **1/2 teaspoon garlic powder**
- **1/2 teaspoon dried thyme**
- **1 cup quick-cooking barley**

In a large resealable plastic bag, combine the flour, salt and 1/4 teaspoon pepper. Add beef and shake to coat. In a Dutch oven, brown beef in oil over medium heat. Remove and set aside.

In the same pan, saute mushrooms until tender. Add the broth, carrots, garlic powder, thyme and remaining pepper; bring to a boil. Add barley and beef. Reduce heat; cover and simmer for 20-25 minutes until the meat, vegetables and barley are tender.

chili macaroni soup

PREP/TOTAL TIME: 30 min.
YIELD: 9 servings (about 2 quarts).

Turn a boxed macaroni dinner into a thick, zesty soup with this recipe. Each helping is chock-full of ground beef, tomatoes, corn and more. flo burtnett // gage, oklahoma

- **1 pound ground beef**
- **1 medium onion, chopped**
- **1/4 cup chopped green pepper**
- **5 cups water**
- **1 can (14-1/2 ounces) diced tomatoes, undrained**
- **1 package (7-1/2 ounces) chili macaroni dinner mix**
- **1 teaspoon chili powder**
- **1/2 teaspoon garlic salt**
- **1/4 teaspoon salt**
- **1 can (8-3/4 ounces) whole kernel corn, drained**
- **2 tablespoons sliced ripe olives**

In a large saucepan, cook the beef, onion and green pepper over medium heat until meat is no longer pink; drain. Add the water, tomatoes, contents of sauce mix from the dinner mix, chili powder, garlic salt and salt. Simmer, uncovered, for 10 minutes.

Add macaroni from the dinner mix, corn and olives. Cover and simmer for 10 minutes or until the macaroni is tender, stirring occasionally.

family vegetable beef soup

PREP: 5 min. • **COOK:** 2 hours 10 min. • **YIELD:** 14 servings (3-1/2 quarts).

My kids aren't excited about vegetables, but in this soup, they love them. It's an easy recipe to make. linda korte // new liskeard, ontario

- **2 pounds ground beef**
- **1 medium onion, chopped**
- **1 can (46 ounces) tomato juice**
- **1 can (28 ounces) diced tomatoes, undrained**
- **1 jar (4-1/2 ounces) sliced mushrooms, drained**
- **2 cups frozen cut green beans**
- **2 cups *each* finely chopped celery, cabbage and carrots**
- **1 teaspoon dried oregano**
- **1 teaspoon dried basil**
- **1/2 teaspoon garlic powder**
- **1 teaspoon salt**
- **1/2 teaspoon pepper**

In a Dutch oven, cook beef and onion over medium heat until meat is no longer pink; drain. Stir in the remaining ingredients. Bring to a boil. Reduce heat; cover and simmer for 2 hours.

easy vegetable soup

PREP: 5 min. • **COOK:** 30 min.
YIELD: 10-12 servings (2-3/4 quarts).

Canned tomatoes and beans and frozen vegetables give you a head start when preparing this crowd-pleaser. Serve tortilla chips with the soup for a fun alternative to crackers.
jan sharp // blue springs, missouri

- **1 pound ground beef**
- **1 medium onion, chopped**
- **1 can (28 ounces) diced tomatoes, undrained**
- **1 package (16 ounces) frozen vegetable blend of your choice**
- **1 can (16 ounces) kidney beans, undrained**
- **1 can (14-1/2 ounces) beef broth**
- **1 envelope taco seasoning**
- **1 garlic clove, minced**
- **Shredded cheddar cheese, optional**

In a large saucepan, cook beef and onion over medium heat until meat is no longer pink; drain. Add the tomatoes, vegetables, beans, broth, taco seasoning and garlic; bring to a boil. Reduce heat; simmer, uncovered, for 10 minutes. Garnish with cheese if desired.

beef barley soup

PREP: 20 min. • **COOK:** 1 hour • **YIELD:** 8 servings (about 2 quarts).

Once a year, I invite my relatives—about 25 people in all—for soup day to honor my late husband's birthday. I make three soups, including comforting beef barley soup. It's loaded with chunks of beef and chopped veggies.

louise laplante // hanmer, ontario

- **2 pounds beef stew meat, cut into 1-inch pieces**
- **1 tablespoon canola oil**
- **5 cups water**
- **4 medium carrots, chopped**
- **4 celery ribs, chopped**
- **1 large onion, chopped**
- **1 can (14-1/2 ounces) diced tomatoes, undrained**
- **2 tablespoons tomato paste**
- **4 teaspoons beef bouillon granules**
- **1 teaspoon *each* dried oregano, thyme, basil and parsley flakes**
- **1/2 teaspoon salt**
- **1/4 teaspoon pepper**
- **1 cup quick-cooking barley**

In a Dutch oven, brown meat in oil on all sides; drain. Add the water, carrots, celery, onion, tomatoes, tomato paste, bouillon and seasonings. Bring to a boil. Reduce heat; cover and simmer for 50 minutes or until meat is tender.

Stir in barley; cover and simmer 10-15 minutes longer or until barley is tender.

DUTCH OVEN BASICS

A Dutch oven is a heavy covered pan that can be used both on the stovetop and in the oven. Available in a variety of sizes, a Dutch oven is handy for browning meats before roasting—you need just one pan and you keep the flavor of the drippings. A heavy fry pan or saucepan may be substituted depending on the recipe.

hearty beef soup

PREP: 1 hour • **COOK:** 40 min.
YIELD: 32 servings (8 quarts).

This quick-to-fix soup feeds a lot of hungry people. The tender sirloin pieces and diced veggies make a filling meal.
marcia severson // hallock, minnesota

- **4 pounds beef top sirloin steak, cut into 1/2-inch cubes**
- **4 cups chopped onions**
- **1/4 cup butter**
- **4 quarts hot water**
- **4 cups sliced carrots**
- **4 cups cubed peeled potatoes**
- **2 cups chopped cabbage**
- **1 cup chopped celery**
- **1 large green pepper, chopped**
- **8 teaspoons beef bouillon granules**
- **1 tablespoon seasoned salt**
- **1 teaspoon dried basil**
- **1 teaspoon pepper**
- **4 bay leaves**
- **6 cups tomato juice**

In two Dutch ovens, brown beef and onions in butter in batches; drain. Add the water, vegetables and seasonings; bring to a boil. Reduce heat; cover and simmer for 20 minutes.

Add tomato juice; cover and simmer 10 minutes longer or until the beef and vegetables are tender. Discard bay leaves.

favorite beef barley soup

PREP: 10 min. • **COOK:** 30 min. • **YIELD:** 4 servings.

My entire family just loves this delicious, comforting soup. Loaded with chunks of tender beef, the rich broth also includes plenty of mushrooms, sliced carrots and quick-cooking barley.
barbara beattie // glen allen, virginia

- **2 tablespoons all-purpose flour**
- **1/2 teaspoon salt**
- **1/4 teaspoon pepper, *divided***
- **1 pound lean beef top sirloin steak, cut into 1/2-inch cubes**
- **1 tablespoon canola oil**
- **2 cups sliced fresh mushrooms**
- **2 cans (14-1/2 ounces *each*) reduced-sodium beef broth**
- **2 medium carrots, sliced**
- **1/4 teaspoon garlic powder**
- **1/4 teaspoon dried thyme**
- **1/2 cup quick-cooking barley**

In a large resealable plastic bag, combine the flour, the salt and 1/8 teaspoon pepper. Add beef and shake to coat. In a Dutch oven, brown beef in oil over medium heat or until the meat is no longer pink. Remove beef and set aside.

In the same pan, saute mushrooms until tender. Add the broth, carrots, garlic powder, thyme and remaining pepper; bring to a boil. Add barley and beef. Reduce heat; cover and simmer for 20-25 minutes until the meat, vegetables and barley are tender.

three's-a-charm shamrock soup

PREP: 10 min. • **COOK:** 40 min. • **YIELD:** 10 servings (2-1/2 quarts).

There's no better way to use up leftover St. Patrick's Day corned beef, cabbage and potatoes than to make a hearty soup. This second-time-around soup is one of my best. deborah mcmirtrey // estes park, colorado

- **6 celery ribs, chopped**
- **4 medium carrots, sliced**
- **2 cups cubed peeled potatoes**
- **5 cups water**
- **3 cups diced cooked corned beef**
- **2 cups chopped cooked cabbage**
- **1 teaspoon dill weed**
- **1 teaspoon salt**
- **1 teaspoon seasoned salt**
- **1/2 teaspoon white pepper**

In a large soup kettle, bring the celery, carrots, potatoes and water to a boil. Reduce heat; cover and simmer until vegetables are tender, about 20 minutes.

Stir in the remaining ingredients. Cover and simmer for 15-20 minutes or until soup is heated through.

beefy vegetable soup

PREP: 20 min. • **COOK:** 1 hour 50 min. • **YIELD:** 9 servings (about 3-1/4 quarts).

This chunky soup is loaded with tender beef stew meat, carrots, potatoes and green beans—and it sure is tasty! A little steak sauce and garlic powder season the broth perfectly. jimmy osmon // upper darby, pennsylvania

- 1-1/2 pounds beef stew meat
- 1 tablespoon canola oil
- 2 cans (14-1/2 ounces *each*) reduced-sodium beef broth
- 1-1/2 cups water
- 2 tablespoons reduced-sodium soy sauce
- 3 medium potatoes, cubed (about 1 pound)
- 3 medium carrots, cubed
- 3 celery ribs, chopped
- 2 tablespoons Worcestershire sauce
- 2 tablespoons steak sauce
- 1 tablespoon garlic powder
- 1/2 teaspoon salt
- 1/4 teaspoon dried oregano
- 1/8 teaspoon ground nutmeg
- 1/8 teaspoon pepper
- 2 cups fresh corn *or* frozen corn
- 1-3/4 cups frozen cut green beans

In a Dutch oven, cook beef over medium heat in oil until no longer pink; drain. Add the broth, water and soy sauce. Bring to a boil. Reduce heat; cover and simmer for 1 hour.

Add the potatoes, carrots, celery, Worcestershire sauce, steak sauce and seasonings. Bring to a boil. Reduce heat; cover and simmer for 30-40 minutes or until the vegetables are just tender.

Add corn and beans. Bring to a boil. Reduce heat; cover and simmer 5-10 minutes longer or until vegetables are tender.

WORCESTERSHIRE SAUCE

Worcestershire sauce is a commercially produced, dark brown sauce used to season meats, gravies and salad dressing or to serve as a condiment. It's made of soy sauce, vinegar, garlic, onions, tamarind, molasses and various seasonings and is widely available in supermarkets. White wine Worcestershire sauce, which is pale in color, is also available.

zesty vegetable beef soup

PREP: 35 min. + cooling • **COOK:** 3-1/2 hours • **YIELD:** 12-14 servings (3-3/4 quarts).

My family loves to come to the table for hot homemade biscuits and a bowl of this flavorful, filling soup. They rave over how good it tastes. A friend shared the recipe with me. brenda wood // portage la prairie, manitoba

BROTH:

- 8 cups water
- 3 pounds bone-in beef short ribs
- 1 large onion, quartered
- 2 medium carrots, quartered
- 2 celery ribs, quartered
- 8 whole allspice
- 2 bay leaves
- 1 tablespoon salt
- 1/2 teaspoon pepper

SOUP:

- 4 cups V8 juice
- 3 celery ribs, sliced
- 2 medium potatoes, peeled and cubed
- 2 medium carrots, sliced
- 1 medium onion, diced
- 2 teaspoons Worcestershire sauce
- 1/2 teaspoon hot pepper sauce
- 1/2 teaspoon dried oregano
- 1/2 teaspoon dried basil
- 1/4 teaspoon chili powder
- 1 cup uncooked noodles

In a Dutch oven or soup kettle, bring broth ingredients to a boil. Reduce heat; cover and simmer for 2 hours or until meat is tender.

Remove ribs; allow to cool. Skim fat and strain broth; discard vegetables and seasonings. Remove meat from bones and cut into bite-size pieces; return to broth. Add the first 10 soup ingredients; bring to a boil. Reduce heat; cover and simmer for 1 hour or until vegetables are tender.

Stir in noodles. Return to a boil; cook, uncovered, for 15 minutes or until the noodles are tender. Discard bay leaves.

POTATO POINTERS

When buying potatoes, look for those that are firm, well shaped and free of blemishes. Avoid potatoes that are wrinkled, cracked or sprouting. If kept in a cool, dark, well-ventilated place, most potatoes will keep for up to 2 weeks. However, new potatoes should be used within 4 days of purchase. Generally, three medium russet potatoes or eight to 10 small new white potatoes equal one pound. One pound of russet potatoes equals approximately 3-1/2 cups chopped or 2 to 3 cups mashed.

four-onion soup

PREP: 35 min. • **COOK:** 50 min. • **YIELD:** 6 servings.

This mellow, rich-tasting onion soup is such a mainstay for our family that I felt compelled to share the recipe. Topped with toasted French bread and melted cheese, it's special to serve. margaret adams // pacific grove, california

- **1 medium yellow onion**
- **1 medium red onion**
- **1 medium leek (white portion only)**
- **5 green onions with tops**
- **1 garlic clove, minced**
- **2 tablespoons butter**
- **2 cans (14-1/2 ounces *each*) beef broth**
- **1 can (10-1/2 ounces) condensed beef consomme, undiluted**
- **1 teaspoon Worcestershire sauce**
- **1/2 teaspoon ground nutmeg**
- **1 cup (4 ounces) shredded Swiss cheese**
- **6 slices French bread (3/4 inch thick), toasted**
- **6 tablespoons grated Parmesan cheese, optional**

Slice all onions 1/4 in. thick. In a large saucepan over medium-low heat, saute onions and garlic in butter for 15 minutes or until tender and golden, stirring occasionally. Add broth, consomme, Worcestershire sauce and nutmeg; bring to a boil. Reduce heat; cover and simmer for 30 minutes.

Sprinkle 1 tablespoon of Swiss cheese in the bottom of six oven-proof 8-oz. bowls. Ladle hot soup into bowls. Top each with a slice of bread. Sprinkle with remaining Swiss cheese and Parmesan cheese if desired.

Broil 6-8 in. from the heat until cheese melts. Serve immediately.

stuffed roast pepper soup

PREP: 25 min. • **COOK:** 1-1/2 hours
YIELD: 14-16 servings (4 quarts).

After sampling a similar soup at a summer resort, my daughter and I invented this version. Using a colorful variety of peppers gives it plenty of eye appeal. betty vig // viroqua, wisconsin

- **2 pounds ground beef**
- **1/2 medium onion, chopped**
- **6 cups water**
- **8 beef bouillon cubes**
- **2 cans (28 ounces *each*) diced tomatoes, undrained**
- **2 cups cooked rice**
- **2 teaspoons salt**
- **1/2 teaspoon pepper**
- **1/2 teaspoon paprika**
- **3 green, sweet yellow *or* red peppers, seeded and chopped**

In a large Dutch oven or soup kettle, cook ground beef with onion until the meat is brown and the onion is tender; drain. Add bouillon cubes, tomatoes, rice and seasonings. Bring to a boil; reduce heat and simmer, covered, for 1 hour.

Add the peppers; cook, uncovered, for 10-15 minutes or just until the peppers are tender.

creole soup

PREP: 10 min. • **COOK:** 40 min.
YIELD: 18 servings (4-1/2 quarts).

Special seasonings set this flavorful soup apart from any others I've tried. It makes a nice big batch, so it's perfect when feeding a crowd. Plus, leftovers freeze well.
del mason // martensville, saskatchewan

- 1 pound ground beef
- 1 medium onion, finely chopped
- 8 cups water
- 1 can (28 ounces) diced tomatoes, undrained
- 3 cups shredded cabbage
- 3 cups cubed peeled potatoes
- 1 can (15-1/2 ounces) pork and beans
- 1 can (10-3/4 ounces) condensed tomato soup, undiluted
- 1 can (4 ounces) mushroom stems and pieces, undrained
- 1 cup sliced carrots
- 1 cup chopped green pepper
- 1 cup frozen peas
- 3 celery ribs with leaves, finely chopped
- 3 chicken bouillon cubes
- 2 tablespoons dried parsley flakes
- 1 teaspoon *each* Cajun seasoning, chili powder, Creole seasoning, pepper, crushed red pepper flakes and Italian seasoning
- 1 bay leaf

In a soup kettle or Dutch oven, cook beef and onion over medium heat until meat is no longer pink; drain.

Add the remaining ingredients; bring to a boil. Reduce heat; simmer, uncovered, for 25 minutes or until vegetables are tender. Discard bay leaf before serving.

EDITOR'S NOTE: The following spices may be substituted for 1 teaspoon Creole seasoning: 1/4 teaspoon each salt, garlic powder and paprika; and a pinch each of dried thyme, ground cumin and cayenne pepper.

family-favorite soup

PREP: 15 min. • **COOK:** 50 min. • **YIELD:** 6-8 servings.

This recipe originally called for chili powder. But one day, I found I didn't have any and used barbecue sauce instead. All of our 10 children ask me to make this recipe whenever they come to visit. caye watson // sangudo, alberta

- 5-1/2 cups water, *divided*
- 1 large onion, chopped
- 1 cup sliced carrots
- 1 cup cubed potatoes
- 1/2 cup sliced celery
- 1/2 teaspoon salt
- 1/2 teaspoon pepper
- 1 can (16 ounces) kidney beans, rinsed and drained
- 1 can (10-3/4 ounces) condensed tomato soup, undiluted
- 1/2 pound ground beef, cooked and drained
- 2 tablespoons barbecue sauce
- 1 teaspoon beef bouillon granules

In a large saucepan, combine 2 cups water, onion, carrots, potatoes, celery, salt and pepper; bring to a boil. Reduce heat; cover and simmer for 15 minutes. Add the remaining ingredients; cover and simmer 30 minutes longer or until vegetables are tender.

EDITOR'S NOTE: Purchase firm, bright-orange carrots without cracks or dry spots. Store in a plastic bag in the refrigerator for up to 2 weeks. Six medium carrots yield about 3 cups sliced.

taco minestrone

PREP/TOTAL TIME: 25 min.
YIELD: 8 servings.

Since my husband and I both work full-time, it's nice to have a winter pick-me-up like this zippy favorite to call on when I need a speedy and filling entree for supper.

carole holder // norman, oklahoma

1/2 pound ground beef
2 cans (15 ounces *each*) ranch style beans (pinto beans in seasoned tomato sauce)
2 cans (10-3/4 ounces *each*) condensed minestrone soup, undiluted
2 cans (10 ounces *each*) diced tomatoes and green chilies, undrained

In a large saucepan, cook beef over medium heat until no longer pink; drain. Stir in the beans, soup and tomatoes. Bring to a boil. Reduce heat; simmer, uncovered for 15-20 minutes or until heated through.

sweet-and-sour beef cabbage soup

PREP/TOTAL TIME: 30 min. • **YIELD:** 8-10 servings (2-3/4 quarts).

This soup has been a favorite of mine from a local restaurant for years. The owner said many people have requested the recipe, so I'm happy to share it with you.

mae lavan // chicago, illinois

8 cups water
3/4 cup cubed cooked roast beef
1 cup chopped onion
1 cup chopped tomatoes
1/2 cup shredded cabbage
1/2 cup sliced celery
1/3 cup chopped carrot
1 cup sugar
1/2 cup cider vinegar
1/4 cup Burgundy wine *or* beef broth, optional
2 tablespoons browning sauce
2 tablespoons Worcestershire sauce
2 teaspoons tomato sauce
6 beef bouillon cubes
1/2 teaspoon garlic powder
1/4 teaspoon dried thyme
Salt and pepper to taste
2 tablespoons all-purpose flour
2 tablespoons canola oil

In a Dutch oven, combine the water, beef, onion, tomatoes, cabbage, celery, carrot, sugar, vinegar and wine or broth if desired. Stir in the browning sauce, Worcestershire, tomato sauce, bouillon and seasonings. Bring to a boil over medium heat. Reduce heat; simmer, uncovered, until vegetables are tender.

Combine flour and oil until smooth; stir into pan. Bring to a boil; cook and stir for about 2 minutes or until slightly thickened. Refrigerate leftovers.

BROWNING SAUCE

Browning sauce is a blend of caramel color, vegetable concentrates and seasonings. Available since the early 1900s, the sauce is used to add a rich, dark color to foods. Traditionally added to gravies and sauces, browning sauce also works well in soups and stews to darken the broth. Today's time-crunched cooks sometimes brush or stir browning sauce into beef, poultry or pork prepared in the microwave to give it an oven-roasted appearance. In some grocery stores, browning sauce is located near the prepared and dry gravy mixes. A little browning sauce goes a long way, so be sure to measure it carefully.

meatball soup

PREP: 15 min. • **COOK:** 35 min. • **YIELD:** 5 servings.

This soup is just like a meal in a bowl. For heartier appetites, serve it with a sandwich. It's great for chilly days.

sue miller // walworth, wisconsin

- **1 egg, lightly beaten**
- **1/4 cup dry bread crumbs**
- **1/4 cup minced fresh parsley**
- **2 tablespoons grated Parmesan cheese**
- **1/4 teaspoon garlic salt, optional**
- **1/8 teaspoon pepper**
- **1/2 pound lean ground beef (90% lean)**
- **4 cups reduced-sodium beef broth**
- **1 can (16 ounces) kidney beans, rinsed and drained**
- **1 can (14-1/2 ounces) stewed tomatoes**
- **1 medium carrot, thinly sliced**
- **1 teaspoon Italian seasoning**
- **1/4 cup uncooked tiny shell pasta**

In a small bowl, combine the first six ingredients. Crumble beef over mixture and mix well. Shape into 1-in. balls. Brown meatballs in a large saucepan; drain. Add broth, beans, tomatoes, carrot and Italian seasoning. Bring to a boil. Reduce heat; cover and simmer for 10 minutes.

Add pasta; simmer 10 minutes longer or until meat is no longer pink and pasta is tender. Freeze in 1-1/2 cup portions for up to 3 months.

beefy minestrone soup

PREP: 20 min. • **COOK:** 3-1/2 hours • **YIELD:** 40 servings (10 quarts).

Here's the perfect soup to put your fresh garden vegetables to good use. It's great for a light meal served with a salad and warm bread. lana rutledge // shepherdsville, kentucky

- **1 boneless beef chuck roast (4 pounds)**
- **4 quarts water**
- **2 bay leaves**
- **2 medium onions, diced**
- **2 cups sliced carrots**
- **2 cups sliced celery**
- **1 can (28 ounces) diced tomatoes, undrained**
- **1 can (15 ounces) tomato sauce**
- **1/4 cup chopped fresh parsley**
- **Salt and pepper to taste**
- **4 teaspoons dried basil**
- **1 teaspoon garlic powder**
- **2 packages (9 ounces *each*) frozen Italian *or* cut green beans**
- **1 package (16 ounces) frozen peas**
- **2 cans (16 ounces *each*) kidney beans, rinsed and drained**
- **2 packages (7 ounces *each*) shell macaroni, cooked and drained**
- **Grated Parmesan cheese**

Place beef roast, water and bay leaves in a large kettle or Dutch oven; bring to a boil. Reduce heat; cover and simmer until meat is tender, about 3 hours.

Remove meat from broth; cool. Add the onions, carrots and celery to broth; cook for 20 minutes or until vegetables are tender.

Cut meat into bite-size pieces; add to broth. Add tomatoes, tomato sauce, parsley, seasonings, beans, peas and kidney beans. Cook until the vegetables are done, about 10 minutes.

Add macaroni and heat through. Remove bay leaves. Ladle into soup bowls; sprinkle with Parmesan cheese.

STORING CELERY

Remove celery from the store bag it comes in, and wrap it in paper towel, then in aluminum foil. Store in the refrigerator. When you need some, break off what your recipe calls for, re-wrap the rest and return to fridge. Celery stored like this stays crisp a very long time.

meatball vegetable soup

PREP/TOTAL TIME: 25 min.
YIELD: 6-8 servings (about 2-1/2 quarts).

This delightful soup uses frozen meatballs. It cooks on the stovetop in half an hour, but I often double the recipe and simmer it in the slow cooker for easy preparation.

marcia piaskowski // plantsville, connecticut

- **2/3 cup uncooked medium pasta shells**
- **4 cups chicken broth**
- **1 can (14-1/2 ounces) diced tomatoes, undrained**
- **1 can (10-1/2 ounces) condensed French onion soup, undiluted**
- **12 frozen fully cooked Italian meatballs (1/2 ounce *each*), thawed and quartered**
- **1-1/2 cups chopped fresh spinach**
- **1 cup frozen sliced carrots, thawed**
- **3/4 cup canned kidney beans, rinsed and drained**
- **3/4 cup garbonzo beans *or* chickpeas, rinsed and drained**

Cook pasta according to package directions.

Meanwhile, combine the remaining ingredients in a Dutch oven or soup kettle. Bring to a boil. Reduce heat; cover and simmer for 15 minutes or until vegetables are tender. Drain pasta and stir into soup.

mexican beef-cheese soup

PREP/TOTAL TIME: 25 min. • **YIELD:** 6 servings.

This hearty soup appeals to all ages and can be spiced up to suit individual tastes. You can also drain the can of tomatoes and add extra beef, serving it as a thick, cheesy dip.

kim gollin // andover, kansas

- **1 pound ground beef**
- **1 medium onion, chopped**
- **1 can (14-1/2 ounces) diced tomatoes with green chilies, undrained**
- **1 can (11 ounces) Mexicorn, drained**
- **1 pound Mexican *or* plain process cheese (Velveeta), cubed**

In a large saucepan, cook beef and onion over medium heat until meat is no longer pink; drain. Stir in the tomatoes, corn and cheese. Cook and stir until cheese is melted.

rich onion beef soup

PREP: 5 min. • **COOK:** 30 min. • **YIELD:** 5 servings.

When you're in the mood for a soup that's big on beef flavor, reach for this robust recipe.

nina hall // spokane, washington

- **2 cups thinly sliced onions**
- **1 tablespoon butter**
- **2 cups cubed cooked roast beef**
- **2 cans (14-1/2 ounces *each*) beef broth**
- **3 tablespoons all-purpose flour**
- **1/2 teaspoon ground mustard**
- **1/2 teaspoon sugar**
- **1/2 cup dry red wine *or* additional beef broth**
- **1 teaspoon browning sauce**

In a large saucepan, cook onions in butter over medium-low heat for 15-20 minutes or until tender and golden brown, stirring occasionally. Add beef and broth. Bring to a boil. Reduce heat; cover and simmer for 10 minutes.

In a small bowl, combine the flour, mustard and sugar; stir in wine or additional broth and browning sauce until smooth. Stir into soup. Bring to a boil; cook and stir for 1-2 minutes or until slightly thickened.

harvest soup

PREP: 10 min. • **COOK:** 25 min. • **YIELD:** 6 servings.

Loaded with ground beef, squash, tomatoes and potatoes, this hearty soup is a great family meal. Substitute any veggies with those that suit your tastes.

janice mitchell // aurora, colorado

- **1 pound lean ground beef (90% lean)**
- **3/4 cup chopped onion**
- **2 garlic cloves, minced**
- **3-1/2 cups water**
- **2-1/4 cups chopped peeled sweet potatoes**
- **1 cup chopped red potatoes**
- **1 cup chopped peeled acorn squash**
- **2 teaspoons beef bouillon granules**
- **2 bay leaves**
- **1/2 teaspoon chili powder**
- **1/2 teaspoon pepper**
- **1/8 teaspoon ground allspice**
- **1/8 teaspoon ground cloves**
- **1 can (14-1/2 ounces) diced tomatoes, undrained**

In a large saucepan, cook beef and onion over medium heat until meat is no longer pink. Add garlic; cook 1 minute longer. Drain. Add the water, potatoes, squash, bouillon, bay leaves, chili powder, pepper, allspice and cloves. Bring to a boil.

Reduce heat; cover and simmer for 15-20 minutes or until vegetables are tender. Add the tomatoes. Cook and stir until heated through. Discard bay leaves.

dilly beef barley soup

PREP: 20 min. • **COOK:** 4 hours
YIELD: 15 servings (3-3/4 quarts).

My mother and grandmother were wonderful cooks who taught me to create foods that were both attractive and full-flavored. This soup from Mom meets those requirements nicely.

phyllis kramer
little compton, rhode island

- **3/4 cup dried baby lima beans**
- **1/2 cup dried yellow split peas**
- **1/2 cup dried green split peas**
- **4 medium carrots, sliced**
- **4 celery ribs, sliced**
- **3 quarts water**
- **2 pounds boneless beef short ribs, cut into 1-inch cubes**
- **2 medium onions, chopped**
- **3/4 cup medium pearl barley**
- **5 chicken bouillon cubes**
- **4 medium potatoes, peeled and cubed**
- **1 tablespoon chopped fresh dill *or* 1 teaspoon dill weed**
- **1-1/2 teaspoons salt, optional**
- **1/4 teaspoon pepper**

In a Dutch oven or soup kettle, combine beans, peas, carrots, celery and water; bring to a boil. Reduce heat; cover and simmer for 1-1/2 hours. Add beef, onions, barley and bouillon; bring to a boil.

Skim foam. Reduce heat; cover and simmer for 2 hours or until meat and beans are tender. Add the potatoes and simmer for 20 minutes. Add the dill, salt if desired and pepper; cook for 5 minutes.

vegetable beef soup

PREP/TOTAL TIME: 30 min. • **YIELD:** 14 servings (3-1/2 quarts).

Just brimming with veggies, this hearty soup will warm family and friends right to their toes! It's especially good served with cornbread, and we think it tastes even better the second day. marie carlisle // sumrall, mississippi

- **4 cups cubed peeled potatoes**
- **6 cups water**
- **1 pound ground beef**
- **5 teaspoons beef bouillon granules**
- **1 can (10-3/4 ounces) condensed tomato soup, undiluted**
- **2 cups frozen corn, thawed**
- **2 cups frozen sliced carrots, thawed**
- **2 cups frozen cut green beans, thawed**
- **2 cups frozen sliced okra, thawed**
- **3 tablespoons dried minced onion**

In a Dutch oven, bring potatoes and water to a boil. Cover and cook for 10-15 minutes or until tender. Meanwhile, in a large skillet, cook beef over medium heat until no longer pink; drain.

Add the bouillon, soup, vegetables, dried minced onion and beef to the undrained potatoes. Bring to a boil. Reduce heat; simmer, uncovered, for 8-10 minutes or until heated through, stirring occasionally.

OKRA SUBSTITUTES

Okra is a vegetable that is popular in the southern United States, where it is often added to soups and stews. It has grayish-green ridged pods that contain numerous small, edible seeds. When okra is sliced, it releases a substance that naturally thickens any liquid it is cooked in. Although the taste and texture of okra is unique, some folks think its mild flavor resembles that of green beans or eggplant. Those two vegetables may be substituted for okra in many soups and stews. However, without okra's natural thickening properties, cornstarch or flour may also have to be added.

louisiana-style taco soup

PREP: 5 min. • **COOK:** 35 min.
YIELD: 13 servings (3 quarts).

This is one of my family's favorite quick and easy soups on cold winter days. With just a few ingredients and your favorite garnish, it's ready to serve in no time.
julie whitlow // alexandria, indiana

- **1 package (8 ounces) red beans and rice mix**
- **1 package (9 ounces) tortilla soup mix**
- **1 pound ground beef**
- **1 cup salsa**
- **1/4 cup sour cream**

Prepare mixes according to package directions. Meanwhile, in a Dutch oven, cook beef over medium heat until no longer pink; drain. Stir in the salsa, prepared rice and soup. Cook, uncovered, for 5 minutes or until heated through. Garnish with sour cream.

EDITOR'S NOTE: This recipe was prepared with Zatarain's New Orleans Style Red Beans and Rice and Bear Creek Tortilla Soup mixes.

ground beef vegetable soup

PREP: 10 min. • **COOK:** 45 min. • **YIELD:** 8 servings.

Chase the chill after a day of raking leaves or running errands by making a batch of this tasty soup. A variety of veggies along with ground beef and macaroni make this a hearty main dish. raymonde bourgeois // swastika, ontario

- **3/4 pound ground beef**
- **2 cans (14-1/2 ounces *each*) beef broth**
- **2 cups water**
- **1 can (28 ounces) diced tomatoes, undrained**
- **3 celery ribs, chopped**
- **2 large carrots, sliced**
- **2 medium onions, sliced**
- **1 medium potato, peeled and cubed**
- **1-1/2 cups fresh cauliflowerets**
- **2 tablespoons minced fresh tarragon *or* 2 teaspoons dried tarragon**
- **1 tablespoon garlic powder**
- **1 tablespoon minced fresh parsley**
- **1/2 teaspoon salt**
- **1/8 teaspoon pepper**
- **3/4 cup uncooked macaroni**

In a Dutch oven, cook beef over medium heat until no longer pink; drain. Add the broth, water, tomatoes, celery, carrots, onions, potato, cauliflower, tarragon, garlic powder, parsley, salt and pepper. Bring to a boil. Reduce heat; cover and simmer for 30 minutes or until vegetables are tender, stirring occasionally.

Cook macaroni according to package directions; drain. Stir into soup; heat through.

country cabbage soup

PREP: 5 min. • **COOK:** 45 min. • **YIELD:** 12-14 servings (3-1/4 quarts).

Here's an old-fashioned favorite that my mother-in-law shared with me. Try stirring in some shredded carrots or frozen mixed vegetables if you like. And to stretch the number of servings a bit, add 2 cups of cooked rice or pasta.

vicky catullo // youngstown, ohio

- **2 pounds ground beef**
- **2 cans (28 ounces *each*) stewed tomatoes**
- **1 medium head cabbage, shredded**
- **2 large onions, chopped**
- **6 celery ribs, chopped**
- **Salt and pepper to taste**

In a large saucepan, cook beef over medium heat until no longer pink; drain. Add the tomatoes, cabbage, onions and celery; bring to a boil. Reduce heat; simmer, uncovered, for 25 minutes or until vegetables are tender. Stir in salt and pepper.

italian wedding soup

PREP: 20 min. • **COOK:** 15 min. • **YIELD:** 12 servings (3 quarts).

No matter when I serve it, this soup always satisfies! I add cooked pasta at the end of the cooking time to keep it from getting mushy. nancy ducharme // deltona, florida

- **1 egg**
- **3/4 cup grated Parmesan cheese**
- **1/2 cup dry bread crumbs**
- **1 small onion, chopped**
- **3/4 teaspoon salt, *divided***
- **1-1/4 teaspoons pepper, *divided***
- **1-1/4 teaspoons garlic powder, *divided***
- **2 pounds ground beef**
- **2 quarts chicken broth**
- **1/3 cup chopped fresh spinach**
- **1 teaspoon onion powder**
- **1 teaspoon dried parsley flakes**
- **1-1/4 cups cooked medium pasta shells**

In a large bowl, combine the egg, cheese, bread crumbs, onion, 1/4 teaspoon salt, 1/4 teaspoon pepper and 1/4 teaspoon garlic powder. Crumble beef over mixture and mix well. Shape into 1-in. balls.

In a Dutch oven, brown meatballs in small batches; drain. Add the broth, spinach, onion powder, parsley and remaining salt, pepper and garlic powder; bring to a boil. Reduce heat; simmer, uncovered, for 5 minutes. Stir in pasta; heat through.

quick pizza soup

PREP: 5 min. • **COOK:** 35 min. • **YIELD:** 16 servings (4 quarts).

My kids first sampled this soup in the school cafeteria. They couldn't stop talking about it, so I knew I had to get the recipe. It's quick and easy to make.

penny lanxon // newell, iowa

1 pound ground beef
2 cans (26 ounces *each*) condensed tomato soup, undiluted
6-1/2 cups water
1 jar (28 ounces) spaghetti sauce
1 tablespoon Italian seasoning
2 cups (8 ounces) shredded cheddar cheese
Additional shredded cheddar cheese, optional

In a soup kettle or Dutch oven, cook beef over medium heat until no longer pink; drain. Add soup, water, spaghetti sauce and Italian seasoning; bring to a boil.

Reduce heat; simmer, uncovered, for 15 minutes. Add cheese; cook and stir until melted. Garnish with additional cheese if desired.

EDITOR'S NOTE: Make Quick Pizza Soup a complete, satisfying meal by serving it with grilled cheese or sub sandwiches.

hamburger vegetable soup

PREP: 10 min. • **COOK:** 40 min.
YIELD: 10 servings (3-3/4 quarts).

Oregano really shines in this hearty soup. It smells delicious while it's cooking and makes a great lunch or dinner. You could use lima beans instead of the green beans, too.

traci wynne // denver, pennsylvania

1 pound ground beef
1 medium onion, chopped
1/2 large green pepper, diced
4 garlic cloves, minced
8 cups beef broth
2 cans (14-1/2 ounces *each*) Italian stewed tomatoes
1 package (9 ounces) frozen cut green beans
1 can (8 ounces) tomato sauce
1 cup ditalini *or* other small pasta
1 tablespoon Worcestershire sauce
2 teaspoons dried oregano
1 teaspoon dried basil
1/2 teaspoon pepper

In a Dutch oven, cook the beef, onion and green pepper over medium heat until meat is no longer pink. Add garlic; cook 1 minute longer. Drain.

Stir in the remaining ingredients. Bring to a boil. Reduce heat; cover and simmer for 30 minutes or until vegetables and pasta are tender.

zesty hamburger soup

PREP/TOTAL TIME: 30 min. • **YIELD:** 10 servings (3-3/4 quarts).

On those very cold winter days, or when I just feel like eating comforting soup, I make this recipe. Jalapeno slices give the beefy mixture an extra-special Southwestern flavor. kelly milan // lake jackson, texas

- **1 pound ground beef**
- **2 cups sliced celery**
- **1 cup chopped onion**
- **2 teaspoons minced garlic**
- **4 cups hot water**
- **2 medium red potatoes, peeled and cubed**
- **2 cups frozen corn**
- **1-1/2 cups uncooked small shell pasta**
- **4 pickled jalapeno slices**
- **4 cups V8 juice**
- **2 cans (10 ounces *each*) diced tomatoes with green chilies**
- **1 to 2 tablespoons sugar**

In a Dutch oven, cook the beef, celery and onion over medium heat until meat is no longer pink. Add garlic, cook 1 minute longer. Drain. Stir in the water, potatoes, corn, pasta and jalapeno.

Bring to a boil. Reduce heat; cover and simmer for 10-15 minutes or until pasta is tender. Stir in the remaining ingredients. Cook and stir until heated through.

GROUND BEEF

When browning ground beef or other ground meat, use a pastry blender to break up larger pieces shortly before the meat is completely cooked. This makes it much more suitable for chili, stews, soups and casseroles.

zippy spanish rice soup

PREP: 25 min. • **COOK:** 4 hours • **YIELD:** 8 servings (about 2 quarts).

I created this recipe after ruining a dinner of Spanish rice. I tried to salvage the dish by adding more water, cilantro and green chiles. It was a hit with the whole family. It's hearty enough to be a main meal with the addition of a garden salad and some corn bread. marilyn schetz // cuyahoga falls, ohio

- **1 pound lean ground beef (90% lean)**
- **1 medium onion, chopped**
- **3 cups water**
- **1 jar (16 ounces) salsa**
- **1 can (14-1/2 ounces) diced tomatoes, undrained**
- **1 jar (7 ounces) roasted sweet red peppers, drained and chopped**
- **1 can (4 ounces) chopped green chilies**
- **1 envelope taco seasoning**
- **1 tablespoon dried cilantro flakes**
- **1/2 cup uncooked converted rice**

In a large skillet, cook the beef and onion over medium heat until meat is no longer pink; drain.

Transfer to a 4- or 5-qt. slow cooker. Add the water, salsa, tomatoes, red peppers, chilies, taco seasoning and cilantro. Stir in rice. Cover and cook on low for 4-5 hours or until rice is tender.

CONVERTED RICE

Also known as parboiled rice, converted rice has gone through a steam-pressure process before milling. This gives it a firmer grain and makes it cook up fluffy and separate.

beefy tomato pasta soup

PREP: 15 min. • **COOK:** 45 min.
YIELD: 10 servings (about 2-1/2 quarts).

If you're a fan of Italian fare, you'll like this chunky combination. I enjoy this savory soup, and it's certainly easier to fix than lasagna.
nancy rollag // kewaskum, wisconsin

- **1 pound ground beef**
- **2 medium green peppers, cut into 1-inch chunks**
- **1 medium onion, cut into chunks**
- **2 garlic cloves, minced**
- **5 to 6 cups water**
- **2 cans (14-1/2 ounces *each*) Italian diced tomatoes, undrained**
- **1 can (6 ounces) tomato paste**
- **1 tablespoon brown sugar**
- **2 to 3 teaspoons Italian seasoning**
- **1 teaspoon salt**
- **1/4 teaspoon pepper**
- **2 cups uncooked spiral pasta**
- **Croutons, optional**

In a Dutch oven, cook the beef, green peppers and onion over medium heat until meat is no longer pink. Add garlic, cook 1 minute longer. Drain. Add the water, tomatoes, tomato paste, brown sugar, Italian seasoning, salt and pepper. Bring to a boil. Add pasta.

Cook for 10-14 minutes or until pasta is tender, stirring occasionally. Serve with croutons if desired.

herbed beef barley soup

PREP/TOTAL TIME: 20 min. • **YIELD:** 4 servings.

Thyme comes through in this colorful soup that's chock-full of tender beef. You can use any combination of vegetables you have on hand, and leftovers reheat especially well. heidee manrose // burns, wyoming

- **2 cups cubed cooked beef**
- **1/2 cup beef broth**
- **3 cups water**
- **1 cup frozen cut green beans**
- **1 cup frozen sliced carrots**
- **1/4 cup quick-cooking barley**
- **1 tablespoon beef bouillon granules**
- **1 teaspoon dried thyme**
- **1/2 teaspoon salt**

In a large saucepan, combine all ingredients. Bring to a boil. Reduce heat; cover and simmer for 10-14 minutes or until vegetables and barley are tender. Let stand for about 5 minutes before serving.

classic beef barley soup

PREP: 30 min. + cooling • **COOK:** 1 hour 55 min. • **YIELD:** 8 servings (2 quarts).

When most folks think of barley, they picture it served up in a delicious soup. I'm no exception! This is a hearty soup that is, without doubt, a satisfying meal in itself. jan spencer // mclean, saskatchewan

- **2 pounds bone-in beef short ribs**
- **5 cups water**
- **1 can (14-1/2 ounces) diced tomatoes, undrained**
- **1 medium onion, chopped**
- **1 to 1-1/2 teaspoons salt, optional**
- **1/8 teaspoon pepper**
- **2 cups sliced carrots**
- **1 cup sliced celery**
- **1 cup chopped cabbage**
- **2/3 cup quick-cooking barley**
- **1/4 cup minced fresh parsley**

In a soup kettle, combine ribs, water, tomatoes, onion, salt if desired and pepper; bring to a boil over medium heat. Reduce heat; cover and simmer for 1-1/2 to 2 hours or until meat is tender. Remove ribs; cool. Skim fat.

Remove meat from bones and cut into bite-size pieces; return to broth. Add carrots, celery and cabbage; bring to a boil. Reduce heat; cover and simmer 15 minutes.

Add barley; return to a boil. Reduce heat; cover and cook 10-15 minutes or until barley and vegetables are tender. Add parsley.

DEFINITION OF SIMMER

To simmer means to cook a combination of ingredients with liquid or liquids alone just under the boiling point (180° to 200°). The surface of the liquid will have some movement and there may be small bubbles around the side of pan.

old-world tomato soup

PREP: 25 min. • **COOK:** 3 hours 10 min.
YIELD: 16-20 servings.

This hearty soup has been in our family for four generations, and I've never seen another recipe like it. Each spoonful brings back memories. linda pandolfo // east haddam, connecticut

- **3 quarts water**
- **4 bone-in beef short ribs (2 pounds)**
- **2 to 3 meaty soup bones, beef shanks *or* short ribs (about 2 pounds)**
- **1 can (28 ounces) diced tomatoes, undrained**
- **3 celery ribs, halved**
- **1 large onion, quartered**
- **1/2 cup chopped fresh parsley, *divided***
- **1 tablespoon salt**
- **1-1/2 teaspoons pepper**
- **4 carrots, cut into 1-inch pieces**
- **2 parsnips, peeled and quartered**
- **2 cups (16 ounces) sour cream**
- **1/2 cup all-purpose flour**
- **1/2 teaspoon ground nutmeg, optional**
- **1 package (8 ounces) egg noodles, cooked and drained**

In a large kettle, combine water, ribs, soup bones, tomatoes, celery, onion, 1/4 cup parsley, salt and pepper. Cover and simmer for 2 hours. Add carrots and parsnips; cover and simmer for 1 hour or until meat and vegetables are tender.

With a slotted spoon, remove meat, bones and vegetables. Strain broth and skim off fat; return all but 1 cup broth to kettle. Set reserved broth aside. Remove meat from the bones; dice and return to kettle. Discard celery and onion. Cut parsnips and carrots into 1/2-in. pieces and return to kettle. Add remaining parsley.

In a large bowl, combine the sour cream, flour, nutmeg if desired and reserved broth; stir into soup. Add noodles. Cook and stir until thickened and heated through (do not boil).

bow tie beef soup

PREP/TOTAL TIME: 30 min.
YIELD: 8 servings (about 2 quarts).

Usually I turn the page when I see a long list of ingredients, but this one didn't seem so bad. I think it's one of the best and easiest one-dish meals I've ever made!
lee anne mcbride // austin, texas

- **2 cups sliced zucchini**
- **1 can (14-1/2 ounces) beef broth**
- **1 cup uncooked bow tie pasta**
- **3/4 cup water**
- **1/2 teaspoon dried oregano**
- **1/4 to 1/2 teaspoon dried thyme**
- **1/4 to 1/2 teaspoon crushed red pepper flakes**
- **1-1/2 pounds ground beef**
- **1 cup chopped onion**
- **2 teaspoons minced garlic**
- **4 plum tomatoes, cut into chunks**
- **1/4 cup minced fresh basil**
- **1/2 cup shredded Parmesan cheese**

In a Dutch oven, combine the first seven ingredients. Bring to a boil. With a spoon, press pasta into broth mixture. Reduce heat; cover and simmer for 15 minutes or until pasta is tender, stirring once.

Meanwhile, in a large skillet, cook the beef, onion and garlic over medium heat until meat is no longer pink; drain.

Add the beef mixture, tomatoes and basil to the broth mixture; heat through. Garnish with Parmesan cheese.

vegetable tortellini soup

PREP/TOTAL TIME: 30 min. • **YIELD:** 10 servings (2-1/2 quarts).

Tomatoes, carrots, green beans, potatoes, corn and celery are the perfect complements to convenient frozen tortellini in this heartwarming soup. Because this soup is like a meal in one, dinner is done in no time.

deborah hutchinson // enfield, connecticut

- **1 large onion, chopped**
- **2 celery ribs, chopped**
- **2 tablespoons canola oil**
- **2 cans (14-1/2 ounces *each*) beef broth**
- **1 cup *each* frozen corn, sliced carrots and cut green beans**
- **1 cup diced uncooked potatoes**
- **1 teaspoon dried basil**
- **1 teaspoon dried thyme**
- **1/2 teaspoon minced chives**
- **2 cans (14-1/2 ounces *each*) diced tomatoes, undrained**
- **2 cups frozen beef *or* cheese tortellini**

In a Dutch oven or soup kettle, saute the onion and celery in oil. Add the broth, corn, carrots, beans, potatoes, basil, thyme and chives; bring to a boil. Reduce heat; cover and simmer for 10-15 minutes or until potatoes are tender.

Add the tomatoes and tortellini. Simmer, uncovered, for 4-5 minutes or until tortellini is heated through.

zucchini beef soup

PREP: 20 min.
COOK: 2-1/4 hours
YIELD: 8 servings (2 quarts).

My garden produces a bumper crop of zucchini—I hate to see even one go to waste! This satisfying soup is a simple solution. The broth is delicious.

robert keith // rochester, minnesota

- **1 pound beef stew meat, cut into 1-inch cubes**
- **1 tablespoon canola oil**
- **6 cups water**
- **1 can (8 ounces) tomato sauce**
- **1 medium onion, chopped**
- **1-1/2 teaspoons salt**
- **3/4 teaspoon dried oregano**
- **1/4 teaspoon pepper**
- **2 cups thinly sliced zucchini**
- **1 cup uncooked broken spaghetti**

In a Dutch oven, brown beef in oil; drain. Add the water, tomato sauce, onion, salt, oregano and pepper. Bring to a boil. Reduce heat; cover and simmer for 2 hours. Add zucchini and spaghetti; return to a boil. Cover and cook for 15-18 minutes or until zucchini and spaghetti are tender.

hearty cabbage soup

PREP/TOTAL TIME: 30 min. • **YIELD:** 6 servings.

I didn't have time to make my favorite cabbage rolls one day, so I just threw together this soup—and I loved it! It's fun to have that old-world flavor in a simple soup. renee leary // citrus springs, florida

- **1 pound ground beef**
- **1 medium onion, chopped**
- **3-1/2 cups shredded cabbage**
- **1 medium zucchini, halved and thinly sliced**
- **1 cup sliced fresh mushrooms**
- **1 carton (18.3 ounces) ready-to-serve sweet red pepper soup**
- **1 can (10 ounces) diced tomatoes and green chilies, undrained**
- **1/4 teaspoon hot pepper sauce**
- **1/4 teaspoon salt**
- **1/4 teaspoon pepper**
- **1/4 cup grated Parmesan cheese**

In a large saucepan, cook beef and onion over medium heat until meat is no longer pink; drain. Add the cabbage, zucchini and mushrooms; cook and stir 8 minutes longer. Stir in the soup, tomatoes, pepper sauce, salt and pepper. Bring to a boil. Reduce heat; cover and simmer for 5 minutes. Sprinkle each serving with 2 teaspoons cheese.

ZUCCHINI

Handle zucchini carefully; they're thin-skinned and easily damaged. To pick the freshest zucchini, look for a firm, heavy squash with a moist stem end and a shiny skin. Smaller squash are generally sweeter and more tender than larger ones. One medium (1/3 pound) zucchini yields about 2 cups sliced or 1-1/2 cups shredded zucchini. Store zucchini in a plastic bag in the refrigerator crisper for 4 to 5 days. Do not wash until ready to use.

lasagna soup

PREP/TOTAL TIME: 30 min.
YIELD: 10 servings (2-1/2 quarts).

Fresh vegetables add color and crunch to a boxed lasagna dinner mix, resulting in a flavorful, fast-to-fix soup.

gladys shaffer // elma, washington

- **1 pound ground beef**
- **1/2 cup chopped onion**
- **1 package (7-3/4 ounces) lasagna dinner mix**
- **5 cups water**
- **1 can (14-1/2 ounces) diced tomatoes, undrained**
- **1 can (7 ounces) whole kernel corn, undrained**
- **2 tablespoons grated Parmesan cheese**
- **1 small zucchini, chopped**

In a Dutch oven or soup kettle, cook beef and onion over medium heat until meat is no longer pink; drain. Add contents of the lasagna dinner sauce mix, water, tomatoes, corn and cheese; bring to a boil. Reduce heat; cover and simmer for 10 minutes, stirring occasionally.

Add the lasagna noodles and zucchini. Cover and simmer for 10 minutes or until noodles are tender. Serve immediately.

beefy zucchini soup

PREP: 20 min. • **COOK:** 20 min. • **YIELD:** 6 servings.

As soon as my homegrown zucchini is plentiful, I make this chunky, fresh-tasting soup. I often double the recipe and freeze the leftovers to enjoy later.

betty claycomb // alverton, pennsylvania

- **1/2 pound lean ground beef (90% lean)**
- **2 celery ribs, thinly sliced**
- **1/3 cup chopped onion**
- **1/2 cup chopped green pepper**
- **1 can (28 ounces) diced tomatoes, undrained**
- **3 medium zucchini, cubed**
- **2 cups water**
- **1-1/2 teaspoons Italian seasoning**
- **1 teaspoon salt, optional**
- **1 teaspoon beef bouillon granules**
- **1/2 teaspoon sugar**
- **Pepper to taste**
- **Shredded Parmesan cheese, optional**

In a large saucepan, cook the beef, celery, onion and green pepper over medium heat until meat is no longer pink and vegetables are tender; drain. Stir in the tomatoes, zucchini, water, Italian seasoning, salt if desired, bouillon, sugar and pepper. Bring to a boil. Reduce heat; cover and simmer for 20-25 minutes or until zucchini is tender. Garnish with Parmesan cheese if desired.

country carrot soup

PREP/TOTAL TIME: 30 min. • **YIELD:** 6-8 servings.

I used ground beef to jazz up a traditional carrot soup recipe. This meaty, creamy meal in a bowl always hits the spot.
marlane jones // allentown, pennsylvania

- **1 pound ground beef**
- **1/4 cup chopped onion**
- **2 cans (10-3/4 ounces *each*) condensed cream of celery soup, undiluted**
- **3 cups tomato juice**
- **2 cups shredded carrots**
- **1 cup water**
- **1 bay leaf**
- **1/2 teaspoon sugar**
- **1/2 teaspoon dried marjoram**
- **1/2 teaspoon salt**
- **1/4 teaspoon garlic powder**
- **1/4 teaspoon pepper**

In a large saucepan, brown beef and onion over medium heat until beef is no longer pink; drain. Add remaining ingredients; bring to a boil. Reduce heat; cover and simmer for 15 minutes or until carrots are tender. Remove bay leaf.

beefy tomato soup

PREP/TOTAL TIME: 30 min. • **YIELD:** 8 servings.

Ground beef and macaroni add heartiness to this yummy soup. Knowing it takes only minutes to put together makes it taste even better! patricia staudt // marble rock, iowa

- **1 pound lean ground beef (90% lean)**
- **4 cups reduced-sodium tomato juice**
- **3 cups water**
- **3/4 cup uncooked elbow macaroni**
- **1 envelope onion soup mix**
- **1/4 teaspoon chili powder**

In a large saucepan, cook beef over medium heat until no longer pink; drain. Add the remaining ingredients. Bring to a boil. Reduce heat; simmer, uncovered, for 15-20 minutes or until macaroni is tender.

hearty hamburger soup

PREP: 10 min. • **COOK:** 30 min.
YIELD: 8 servings (2 quarts).

At family get-togethers, our children always request this spirit-warming soup along with a fresh loaf of homemade bread and tall glasses of milk. It has robust flavor, shows off plenty of colorful vegetables and is easy to make.
barbara brown // janesville, wisconsin

- **1 pound ground beef**
- **4 cups water**
- **1 can (14-1/2 ounces) diced tomatoes, undrained**
- **3 medium carrots, sliced**
- **2 medium potatoes, peeled and cubed**
- **1 medium onion, chopped**
- **1/2 cup chopped celery**
- **4 teaspoons beef bouillon granules**
- **1-1/2 teaspoons salt**
- **1/4 teaspoon pepper**
- **1/4 teaspoon dried oregano**
- **1 cup cut fresh *or* frozen green beans**

In a large saucepan, brown beef; drain. Add the next 10 ingredients; bring to a boil.

Reduce the heat; cover and simmer for 15 minutes or until the potatoes and carrots are tender. Add the beans. Cover and simmer 15 minutes longer or until the beans are tender.

simple taco soup

PREP/TOTAL TIME: 25 min. • **YIELD:** 6-8 servings (about 2 quarts).

We first sampled this chili-like soup at a church dinner. It's a warm dish on a blustery cold day, and since it uses packaged seasonings and several cans of vegetables, it's a snap to prepare. glenda taylor // sand springs, oklahoma

- **2 pounds ground beef**
- **1 envelope taco seasoning**
- **1-1/2 cups water**
- **1 can (16 ounces) mild chili beans, undrained**
- **1 can (15-1/4 ounces) whole kernel corn, drained**
- **1 can (15 ounces) pinto beans, rinsed and drained**
- **1 can (14-1/2 ounces) stewed tomatoes**
- **1 can (10 ounces) diced tomatoes with green chilies**
- **1 can (4 ounces) chopped green chilies, optional**
- **1 envelope ranch salad dressing mix**

In a Dutch oven, cook beef over medium heat until no longer pink; drain. Add taco seasoning and mix well. Stir in the remaining ingredients. Bring to a boil. Reduce heat; simmer, uncovered, for 15 minutes or until heated through, stirring occasionally.

TRANSPORTING SOUP

Whenever you're bringing a stew, soup or chili to a potluck, you'll find it can be easily transported in a 5-quart slow cooker.

pronto taco soup

PREP/TOTAL TIME: 30 min. • **YIELD:** 8 servings (2 quarts).

When out-of-state friends dropped by, I invited them to stay for dinner, knowing that I could put together this mild, chili-flavored soup in a jiffy. I served it with cornmeal muffins and a crisp salad for a filling meal everyone loved. My guests even asked for the recipe before leaving!

priscilla gilbert // indian harbour beach, florida

- **1 pound ground beef**
- **1 medium onion, chopped**
- **2 garlic cloves, minced**
- **2 cans (14-1/2 ounces *each*) beef broth**
- **1 can (14-1/2 ounces) diced tomatoes, undrained**
- **1-1/2 cups picante sauce**
- **1 cup uncooked spiral *or* small shell pasta**
- **1 medium green pepper, chopped**
- **2 teaspoons chili powder**
- **1 teaspoon dried parsley flakes**
- **Shredded cheddar cheese and tortilla chips**

In a large saucepan, cook the beef, onion and garlic until meat is no longer pink; drain. Add the broth, tomatoes, picante sauce, pasta, green pepper, chili powder and parsley. Bring to a boil, stirring occasionally.

Reduce heat; cover and simmer for 10-15 minutes or until pasta is tender. Garnish with cheese and tortilla chips.

pasta cheeseburger soup

PREP/TOTAL TIME: 30 min.
YIELD: 3 servings.

'This tastes just like a cheeseburger' is what I always hear when I serve this satisfying soup. And it's so simple to make! Just combine ground beef and small shell pasta with some popular burger toppings.

darlene brenden // salem, oregon

- **1 pound ground beef**
- **1/2 cup chopped onion**
- **3 cups water**
- **1 can (10-3/4 ounces) condensed cheddar cheese soup, diluted**
- **1 can (10-3/4 ounces) condensed tomato soup, undiluted**
- **3 tablespoons dill pickle relish**
- **1 cup uncooked small shell pasta**
- **Ketchup and mustard**

In a large saucepan, cook beef and onion over medium heat until meat is no longer pink; drain. Stir in the water, soups and relish. Bring to a boil. Reduce heat; add the pasta. Cook, uncovered for 15-20 minutes or until the pasta is tender, stirring occasionally. Carefully drizzle each serving with ketchup and mustard.

beef vegetable soup

PREP: 15 min. • **COOK:** 9 hours • **YIELD:** 7 servings.

This nicely seasoned soup tastes so good. It's convenient, too, since it simmers all day in the slow cooker.

jean hutzell // dubuque, iowa

- **1 pound lean ground beef (90% lean)**
- **1 medium onion, chopped**
- **1/2 teaspoon salt**
- **1/4 teaspoon pepper**
- **3 cups water**
- **3 medium potatoes, peeled and cut into 3/4-inch cubes**
- **1 can (14-1/2 ounces) Italian diced tomatoes, undrained**
- **1 can (11-1/2 ounces) V8 juice**
- **1 cup chopped celery**
- **1 cup sliced carrots**
- **2 tablespoons sugar**
- **1 tablespoon dried parsley flakes**
- **2 teaspoons dried basil**
- **1 bay leaf**

In a nonstick skillet, cook beef and onion over medium heat until meat is no longer pink; drain. Stir in salt and pepper.

Transfer to a 5-qt. slow cooker. Add the remaining ingredients. Cover and cook on low for 9-11 hours or until vegetables are tender. Discard bay leaf before serving.

PREPARING POTATOES

Scrub with a vegetable brush under cold water. Remove eyes or sprouts. When working with lots of potatoes, peel and place in cold water to prevent discoloration. Before baking a whole potato, pierce with a fork.

chives
baby dill
RIVAL®
CROCK·POT®
STONEWARE SLOW COOKER
Off
Low
High

TORTILLA-VEGETABLE CHICKEN SOUP, PG. 66

SOUPS

chicken & turkey

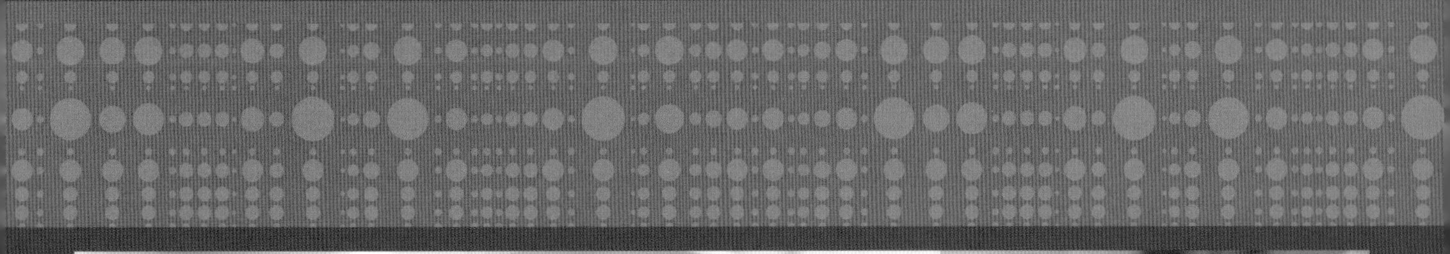

CHICKEN NOODLE SOUP, PG. 73

CURRY CHICKEN SOUP, PG. 100

SAUSAGE KALE SOUP, PG. 103

peasant soup for one

PREP: 15 min. • **COOK:** 20 min.
YIELD: 1 serving.

This recipe makes a tasty small batch of soup that's perfect for one person. kay harris // amarillo, texas

- **1 boneless skinless chicken breast half (4 ounces), cubed**
- **1/4 cup chopped onion**
- **1 small potato, cubed**
- **1 small carrot, sliced**
- **1 cup chicken broth**
- **1 garlic clove, minced**
- **1/4 teaspoon dried tarragon, crushed**
- **1/8 teaspoon salt, optional**
- **Dash pepper**
- **2 teaspoons chopped fresh parsley**

Coat a saucepan with cooking spray; brown chicken over medium-high heat. Add the next eight ingredients; bring to a boil. Reduce heat. Cover and simmer for 20-25 minutes or until vegetables are tender. Sprinkle with parsley.

corny chicken soup

PREP: 10 min. • **COOK:** 1-1/4 hours • **YIELD:** 8 servings.

The spices really liven up the flavor in this filling soup. This recipe is easily doubled and freezes well. anne smithson // cary, north carolina

- **1 carton (32 ounces) reduced-sodium chicken broth plus 1 can (14-1/2 ounces) reduced-sodium chicken broth**
- **1 can (14-1/2 ounces) crushed tomatoes, undrained**
- **1 can (14-1/2 ounces) diced tomatoes, undrained**
- **1 pound boneless skinless chicken breast, cut into 1/2-inch cubes**
- **1 large onion, chopped**
- **1/3 cup minced fresh cilantro**
- **1 can (4 ounces) chopped green chilies**
- **1 garlic clove, minced**
- **1 teaspoon chili powder**
- **1 teaspoon ground cumin**
- **1/2 teaspoon dried oregano**
- **1/4 teaspoon cayenne pepper**
- **3 cups frozen corn, thawed**
- **Tortilla chips**
- **1 cup (4 ounces) shredded reduced-fat cheddar *or* Mexican cheese blend**

In a large saucepan, combine the first 12 ingredients. Bring to a boil. Reduce heat; cover and simmer for 1 hour. Add corn; cook 10 minutes longer. Top each serving with tortilla chips; sprinkle with cheese.

wild rice chicken soup

PREP/TOTAL TIME: 30 min. • **YIELD:** 5 servings.

Wild rice gives soup extra appeal. This hearty blend is chock-full of tender thigh meat and veggies and pleasantly seasoned with savory and garlic. taste of home test kitchen

- **1/4 cup *each* chopped carrot, celery, green pepper and onion**
- **1/4 cup chopped peeled parsnip**
- **2 teaspoons canola oil**
- **2 cans (14-1/2 ounces *each*) chicken broth**
- **3/4 pound bone-in chicken thighs, skin removed**
- **1/2 teaspoon dried savory**
- **1 garlic clove, minced**
- **1/8 teaspoon salt**
- **1/8 teaspoon pepper**
- **1 cup cooked long grain and wild rice**

In a large saucepan, saute the carrot, celery, green pepper, onion and parsnip in oil for 3 minutes or until crisp-tender. Add the broth, chicken, savory, garlic, salt and pepper. Bring to a boil. Reduce heat; cover and simmer for 15 minutes or until chicken is no longer pink.

Remove chicken from broth. When cool enough to handle, remove meat from bones and cut into bite-size pieces. Discard bones. Add chicken and rice to soup; heat through.

simple chicken soup

PREP/TOTAL TIME: 20 min. • **YIELD:** 6 servings.

I revised a chicken soup recipe that my family loved so it would be lighter and easier to make. My version is a healthy meal when you add a green salad and fresh bread. sue west // alvord, texas

- **2 cans (14-1/2 ounces *each*) reduced-sodium chicken broth**
- **1 tablespoon dried minced onion**
- **1 package (16 ounces) frozen mixed vegetables**
- **2 cups cubed cooked chicken breast**
- **2 cans (10-3/4 ounces *each*) reduced-fat reduced-sodium condensed cream of chicken soup, undiluted**

In a large saucepan, bring broth and onion to a boil. Reduce heat. Add the vegetables; cover and cook for 6-8 minutes or until crisp-tender. Stir in the chicken and soup; heat through.

ONION OPTIONS

If you don't have dried minced onion for this recipe, substitute fresh onion. One tablespoon of dried minced onion equals 1/4 cup minced raw onion. These choices will produce the best flavor, but if you're out of both dried and fresh onion, use 3/4 teaspoon of onion powder for similar results.

stone soup

PREP: 15 min. • **COOK:** 40 min. • **YIELD:** 12 servings.

We enjoyed concocting our own version of the folktale classic. It's loaded with veggies and other ingredients, so all your guests can bring something to add to the fun and flavor! taste of home test kitchen

- **4 cans (14-1/2 ounces *each*) chicken broth**
- **4 medium red potatoes, cut into eighths**
- **1 yellow summer squash, chopped**
- **2 medium carrots, chopped**
- **1 medium onion, chopped**
- **2 celery ribs, chopped**
- **1 teaspoon dried thyme**
- **1/2 teaspoon pepper**
- **4 cups cubed cooked chicken**
- **1 cup frozen cut green beans**
- **1/2 cup quick-cooking barley**
- **1 can (14-1/2 ounces) diced tomatoes, undrained**
- **4 cups salad croutons**
- **1 cup shredded Parmesan cheese**

In a Dutch oven, combine the first eight ingredients. Bring to a boil. Reduce heat; cover and simmer for 10-15 minutes or until vegetables are crisp-tender.

Stir in the chicken, beans and barley. Bring to a boil. Reduce heat; cover and simmer for 10-12 minutes or until vegetables and barley are tender. Add tomatoes; heat through. Serve with croutons and cheese.

home-style chicken soup

PREP: 15 min.
COOK: 6 hours 10 min.
YIELD: 4 servings.

I've relied on this easy soup many times over the years. Mom gave me the recipe, and we love it so much that we eat it year-round.
kathy rairigh // milford, indiana

- **1 can (14-1/2 ounces) chicken broth**
- **1 can (14-1/2 ounces) diced tomatoes, undrained**
- **1 cup cubed cooked chicken**
- **1 can (8 ounces) mushroom stems and pieces, drained**
- **1/4 cup sliced fresh carrot**
- **1/4 cup sliced celery**
- **1 bay leaf**
- **1/8 teaspoon dried thyme**
- **3/4 cup cooked egg noodles**

In a 1-1/2-qt. slow cooker, combine the first eight ingredients. Cover and cook on low for 6 hours. Stir in noodles; cover and cook on high for 10 minutes. Discard bay leaf.

tortilla-vegetable chicken soup

PREP: 20 min. • **COOK:** 15 min. • **YIELD:** 6 servings.

Surprisingly, this recipe is a snap. Don't worry about the long list of ingredients; most of them are already in your pantry.

jan peri-wyrick // fort worth, texas

- **3 flour tortillas (6 inches), cut into 1-inch strips**
- **1/4 cup chicken drippings, optional**
- **1 cup chopped celery**
- **3/4 cup finely chopped carrot**
- **1/2 cup chopped red onion**
- **2 tablespoons olive oil**
- **3 cans (14-1/2 ounces *each*) reduced-sodium chicken broth**
- **1 can (15 ounces) black beans, rinsed and drained**
- **1 can (14-1/2 ounces) beef broth**
- **1 can (10 ounces) diced tomatoes with mild green chilies**
- **2 cups cubed cooked chicken breast**
- **2 cups frozen corn**
- **2 teaspoons dried parsley flakes**
- **1 teaspoon garlic powder**
- **1 teaspoon dried basil**
- **1 teaspoon ground cumin**
- **1 teaspoon ground coriander**
- **Shredded Monterey Jack cheese, optional**

Place tortilla strips on a baking sheet coated with cooking spray; bake at 350° for 8-10 minutes or until lightly browned. Set aside.

Meanwhile, skim fat from drippings. In a Dutch oven, saute the celery, carrot and onion in oil until tender. Stir in chicken broth, black beans, beef broth, tomatoes, chicken, corn, seasonings and drippings if desired. Bring to a boil. Reduce heat; simmer, uncovered, for 15 minutes.

Serve with cheese if desired and tortilla strips.

HANDY CUBED COOKED CHICKEN

To make cubed cooked chicken for recipes, simmer some boneless chicken breasts in a little water seasoned with salt, pepper and your favorite herbs. Cool and dice; keep this handy chicken in the freezer for use later. Consider freezing it in 1-cup portions.

florentine chicken soup

PREP/TOTAL TIME: 30 min. • **YIELD:** 5 cups.

My husband loves Alfredo sauce, so I'm always looking for new variations. This soup comes together quickly, and it's wonderful with crusty Italian bread and a tomato-mozzarella-basil salad. Best of all, it's the perfect amount for the two of us.

cindie henf // sebastian, florida

- **1 cup uncooked penne pasta**
- **1 package (6 ounces) ready-to-use chicken breast cuts**
- **4 cups chopped fresh spinach**
- **1 jar (7 ounces) roasted sweet red peppers, drained and sliced**
- **3 fresh rosemary sprigs, chopped**
- **1/2 teaspoon garlic powder**
- **1/4 teaspoon pepper**
- **1 tablespoon butter**
- **1-1/2 cups reduced-sodium chicken broth**
- **3/4 cup Alfredo sauce**
- **3 tablespoons prepared pesto**
- **2 tablespoons pine nuts, toasted**
- **1 tablespoon shredded Parmesan cheese**

Cook pasta according to package directions. Meanwhile, in a large saucepan, saute the chicken, spinach, red peppers, rosemary, garlic powder and pepper in butter until the spinach is wilted. Stir in the broth, Alfredo sauce and pesto; cook for 4-5 minutes or until heated through.

Drain pasta and add to the soup. Sprinkle with pine nuts and cheese.

WHAT'S A PINE NUT?

Also know as pignolia or pinon, the pine nut is a small seed from one of several varieties of pine trees. The elongated ivory-colored nuts measure about 3/8 inch and have a soft texture and buttery flavor. Frequently used in Italian dishes and sauces such as pesto, pine nuts are often toasted to enhance their flavor.

chinese chicken soup

PREP/TOTAL TIME: 25 min.
YIELD: 6 servings.

This attractive, simple soup begins with frozen stir-fry vegetables. Consider using convenient refrigerated minced gingerroot for easy Asian flavor.
taste of home test kitchen

- **3 cans (14-1/2 ounces *each*) chicken broth**
- **1 package (16 ounces) frozen stir-fry vegetable blend**
- **2 cups cubed cooked chicken**
- **1 teaspoon minced fresh gingerroot**
- **1 teaspoon soy sauce**
- **1/4 teaspoon sesame oil**

In a large saucepan, combine all the ingredients. Bring to a boil. Reduce heat; cover and simmer for 15 minutes or until heated through.

swedish potato dumpling soup

PREP: 20 min. • **COOK:** 30 min. + simmering
YIELD: 12 servings (3 quarts).

Family and friends gather around our table throughout the year to enjoy good company and great food. As part of our traditional Christmas Eve meal, I serve this hearty soup. margaret peterson // genoa, nebraska

- **1 broiler/fryer chicken (3-1/2 to 4 pounds), cut up**
- **6-1/2 cups water**
- **2 teaspoons salt, optional**
- **2 celery ribs, quartered**
- **1 medium carrot, quartered**
- **1 small onion, peeled**
- **4 whole peppercorns**
- **2 whole cloves**
- **2 whole allspice**
- **2 chicken bouillon cubes**
- **1 package (9 ounces) frozen cut green beans**
- **1 package (12 ounces) frozen noodles**

DUMPLINGS:

- **2 medium potatoes, cooked and mashed (without added milk *or* butter)**
- **1 egg, beaten *or* egg substitute equivalent**
- **2 tablespoons half-and-half cream**
- **1 teaspoon sugar**
- **1/4 teaspoon salt, optional**
- **1/2 cup all-purpose flour**

In a 5-qt. soup kettle, combine the first 10 ingredients. Cover and slowly bring to a boil. Reduce heat; simmer for 3 hours. Remove chicken; set aside until cool enough to handle.

Strain broth, discarding vegetables and seasonings. Add enough water to make 8 cups; return to kettle. Remove chicken from bones; discard bones and skin. Cut chicken into chunks; add to kettle along with beans and noodles. Bring to a boil; cook for 20 minutes.

For dumplings, combine the potatoes, egg, cream, sugar and salt if desired in a medium bowl. Gradually add flour to make a stiff dough (it should form a peak when spoon is lifted). Drop by teaspoons into boiling soup. Cover and simmer for 3 minutes.

chunky chicken noodle soup

PREP/TOTAL TIME: 25 min. • **YIELD:** 6 servings.

Marjoram and thyme come through nicely in this old-fashioned soup that tastes just like the one Grandma used to make. You can modify the recipe to include vegetables your family enjoys. My kids love carrots, so I always toss in extra.

coleen martin // brookfield, wisconsin

- **1/2 cup diced carrot**
- **1/4 cup diced celery**
- **1/4 cup chopped onion**
- **1 teaspoon butter**
- **6 cups chicken broth**
- **1-1/2 cups diced cooked chicken**
- **1 teaspoon salt**
- **1/2 teaspoon dried marjoram**
- **1/2 teaspoon dried thyme**
- **1/8 teaspoon pepper**
- **1-1/4 cups uncooked medium egg noodles**
- **1 tablespoon minced fresh parsley**

In a large saucepan, saute the carrot, celery and onion in butter until tender. Stir in the broth, chicken and seasonings; bring to a boil. Reduce heat. Add noodles; cook for 10 minutes or until noodles are tender. Sprinkle with parsley.

ONION AT THE READY

I keep a peeled onion in a glass jar in my refrigerator. It's handy when I need a small amount of chopped onion for a recipe or my husband wants a slice of onion on a sandwich. It stays fresh in the jar, eliminating waste.

dorothy g. // tewksbury, massachusetts

chicken noodle soup

PREP: 1 hour • **COOK:** 2-1/2 hours • **YIELD:** 64 servings (1 cup each).

This classic comfort food is perfect for those days when someone you love feels under the weather. It makes a big batch, so you can freeze the leftovers to have on hand when you're rushed for time. stacey christensen // west valley city, utah

- **4 whole broiler/fryer chickens (3 to 4 pounds *each*)**
- **10 quarts water**
- **3 bunches celery, chopped**
- **2 pounds carrots, sliced**
- **2 large onions, chopped**
- **2 jars (8 ounces *each*) chicken base**
- **1/4 cup dried parsley flakes**
- **Salt and pepper to taste**
- **2-1/2 pounds uncooked fine egg noodles**

Divide chickens and water between two stockpots. Slowly bring to a boil over low heat. Cover and simmer for 2 hours or until meat is tender, skimming the surface as foam rises. Remove chickens from broth; set aside until cool enough to handle.

Add the celery, carrots, onions, chicken base and parsley to the pots; season with salt and pepper. Cover and simmer for 15-20 minutes or until vegetables are tender.

Cook noodles according to package directions; drain. Stir into soup. Remove chicken meat from bones; cut into bite-size pieces. Add to soup; heat through. Serve desired amount. Cool remaining soup; transfer to freezer containers. Freeze for up to 3 months.

TO USE FROZEN SOUP: Thaw in the refrigerator overnight. Place in a saucepan and heat through.

EDITOR'S NOTE: Look for chicken base near the broth and bouillon.

FREEZE SOUPS FOR FUTURE MEALS

Make soups when you have time, then freeze them for fast future meals. Here are some hints for freezing: To cool soup quickly before freezing, place the kettle in a sink filled with ice water. When cool, transfer to airtight freezer-safe containers, leaving 1/4 inch of headspace for expansion. Most soups freeze nicely. The exceptions are those made with cream and potatoes, which are better when eaten fresh. Pasta in soup can get mushy in the freezer. It's best to add the pasta when you're ready to eat, not before freezing. To help retain a soup's flavor, don't freeze for longer than three months. Thaw frozen soup completely in the refrigerator and reheat in a saucepan.

best chicken noodle soup

PREP: 2 hours • **COOK:** 30 min.
YIELD: 10 servings (2-3/4 quarts).

For years, I worked at making a chicken soup that tasted just like my mother's. When I realized I couldn't, I decided to come up with my own recipe. It was an immediate hit! People enjoy the vegetables, noodles and the flavor of rosemary.
cheryl rogers // ames, iowa

- **1 tablespoon dried rosemary, crushed**
- **2 teaspoons garlic powder**
- **2 teaspoons pepper**
- **2 teaspoons seasoned salt**
- **2 broiler/fryer chickens (3 to 3-1/2 pounds *each*)**
- **5 cups chicken broth**
- **2-1/4 cups sliced fresh mushrooms**
- **1/2 cup chopped celery**
- **1/2 cup sliced carrots**
- **1/2 cup chopped onion**
- **1/4 teaspoon pepper**

NOODLES:

- **2-1/4 cups all-purpose flour**
- **1 teaspoon salt**
- **2 eggs**
- **1 can (5 ounces) evaporated milk**
- **1 tablespoon olive oil**

Combine the first four ingredients; rub over chickens. Place in an ungreased 13-in. x 9-in. baking pan. Cover and bake at 350° for 1-1/4 hours or until a meat thermometer reads 180°. Drain and reserve drippings. Skim fat. When cool enough to handle, remove meat from bones; discard bones. Cut meat into bite-size pieces. Cover chicken and refrigerate.

In a Dutch oven or soup kettle, bring chicken broth and reserved drippings to a boil. Add the mushrooms, celery, carrots, onion and pepper; simmer for 30 minutes or until vegetables are tender.

In a large bowl, combine flour and salt. Make a well in the center. Beat eggs, milk and oil; pour into well. Stir together, forming a dough. Turn dough onto a floured surface; knead 8-10 times. Divide dough into thirds. Roll out each portion to 1/8-in. thickness; cut to desired width.

Freeze two portions to use at another time. Bring soup to a boil. Add one portion of noodles; cook for 7-9 minutes or until noodles are almost tender. Add chicken; heat through.

soothing chicken soup

PREP/TOTAL TIME: 20 min.
YIELD: 16 servings (4 quarts).

I made a few improvements to a fast-to-fix recipe to create this comforting soup. It's easy to stir up with broth, soup mix and instant rice. kris countryman // joliet, illinois

- **2 cups sliced celery**
- **3 quarts chicken broth**
- **4 cups cubed cooked chicken**
- **1 can (10-3/4 ounces) condensed cream of mushroom soup, undiluted**
- **1 cup uncooked instant rice**
- **1 envelope onion soup mix**
- **1 teaspoon poultry seasoning**
- **1/2 teaspoon seasoned salt**
- **1/2 teaspoon dried thyme**
- **1/2 teaspoon pepper**

In a Dutch oven or soup kettle, simmer celery in broth until tender. Stir in the remaining ingredients. Bring to a boil. Reduce heat; cover and simmer for 6-8 minutes or until the rice is tender.

flower garden soup

PREP: 15 min. • **COOK:** 30 min. • **YIELD:** 8 servings (2 quarts).

Fresh vegetables flavor traditional chicken soup in this bountiful blend. To add seasonal fun, cut notches in the carrots and zucchini to make "petals" before slicing them, then simmer up bowls of blooms! taste of home test kitchen

- **6 medium carrots**
- **1 medium zucchini**
- **4 celery ribs, chopped**
- **1 medium onion, chopped**
- **8 cans (14-1/2 ounces *each*) chicken broth**
- **1 teaspoon dried basil**
- **1 teaspoon dried oregano**
- **4 cups cubed cooked chicken**

Using a zest stripper or paring knife, cut a lengthwise strip on each carrot, forming a notch. Repeat at equal intervals around carrot. Repeat with zucchini. Cut carrots and zucchini into 1/4-in. slices; set zucchini aside.

In a Dutch oven or soup kettle, combine the carrots, celery, onion, broth, basil and oregano. Bring to a boil. Reduce heat; cover and simmer for 20-30 minutes or until vegetables are crisp-tender.

Add chicken and reserved zucchini; simmer, uncovered, for 10 minutes or until the zucchini is tender.

turkey noodle soup

PREP: 10 min. • **COOK:** 35 min.
YIELD: 7 servings.

Homemade taste makes this chunky, budget-friendly soup a favorite of mine. We enjoy it with hot bread in winter and with salad in summer.
elaine bickford // las vegas, nevada

- **2 cans (14-1/2 ounces *each*) chicken broth**
- **3 cups water**
- **1-3/4 cups sliced carrots**
- **1/2 cup chopped onion**
- **2 celery ribs, sliced**
- **1 package (12 ounces) frozen egg noodles**
- **3 cups chopped cooked turkey**
- **1 package (10 ounces) frozen peas**
- **2 envelopes chicken gravy mix**
- **1/2 cup cold water**

In a large saucepan, bring the broth, water, carrots, onion and celery to a boil. Reduce heat; cover and simmer for 4-6 minutes or until vegetables are crisp-tender. Add the noodles. Simmer, uncovered, for 20 minutes or until the noodles are tender.

Stir in turkey and peas. Combine gravy mixes and cold water until smooth; stir into soup. Bring to a boil; cook and stir for 2 minutes or until thickened.

tasty tortilla soup

PREP: 20 min. • **COOK:** 40 min. • **YIELD:** 7 servings.

Switch out the ingredients to match your own personal tastes. You can use packaged mesquite-flavored chicken, add more tomatoes and onions, or get creative with the cheeses. Luckily for me, though, when I entered this in a recipe contest, the judges absolutely loved it just the way it is! jennifer giles // des moines, iowa

- 1 large onion, chopped
- 2 green onions, thinly sliced
- 2 tablespoons butter
- 4 garlic cloves, minced
- 2 tablespoons all-purpose flour
- 4-1/2 cups reduced-sodium chicken broth
- 2 cans (14-1/2 ounces *each*) no-salt-added diced tomatoes, undrained
- 1 can (8 ounces) no-salt-added tomato sauce
- 1 can (4 ounces) chopped green chilies
- 1 tablespoon minced fresh oregano *or* 1 teaspoon dried oregano
- 2 teaspoons ground cumin
- 1/4 teaspoon pepper
- 3 cups cubed cooked chicken breast
- 2 tablespoons minced fresh cilantro
- 1-1/3 cups crushed baked tortilla chip scoops
- 7 tablespoons shredded reduced-fat cheddar cheese

In a Dutch oven, saute onion and green onions in butter until tender. Add garlic; cook 1 minute longer.

Stir in flour until blended; gradually add broth. Stir in the tomatoes, tomato sauce, chilies, oregano, cumin and pepper. Bring to a boil. Reduce heat; cover and simmer for 20 minutes. Add chicken and cilantro; heat through.

For each serving, place 2 tablespoons chips in a soup bowl. Top with 1-1/2 cups soup. Garnish each serving with 1 tablespoon each of cheese and more chips.

SPEEDY SLICED GREEN ONIONS

I recently tried a recipe that called for 3/4 cup green onions. Instead of using a knife, I snipped the onions with a pair of kitchen scissors. I had chopped onions in only a few seconds. kristy b. // kelowna, british columbia

old-fashioned turkey soup

PREP: 25 min. • **COOK:** 2-3/4 hours
YIELD: 22 servings (5-1/2 quarts).

For added convenience, freeze some of this delicious big-batch soup in individual serving-size portions.

linda sand // winsted, connecticut

- 1 leftover turkey carcass (from a 12-pound turkey)
- 5 quarts water

SOUP:

- 3 cups cubed cooked turkey
- 1 can (28 ounces) stewed tomatoes
- 1 large onion, chopped
- 2 large carrots, shredded
- 1 cup chopped celery
- 1 package (10 ounces) frozen chopped spinach, thawed
- 3/4 cup fresh *or* frozen peas
- 3/4 cup uncooked long grain rice
- 4 teaspoons chicken bouillon granules
- 2 teaspoons salt
- 3/4 teaspoon pepper
- 1/2 teaspoon dried marjoram
- 1/2 teaspoon dried thyme

Place the turkey carcass and water in a Dutch oven or soup kettle; slowly bring to a boil over low heat. Cover and simmer for 1-1/2 hours.

Remove carcass and discard. Strain broth through a cheesecloth-lined colander. If using immediately, skim fat or refrigerate for 8 hours or overnight; remove fat from surface. Stock may be refrigerated for up to 3 days or frozen for 4 to 6 months.

For soup, return strained broth to pan. Add turkey, vegetables, rice, bouillon and seasonings; bring to a boil. Reduce heat; cover and simmer for 30 minutes or until the rice and vegetables are tender.

TURKEY BARLEY SOUP: Prepare stock as directed. For soup, omit stewed tomatoes and rice. Bring stock to a boil; add 1 cup uncooked medium pearl barley. Reduce heat; cover and simmer for 30 minutes. Add remaining ingredients. Cook, uncovered, for 20-25 minutes or until barley and vegetables are tender.

chicken gumbo

PREP: 40 min. • **COOK:** 35 min.
YIELD: 48 servings (1 cup each).

Chicken, ham, shrimp, rice and a whole host of good-for-you vegetables make this gumbo a surefire people-pleaser.

willa govoro // st. clair, missouri

- 6 celery ribs, chopped
- 3 medium green peppers, chopped
- 3 medium onions, chopped
- 3/4 cup butter, cubed
- 10 quarts chicken broth
- 7 cans (14-1/2 ounces *each*) diced tomatoes, undrained
- 3 bay leaves
- 2 tablespoons minced fresh parsley
- 1 tablespoon pepper
- 2 to 3 tablespoons garlic powder
- 2 teaspoons salt
- 2 cups uncooked long grain rice
- 10 cups cubed cooked chicken
- 6 cups cubed fully cooked ham
- 1 package (16 ounces) frozen chopped okra
- 2 pounds cooked small shrimp, peeled and deveined, optional

In several large stock pots, saute celery, green peppers and onions in butter until tender. Add the next seven ingredients; bring to a boil. Stir in rice. Reduce heat; cover and simmer for 15-20 minutes or until rice is tender.

Stir in chicken, ham, okra and shrimp if desired. Simmer for 8-10 minutes or until the shrimp turn pink and okra is tender. Discard bay leaves.

turkey tomato soup

PREP: 10 min. • **COOK:** 2-1/2 hours • **YIELD:** 12 servings (3 quarts).

Turkey and tomatoes are high on my list of favorite foods, and I created this recipe to showcase both ingredients. It's wonderful any time of year, but I prefer to make it when the tomatoes, green peppers, basil and garlic are all fresh from our garden. It helps that my husband grows the best tomatoes ever. carol brunelle // ascutney, vermont

- **4 pounds tomatoes, seeded and chopped (about 8 large tomatoes)**
- **3 medium green peppers, chopped**
- **2 cans (14-1/2 ounces *each*) reduced-sodium chicken broth**
- **1 can (14-1/2 ounces) vegetable broth**
- **1-1/2 cups water**
- **1-1/2 teaspoons beef bouillon granules**
- **2 garlic cloves, minced**
- **1 teaspoon dried oregano**
- **1 teaspoon dried basil**
- **1/2 teaspoon pepper**
- **3 cups cubed cooked turkey breast**
- **3 cups cooked elbow macaroni**
- **Minced fresh basil, optional**

In a Dutch oven, combine the first 10 ingredients. Bring to a boil. Reduce heat; cover and simmer for 2 hours. Stir in turkey and macaroni; heat through. Garnish with fresh basil if desired.

SEEDING A TOMATO

To seed a tomato, cut it in half and gently squeeze each half. Seeding a tomato this way not only removes the seeds, it also eliminates some of the juice that can make a dish too watery. If you don't want to lose as much juice, try using a small spoon to scoop out the seeds.

santa fe cheese soup

PREP/TOTAL TIME: 25 min.
YIELD: 6-8 servings (2 quarts).

My husband and I are retired, but I still look for shortcut recipes like this one I received from a great-niece. You'll likely have the majority of ingredients for this colorful soup in your pantry. To save time, I start warming the canned ingredients on the stove while I cube the cheese. modie phillips // lubbock, texas

1 can (15-1/4 ounces) whole kernel corn, drained
1 can (15 ounces) pinto beans, rinsed and drained
1 can (14-1/2 ounces) chicken broth
1 can (10 ounces) diced tomatoes and green chilies, undrained
1 can (10 ounces) premium chunk white chicken, drained
1 can (4 ounces) chopped green chilies
1 pound process American cheese (Velveeta), cubed
Crushed tortilla chips, optional

In a 3-qt. saucepan, combine the first seven ingredients. Cook and stir until cheese is melted. Garnish with tortilla chips if desired.

harvest turkey soup

PREP: 20 min. simmering • **COOK:** 40 min.
YIELD: 12 servings (1-1/3 cups each).

This hearty, chunky soup is the perfect answer to your Turkey Day leftovers. Combining the earthy flavors of curry and cumin, no one will mistake it for canned soup! jane scanlon // marco island, florida

1 leftover turkey carcass (from a 12- to 14-pound turkey)
4-1/2 quarts water
1 medium onion, quartered
1 medium carrot, cut into 2-inch pieces
1 celery rib, cut into 2-inch pieces

SOUP:

2 cups shredded cooked turkey
4 celery ribs, chopped
2 cups fresh *or* frozen corn
2 medium carrots, sliced
1 large onion, chopped
1 cup uncooked orzo pasta
2 tablespoons minced fresh parsley
4 teaspoons chicken bouillon granules
1 teaspoon salt
1 teaspoon curry powder
1/2 teaspoon ground cumin
1/2 teaspoon pepper

Place the turkey carcass in a stockpot; add the water, onion, carrot and celery. Slowly bring to a boil over low heat; cover and simmer for 1-1/2 hours.

Discard carcass. Strain broth through a cheesecloth-lined colander. If using immediately, skim fat. Or cool, then refrigerate for 8 hours or overnight; remove fat from surface before using. (Broth may be refrigerated for up to 3 days or frozen for 4-6 months.)

Place the soup ingredients in a stockpot; add the broth. Bring to a boil. Reduce heat; cover and simmer for 30 minutes or until pasta and vegetables are tender.

chicken soup with beans

PREP: 15 min. • **COOK:** 6 hours
YIELD: 12 servings (3 quarts).

I put lime-flavored tortilla chips at the bottom of individual bowls before ladling in this Southwestern soup. Loaded with chicken, beans, corn, tomatoes and green chilies, it's satisfying and fuss-free. penny peronia // west memphis, arkansas

- **1 large onion, chopped**
- **1 tablespoon canola oil**
- **2 garlic cloves, minced**
- **1-1/4 pounds boneless skinless chicken breasts, cooked and cubed**
- **2 cans (15-1/2 ounces *each*) great northern beans, rinsed and drained**
- **3 cans (7 ounces *each*) white *or* shoepeg corn, drained**
- **1 can (10 ounces) diced tomatoes and green chilies, undrained**
- **3 cups water**
- **1 can (4 ounces) chopped green chilies**
- **2 tablespoons lime juice**
- **1 teaspoon lemon-pepper seasoning**
- **1 teaspoon ground cumin**
- **1/4 teaspoon salt**
- **1/4 teaspoon pepper**

In a small skillet, saute onion in oil until tender. Add garlic; cook 1 minute longer.

Transfer to a 5-qt. slow cooker. Stir in the chicken, beans, corn, tomatoes, water, chopped green chilies, lime juice and seasonings. Cover and cook on low for 6-7 hours or until heated through.

mom's tomato vegetable soup

PREP: 15 min. • **COOK:** 3-1/4 hours
YIELD: 18 servings (4-1/2 quarts).

I created this vegetable-based soup using a recipe my mom used when I was a child. The robust, down-home taste brings back memories of growing up on the farm.
sandra davis // brownsville, tennessee

- **1 broiler/fryer chicken (3 to 3-1/2 pounds), cut up**
- **8 cups water**
- **1 celery rib, halved**
- **1 medium onion, halved**
- **3 medium potatoes, peeled and cut into 1/2-inch cubes**
- **2 cups tomato juice**
- **1 can (15 ounces) mixed vegetables, drained**
- **1 can (15-1/2 ounces) black-eyed peas, rinsed and drained**
- **1 can (14-1/2 ounces) stewed tomatoes**
- **1/2 cup chopped onion**
- **2-1/2 teaspoons salt, optional**
- **1 teaspoon pepper**
- **1/2 pound lean ground beef (90% lean)**
- **1 can (15 ounces) cream-style corn**

In an 8-qt. soup kettle, place chicken, water, celery and onion. Cover and slowly bring to a boil; skim fat. Reduce heat; cover and simmer for 1-1/2 hours or until chicken falls off the bones.

Strain broth and skim fat; return broth to kettle. Add the next eight ingredients. Debone chicken and cut into chunks; return to kettle. Bring to a boil.

Meanwhile, in a medium skillet, cook the beef until no longer pink; drain and add to soup. Reduce heat; cover and simmer for 1 hour. Stir in the corn; cook, uncovered, for 30 minutes, stirring occasionally.

red bean 'n' sausage soup

PREP: 10 min. • **COOK:** 55 min.
YIELD: 8 servings (2 quarts).

We have many cold months in the northwest, and hearty soups served with hot rolls help warm us up. My mom got the recipe for this delicious soup—brimming with kidney beans, apples and turkey sausage—at a country restaurant nearby. Guests always ask for a copy. tami christman // lima, montana

- **1 pound turkey Italian sausage links, casings removed**
- **1 medium onion, diced**
- **3 cups chicken broth**
- **3 medium tart apples, peeled and chopped**
- **1 can (14-1/2 ounces) crushed tomatoes, undrained**
- **2 tablespoons cider vinegar**
- **2 tablespoons chopped green pepper**
- **2 tablespoons chopped sweet red pepper**
- **2 tablespoons brown sugar**
- **1/2 teaspoon seasoned salt**
- **1/2 teaspoon ground mustard**
- **1/4 teaspoon rubbed sage**
- **1/4 teaspoon chili powder**
- **1/4 teaspoon pepper**
- **1 can (16 ounces) kidney beans, rinsed and drained**

In a large saucepan or soup kettle, cook the sausage and onion until meat is no longer pink; drain. Add the next 12 ingredients. Bring to a boil. Reduce heat; cover and simmer for 45 minutes, stirring occasionally. Add beans; heat through.

tuscan turkey sausage soup

PREP/TOTAL TIME: 30 min. • **YIELD:** 8 servings.

While trying to reproduce my favorite soup from an Italian restaurant's menu, I hit upon this tasty combination of turkey sausage, broth and mushrooms. Fennel, caraway seeds and the herb seasoning provide ample flavor without adding salt. Serve this soup steaming hot alongside a crisp salad and bread for a well-rounded meal.
thomas licking // green lake, wisconsin

- **12 ounces turkey Italian sausage links**
- **4 cups reduced-sodium chicken broth**
- **1 can (10-3/4 ounces) reduced-fat reduced-sodium condensed cream of chicken soup, undiluted**
- **1 can (8 ounces) mushroom stems and pieces, drained**
- **1 small onion, chopped**
- **1 tablespoon Italian seasoning**
- **1/4 teaspoon salt-free garlic and herb seasoning**
- **1/8 teaspoon caraway seeds**
- **1/8 teaspoon fennel seed, crushed**
- **1 can (15-1/2 ounces) great northern beans, rinsed and drained**
- **1 small leek (white portion only), cut into 1-inch strips**

In a nonstick skillet coated with cooking spray, cook sausage over medium heat until no longer pink; drain. Let cool and slice.

In a large saucepan, whisk together the broth, soup, mushrooms, onion, Italian seasoning, garlic and herb seasoning, caraway seeds and fennel seed. Add sausage. Bring to a boil.

Reduce heat; simmer, uncovered, for 5 minutes. Add beans and leek. Simmer 10 minutes longer or until vegetables are tender.

barley turkey soup

PREP: 15 min. • **COOK:** 30 min. • **YIELD:** 9 servings.

A steaming bowl of soup takes the bite out of the winter chill. I often make homemade stock using our leftover holiday turkey, so I sometimes substitute that for the broth in this recipe.

warrens constans // fruitland, idaho

8 cups chicken broth
1-1/2 cups diced celery
1 cup medium pearl barley
1 medium onion, diced
3/4 cup diced carrots
1/4 teaspoon salt
1/2 teaspoon dried thyme
1 bay leaf
1/8 teaspoon ground allspice
1/8 teaspoon pepper
Dash cayenne pepper
2 cups cubed cooked turkey
1/4 cup minced fresh parsley, optional

In a Dutch oven or soup kettle, combine the first 11 ingredients. Bring to a boil. Reduce heat; simmer, uncovered, for 30-40 minutes or until vegetables and barley are tender.

Stir in the turkey and parsley if desired; heat through. Discard bay leaf.

southern chicken rice soup

PREP: 25 min. • **COOK:** 2-1/2 hours + cooling
YIELD: 10 servings (about 2-1/2 quarts).

This is always on the menu when we have soup night at our church. My husband concocted the recipe after he retired. I frequently find it on the table when I get home from work.

rosalie biar // thorndale, texas

1 broiler/fryer chicken (about 3 pounds)
10 cups water
2 teaspoons salt
1/2 cup uncooked long grain rice
1/2 cup chopped onion
1/2 cup chopped celery
1/2 cup thinly sliced carrots
1/2 cup sliced fresh *or* frozen okra
1 can (14-1/2 ounces) stewed tomatoes, diced
1 tablespoon chopped green chilies
1 garlic clove, minced
1-1/2 teaspoons chili powder
1 teaspoon seasoned salt
1/2 teaspoon lemon-pepper seasoning
1/2 teaspoon Creole seasoning

Place chicken, water and salt in a Dutch oven or soup kettle. Slowly bring to a boil; skim foam. Reduce heat; cover and simmer for 45-60 minutes or until the chicken is tender.

Remove the chicken and set side until cool enough to handle. Remove meat from bones and discard bones and skin. Cut chicken into bite-size pieces. Skim fat from broth. Add the rice, vegetables and seasonings. Cook, uncovered, over medium heat for 30 minutes.

Add the chicken. Simmer for 30 minutes or until the vegetables are tender.

EDITOR'S NOTE: This spice mixture may be substituted for the Creole seasoning: 1/2 teaspoon each paprika and garlic powder, and a pinch each of cayenne pepper, dried thyme and ground cumin.

chicken tortilla soup

PREP/TOTAL TIME: 30 min. • **YIELD:** 6 servings.

The fresh lime and cilantro in this zesty soup reminds me of warmer climates—a nice bonus on blustery days here in northern Michigan. I lightened up the original recipe by baking the tortilla strips rather than frying them.

marianne morgan // traverse city, michigan

- **3 corn tortillas (6 inches), cut into 1/4-inch strips**
- **4 teaspoons olive oil, *divided***
- **1/4 teaspoon salt**
- **3/4 pound boneless skinless chicken breasts, cut into 1/2-inch chunks**
- **1 large onion, chopped**
- **5 cups reduced-sodium chicken broth**
- **1 pound red potatoes, cut into 1/2-inch cubes**
- **1 cup frozen corn**
- **1 can (4 ounces) chopped green chilies**
- **1/4 cup minced fresh cilantro**
- **1/4 teaspoon pepper**
- **3 tablespoons lime juice**

In a large resealable plastic bag, combine tortilla strips, 1 teaspoon oil and salt. Seal bag and shake to coat. Arrange tortilla strips on an ungreased baking sheet. Bake at 400° for 8-10 minutes or until crisp, stirring once. Remove to paper towels to cool.

In a large saucepan, saute chicken in remaining oil until no longer pink and lightly browned. Add onion; cook and stir until onion is tender. Add broth and potatoes.

Bring to a boil. Reduce heat; cover and simmer for 10 minutes. Add corn, chilies, cilantro and pepper. Cook until heated through. Stir in lime juice. Garnish with tortilla strips.

CILANTRO HINTS

With its slightly sharp flavor, cilantro—also known as Chinese parsley—gives a distinctive taste to Mexican, Latin American and Asian dishes. (The spice coriander comes from the seed of the cilantro plant.) Like all other fresh herbs, cilantro should be used as soon as possible. For short-term storage, immerse the freshly cut stems in water about 2 inches deep. Cover leaves loosely with a plastic bag and refrigerate for several days. Wash just before using.

italian sausage soup

PREP: 10 min. • **COOK:** 45 min. • **YIELD:** 8 servings.

This full-bodied soup will satisfy even the heartiest of appetites. Italian sausage gives the dish a wonderful rich flavor.
taste of home test kitchen

- **1 can (49-1/2 ounces) chicken broth**
- **2 cups cut fresh green beans**
- **1 can (15 ounces) cannellini *or* white kidney beans, rinsed and drained**
- **1 can (14-1/2 ounces) Italian diced tomatoes**
- **1 cup chopped onion**
- **1 cup chopped celery**
- **1 cup chopped fennel bulb**
- **1 can (6 ounces) tomato paste**
- **1 teaspoon dried oregano**
- **1/2 teaspoon white pepper**
- **5 Italian sausage links**
- **1 tablespoon olive oil**
- **3 cups coarsely chopped fresh spinach**
- **Shredded Parmesan cheese, optional**

In a Dutch oven, combine the first 10 ingredients. Bring to a boil. Reduce heat; cover and simmer for 20 minutes.

Meanwhile, in a large skillet, brown sausage in oil over medium heat. Add a small amount of hot water. Cover and cook until sausage is no longer pink; drain. Cut into 1/4-in. slices and add to soup. Simmer, uncovered, for 15 minutes.

Add spinach. Simmer, uncovered, for 5 minutes or until spinach is wilted. Garnish with Parmesan cheese if desired.

CELERY CUBES

When I have a bit of extra time, I chop a few stalks of celery. After sauteing them in a bit of margarine, I spoon them into ice cube trays, freeze, then pop the frozen "celery cubes" into a labeled freezer bag to store. They are an invaluable addition to soups or casseroles when I'm in a hurry. sally m. // neligh, nebraska

mulligatawny soup

PREP: 20 min. • **COOK:** 6 hours
YIELD: 8 servings (2 quarts).

I always try to use fresh fruits, herbs and vegetables in recipes. This is a delicious and satisfying soup that I make with chicken or any other meat I have left over.

mary ann marino
west pittsburg, pennsylvania

- **1 carton (32 ounces) chicken broth**
- **1 can (14-1/2 ounces) diced tomatoes**
- **2 cups cubed cooked chicken**
- **1 large tart apple, peeled and chopped**
- **1/4 cup finely chopped onion**
- **1/4 cup chopped carrot**
- **1/4 cup chopped green pepper**
- **1 tablespoon minced fresh parsley**
- **2 teaspoons lemon juice**
- **1 teaspoon salt**
- **1 teaspoon curry powder**
- **1/2 teaspoon sugar**
- **1/4 teaspoon pepper**
- **2 whole cloves**

In a 3- or 4-qt. slow cooker, combine all ingredients. Cover and cook on low for 6-8 hours or until vegetables are tender. Discard cloves.

italian chicken soup

PREP: 10 min. • **COOK:** 45 min. • **YIELD:** 4 servings.

This satisfying soup gets its Italian flair from fennel, thyme, basil and orzo pasta. If you don't start with a low-sodium or sodium-free stock, you might want to decrease the amount of salt called for in the recipe.

taste of home test kitchen

- **1 fennel bulb, chopped**
- **1/2 cup chopped onion**
- **2 teaspoons olive oil**
- **2 cups hot water**
- **4 cups reduced-sodium chicken broth**
- **1-1/2 cups chopped carrots**
- **1 teaspoon salt**
- **1/4 teaspoon dried thyme**
- **1/4 teaspoon dried basil**
- **1/4 teaspoon pepper**
- **2 cups cubed cooked chicken breast**
- **1/2 cup uncooked orzo pasta**
- **2 tablespoons finely chopped fennel fronds**

In a Dutch oven, saute fennel bulb and onion in oil until fennel is tender. Add the next seven ingredients. Bring to a boil. Reduced heat; cover and simmer for 15 minutes.

Stir in chicken and orzo. Cover and cook for 20 minutes or until orzo is tender. Stir in fennel fronds.

tuscan turkey soup

PREP/TOTAL TIME: 30 min. • **YIELD:** 8 servings (2 quarts).

Use your leftover holiday turkey to make this quick, creamy soup full of pumpkin and beans to feed hungry family and friends. It's simply fabulous! marie mcconnell // shelbyville, illinois

- **1 cup chopped onion**
- **1 cup chopped celery**
- **2 tablespoons olive oil**
- **1 teaspoon minced garlic**
- **2 cans (14-1/2 ounces *each*) chicken broth**
- **2 cups cubed cooked turkey**
- **1 can (15 ounces) solid-pack pumpkin**
- **1 can (15 ounces) white kidney *or* cannellini beans, rinsed and drained**
- **1/2 teaspoon salt**
- **1/2 teaspoon dried basil**
- **1/4 teaspoon pepper**
- **Shredded Parmesan cheese, optional**

In a large saucepan, saute onion and celery in oil until tender. Add the garlic; cook 1 minute longer. Stir in the broth, turkey, pumpkin, beans, salt, basil and pepper. Bring to a boil.

Reduce heat; simmer, uncovered, for 10-15 minutes or until heated through, stirring occasionally. Serve with cheese if desired.

HOMEMADE PUMPKIN PUREE

In the fall, pumpkins are usually inexpensive. I like to take advantage of this by purchasing several pie pumpkins and seeding and slicing them. I cook the slices in my pressure cooker until soft. When cool, I discard the skins, puree the pumpkin and put it in measured amounts in freezer containers. By storing the pumpkin in the freezer, it is readily available for making soups, casseroles, side dishes and pies. ruth b. // priest river, idaho

farmhouse chicken soup

PREP: 30 min. • **COOK:** 70 min. • **YIELD:** 10-12 servings (about 3 quarts).

Over the years, I've changed this recipe bit by bit until my family said it was perfect. I hope your family enjoys it as much as we do! janice mitchell // aurora, colorado

- 1 broiler/fryer chicken (3 to 3-1/2 pounds)
- 2 quarts water
- 1 large onion, chopped
- 1/2 cup chopped celery
- 1 cup diced carrots
- 2 garlic cloves, minced
- 2 teaspoons salt
- 1/2 teaspoon pepper
- 1/2 teaspoon poultry seasoning
- 1/4 teaspoon crushed red pepper flakes

SPAETZLE:

- 1-1/2 cups all-purpose flour
- 1/2 teaspoon salt
- 1/8 teaspoon baking powder
- 1/8 teaspoon ground nutmeg
- 2 eggs, well beaten
- 1/2 cup milk
- 1 tablespoon minced fresh parsley

Place the chicken and water in a Dutch oven. Bring to a boil; reduce heat. Add the onion, celery, carrots, garlic, salt, pepper, poultry seasoning and red pepper flakes. Cover and simmer for 1 hour or until chicken is tender.

Remove chicken from broth; cool. Skim fat from broth. Remove meat from bones; discard bones and skin. Cut meat into bite-size pieces; return to broth. Cover and simmer.

For spaetzle, combine the flour, salt, baking powder and nutmeg in a small bowl. Stir in the eggs, milk and parsley; blend well. With a rubber spatula, push batter through a large-hole grater or colander into simmering soup. Simmer, uncovered, for 10 minutes or until spaetzle float to the top.

WHAT IS SPAETZLE?

Spaetzle is a German noodle or dumpling made of flour, eggs, water or milk, salt and sometimes a little nutmeg. The dough is firm enough to roll out and cut into narrow strips and soft enough to force through a colander or spaetzle maker. The dough is then boiled in water, broth or soup for a very short time. If cooked alone, it can be tossed with butter or used in other side or main dishes.

gumbo in a jiffy

PREP/TOTAL TIME: 20 min. • **YIELD:** 6 servings.

This gumbo recipe could not be any easier to make. Try it on a busy weeknight with a side of crusty bread for dipping!

amy flack // homer city, pennsylvania

- **3 Italian turkey sausage links, sliced**
- **1 can (14-1/2 ounces) diced tomatoes with green peppers and onions, undrained**
- **1 can (14-1/2 ounces) reduced-sodium chicken broth**
- **1/2 cup water**
- **1 cup uncooked instant rice**
- **1 can (7 ounces) whole kernel corn, drained**

In a large saucepan, cook sausage until no longer pink; drain. Stir in the tomatoes, broth and water; bring to a boil. Stir in rice and corn; cover and remove from the heat. Let stand for 5 minutes.

INSTANT OR REGULAR RICE?

Instant rice (which is precooked before packaging) and long grain rice require different amounts of liquid during cooking, so they cannot be substituted measure for measure. Once prepared, you can use either kind of rice interchangeably in a recipe that calls for cooked rice.

minestrone with turkey

PREP/TOTAL TIME: 30 min. • **YIELD:** 6 servings (2 quarts).

I remember my mom making this soup; now I make it as often as I can. It's a good way to use up leftover vegetables. Sometimes I add a can of rinsed and drained kidney or garbanzo beans. angela goodman // kaneohe, hawaii

- **1 medium onion, chopped**
- **1 medium carrot, sliced**
- **1 celery rib, sliced**
- **1 garlic clove, minced**
- **1 tablespoon olive oil**
- **4 cups chicken broth *or* homemade turkey stock**
- **1 can (14-1/2 ounces) diced tomatoes, undrained**
- **2/3 cup *each* frozen peas, corn and cut green beans, thawed**
- **1/2 cup uncooked elbow macaroni**
- **1 teaspoon salt**
- **1/4 teaspoon dried basil**
- **1/4 teaspoon dried oregano**
- **1/4 teaspoon pepper**
- **1 bay leaf**
- **1 cup cubed cooked turkey**
- **1 small zucchini, halved lengthwise and cut into 1/4-inch slices**
- **1/4 cup grated Parmesan cheese, optional**

In a Dutch oven, saute the onion, carrot, celery and garlic in oil until tender. Add the broth, vegetables, macaroni and seasonings.

Bring to a boil. Reduce heat; simmer, uncovered, for 5 minutes. Add turkey and zucchini; cook until zucchini is crisp-tender. Discard bay leaf. Serve with Parmesan cheese if desired.

turkey cabbage soup

PREP: 15 min. • **COOK:** 20 min.
YIELD: 10 servings (about 3-1/2 quarts).

I learned to cook from my mother, who comes from Germany. She made this soup frequently when I was younger. The turkey is my addition to the recipe.
marlene schieferstein
decatur, indiana

- **1 pound lean ground turkey**
- **2 medium onions, chopped**
- **1 tablespoon canola oil**
- **3 pounds potatoes, peeled and cut into 1-inch pieces**
- **3 medium carrots, sliced**
- **1 small head cabbage, chopped**
- **1 can (49-1/2 ounces) reduced-sodium chicken broth**
- **1 tablespoon prepared Dijon mustard**
- **1-1/2 teaspoons prepared horseradish**
- **3/4 teaspoon salt**
- **1/2 teaspoon pepper**
- **2 teaspoons cornstarch**
- **1 tablespoon cold water**

In a Dutch oven, cook turkey and onions in oil over medium heat until turkey is no longer pink; drain. Add potatoes, carrots, cabbage, broth, mustard, horseradish, salt and pepper; bring to a boil. Reduce heat; cover and simmer for 15-20 minutes or until potatoes are tender, stirring occasionally.

Combine cornstarch and cold water until smooth; gradually stir into the soup. Bring to a boil; cook and stir for 2 minutes or until slightly thickened.

lemony chicken soup

PREP/TOTAL TIME: 25 min. • **YIELD:** 8 servings (2 quarts).

While living in California, I enjoyed a delicious chicken-lemon soup at a local restaurant. When I returned to Texas, I longed for it but never came across a recipe. I experimented with many versions before creating this one.

brenda tollett // san antonio, texas

1/3 cup butter, cubed
3/4 cup all-purpose flour
6 cups chicken broth
1 cup milk
1 cup half-and-half cream
1-1/2 cups cubed cooked chicken
1 tablespoon lemon juice
1/2 teaspoon salt
1/8 teaspoon pepper
Dash ground nutmeg
8 lemon slices

In a Dutch oven or large saucepan, melt butter. Stir in flour until smooth; gradually add the broth, milk and cream. Bring to a boil; cook and stir for 2 minutes or until thickened.

Stir in the chicken, lemon juice, salt, pepper and nutmeg. Cook over medium heat until heated through, stirring occasionally. Garnish each serving with a lemon slice.

MORE LEMON JUICE

To get more juice from a lemon, I soak the fruit in hot water for 15 minutes, then roll it on my kitchen counter. When I halve the lemon and squeeze it, the juice comes out more easily. anna victoria r. // albuquerque, new mexico

rainy day soup

PREP: 20 min.
COOK: 1-1/4 hours
YIELD: 12 servings (3 quarts).

One rainy day a few years back, the organizers of a local arts and crafts bazaar served this soup to visitors. Now my family members request it when they're feeling blue.
laine fengarinas // palm harbor, florida

- **1 pound ground turkey**
- **1 can (46 ounces) V8 juice**
- **1 jar (16 ounces) thick and chunky salsa**
- **1 can (14-1/2 ounces) chicken broth**
- **1 can (16 ounces) kidney beans, rinsed and drained**
- **1 package (10 ounces) frozen mixed vegetables**
- **4 cups shredded cabbage**
- **1 cup chopped onion**
- **1/2 cup cubed peeled potatoes**
- **1/3 cup medium pearl barley**

In a Dutch oven coated with cooking spray, cook turkey over medium heat until no longer pink; drain. Add the remaining ingredients; bring to a boil. Reduce heat; cover and simmer for 60-70 minutes or until the vegetables and barley are tender.

chicken vegetable soup

PREP: 10 min. • **COOK:** 40 min. • **YIELD:** 4 servings.

I'm always looking for recipes that are low in fat but don't taste like it. Even my picky son likes this healthy soup! anna overton // lakewood, california

- **1 pound boneless skinless chicken breasts, cut into cubes**
- **2 cups chicken broth, *divided***
- **1 teaspoon Italian seasoning**
- **1 garlic clove, minced**
- **1/4 teaspoon paprika**
- **4 small red potatoes, cut into 1-inch pieces**
- **3 small carrots, cut into 1/2-inch pieces**
- **5 celery ribs, cut into 1/2-inch pieces**
- **1 medium onion, cut into wedges**
- **2 tablespoons chopped celery leaves**
- **2 tablespoons all-purpose flour**
- **2 tablespoons minced fresh parsley**
- **1-1/2 teaspoons lemon juice**

In a large saucepan, combine the chicken, 1-3/4 cups broth, Italian seasoning, garlic and paprika. Bring to a boil. Reduce heat; cover and simmer for 10 minutes. Add the potatoes, carrots, celery, onion and celery leaves. Bring to a boil. Reduce heat; cover and simmer for 20-25 minutes or until vegetables are tender.

In a small bowl, combine flour and remaining broth until smooth; gradually add to pan. Bring to a boil; cook and stir for 2 minutes or until thickened. Stir in parsley and lemon juice.

spicy kielbasa soup

PREP: 15 min. • **COOK:** 8 hours • **YIELD:** 5 servings.

Red pepper flakes bring a little zip to this healthful and hearty soup. If you have any of it left over, it's delicious reheated, after the flavors have had some time to blend. I like to serve it piping hot with a good loaf of rye bread.
carol custer // clifton park, new york

- **1/2 pound reduced-fat smoked turkey kielbasa, sliced**
- **1 medium onion, chopped**
- **1 medium green pepper, chopped**
- **1 celery rib with leaves, thinly sliced**
- **4 garlic cloves, minced**
- **2 cans (14-1/2 ounces *each*) reduced-sodium chicken broth**
- **1 can (15-1/2 ounces) great northern beans, rinsed and drained**
- **1 can (14-1/2 ounces) stewed tomatoes, cut up**
- **1 small zucchini, sliced**
- **1 medium carrot, shredded**
- **1 tablespoon dried parsley flakes**
- **1/4 teaspoon crushed red pepper flakes**
- **1/4 teaspoon pepper**

In a nonstick skillet, cook kielbasa over medium heat until lightly browned. Add the onion, green pepper, celery and garlic. Cook and stir for 5 minutes or until vegetable are tender.

Transfer to a 5-qt. slow cooker. Stir in the remaining ingredients. Cover and cook on low for 8-9 hours.

turkey barley soup

PREP: 15 min. • **COOK:** 55 min.
YIELD: 10 servings (3 quarts).

This satisfying dish has an interesting blend of flavors—and it's very nutritious, too. I like using this recipe to use up leftover holiday turkey. betty kleberger // florissant, missouri

- **2 cans (one 49-1/2 ounces, one 14-1/2 ounces) chicken broth**
- **4 cups cubed cooked turkey**
- **2 medium carrots, halved and thinly sliced**
- **1 large potato, peeled and cubed**
- **2 cups frozen cut green beans**
- **1 medium green pepper, chopped**
- **1 celery rib, chopped**
- **3 garlic cloves, minced**
- **1/2 cup uncooked medium pearl barley**
- **2 bay leaves**
- **1 teaspoon dried thyme**
- **1 teaspoon rubbed sage**
- **1/2 teaspoon salt**

In a Dutch oven, combine all the ingredients. Bring to a boil. Reduce heat; simmer, uncovered, for 45-55 minutes or until barley and vegetables are tender. Discard bay leaves.

EDITOR'S NOTE: This soup may be frozen for up to 3 months.

summer vegetable soup

PREP/TOTAL TIME: 30 min. • **YIELD:** 4 servings.

This vegetable soup brims with goodies from the garden, from celery and green beans to potatoes and zucchini, but it's the turmeric that gives it a tasty new twist. edith ruth muldoon // baldwin, new york

- **1 small onion, quartered and thinly sliced**
- **1 tablespoon olive oil**
- **4 cups reduced-sodium chicken *or* vegetable broth**
- **1 cup sliced zucchini**
- **1 can (15-1/2 ounces) navy beans, rinsed and drained**
- **1/2 cup diced peeled red potato**
- **1/2 cup cut fresh green beans (2-inch pieces)**
- **1/2 cup chopped peeled tomato**
- **1/4 teaspoon pepper**
- **1/8 teaspoon ground turmeric**
- **1/4 cup chopped celery leaves**
- **2 tablespoons tomato paste**

In a large saucepan, saute onion in oil until tender. Add the next eight ingredients. Bring to a boil. Reduce heat; cover and simmer for 20-30 minutes or until vegetables are tender.

Stir in the celery leaves and tomato paste. Cover and let stand for 5 minutes before serving.

TOMATO PEELING MADE EASY

To peel tomatoes quickly and easily, cut a shallow "X" on the bottom of each tomato. Put them into a pot of boiling water for about a minute, then rinse under cold water. The skin will peel right off.

claire g.// murphy, north carolina

matzo ball soup

PREP: 10 min. • **COOK:** 2-3/4 hours
YIELD: 18 servings (4-1/2 quarts).

My mother is of Russian descent and always made this for Friday night dinner while I was growing up. It's a very comforting meal that brings back many happy memories. bernice polak // new smyrna beach, florida

- 1 broiler/fryer chicken (3-1/2 to 4 pounds), cut up
- 8 cups water
- 6 carrots, cut in half lengthwise, then into 2-inch pieces
- 1 large onion, peeled
- 2 celery ribs, cut in half
- 2 sprigs fresh dill (3-inch pieces)
- 1 can (49-1/2 ounces) chicken broth
- 2 teaspoons salt
- 1/2 teaspoon pepper
- 2 cups cooked noodles

MATZO BALLS:

- 2 eggs
- 1 cup matzo meal
- 2 tablespoons rendered chicken fat *or* canola oil
- 2 tablespoons minced fresh parsley
- 2 teaspoons salt
- Dash pepper
- 1/2 to 1 cup cold water

Place chicken and water in a 8-qt. stockpot. Cover and slowly bring to a boil; skim fat. Add carrots, onion and celery. Fold dill in half and wrap many times with kitchen string; add to soup. Bring to a boil. Reduce heat to medium-low; cover but keep lid ajar and simmer for 2-1/2 hours.

Meanwhile, combine first six matzo ball ingredients in a medium bowl. Add enough water to make a thick pancake-like batter. Refrigerate for 2 hours (mixture thickens as it stands).

Remove and discard onion, celery and dill from broth. Remove chicken and allow to cool; debone and cut into chunks. Skim fat from broth. Return chicken to kettle. Add the broth, salt and pepper; bring to a boil. Reduce heat; cover and simmer.

To complete matzo balls, bring 4 quarts water to a boil in a 5-qt. Dutch oven. With very wet hands, form heaping teaspoonfuls of batter into balls. If mixture is too thin, stir in 1-2 tablespoons of matzo meal.

Drop balls into boiling water. They will sink when dropped but will rise in a few minutes. Cook for 10 minutes. Remove with slotted spoon and add to simmering soup. Add noodles; heat through.

country sausage soup

PREP/TOTAL TIME: 20 min.
YIELD: 4 servings.

Savory pork sausage, two kinds of beans and diced tomatoes make this soup a standby. I prepare it time and again, especially on nights when I don't know what to make for supper.
grace meyer // galva, kansas

- 3/4 pound bulk pork sausage
- 1 can (14-1/2 ounces) diced tomatoes, undrained
- 1 can (14-1/2 ounces) chicken broth
- 1 teaspoon dried thyme
- 3/4 to 1 teaspoon dried rosemary, crushed
- 1/4 teaspoon pepper
- 1 can (15-1/2 ounces) great northern beans, rinsed and drained
- 1 can (15 ounces) garbanzo beans *or* chickpeas, rinsed and drained

In a large saucepan, cook sausage over medium heat until no longer pink; drain. Stir in the tomatoes, broth, thyme, rosemary and pepper. Bring to a boil. Stir in the beans; heat through.

curry chicken soup

PREP: 20 min. • **COOK:** 20 min. • **YIELD:** 4 servings.

Despite the longer ingredient list, this yummy soup is quick and easy to prepare. What a fantastic way to eat up your fruits and veggies! jane hacker // milwaukee, wisconsin

- **1/2 pound boneless skinless chicken breast, cut into 1/2-inch cubes**
- **3 teaspoons canola oil, *divided***
- **3/4 cup chopped onion**
- **1/2 cup chopped carrot**
- **1/2 cup chopped celery**
- **1/2 cup chopped green pepper**
- **1 cup chopped peeled apple**
- **2 tablespoons all-purpose flour**
- **1/4 teaspoon salt**
- **2 cans (14-1/2 ounces *each*) reduced-sodium chicken broth**
- **1/4 cup tomato paste**
- **2 to 3 teaspoons curry powder**
- **1 teaspoon ground ginger**
- **1/4 to 1/2 teaspoon crushed red pepper flakes**
- **2 tablespoons minced fresh parsley**

In a large saucepan coated with cooking spray, cook the chicken in 1 teaspoon oil for 4-5 minutes or until no longer pink. Remove chicken and set aside.

In the same saucepan, saute the onion, carrot, celery and green pepper in remaining oil for 4 minutes. Add apple; cook 2 minutes longer. Combine flour and salt. Sprinkle over vegetable mixture; cook and stir for 1 minute. Gradually stir in broth and tomato paste. Bring to a boil; cook and stir 1-2 minutes longer or until slightly thickened.

Stir in the curry, ginger and pepper flakes. Return chicken to saucepan and bring to a boil. Reduce heat; simmer, uncovered, for 8-10 minutes or until vegetables are tender. Sprinkle with parsley.

CURRY POWDER

Curry powder is a blend of many different ground spices used to replicate the individual spices combined in the cuisine of India. Curry powder imparts a distinctive flavor and rich golden color to recipes and is available in both mild and hot versions. Most cooks season dishes lightly with curry powder and gradually add more as desired to reach an acceptable spice level.

slow cooker chicken soup

PREP: 5 min. • **COOK:** 6 hours
YIELD: 8 servings (2 quarts).

My savory chicken soup includes a couple of unusual ingredients—lentils and Worcestershire sauce. Try it!
connie thomas // jensen, utah

- **1 can (28 ounces) diced tomatoes, undrained**
- **2 cups reduced-fat reduced-sodium chicken broth**
- **2 cups cubed cooked chicken breast**
- **1 cup frozen corn**
- **2 celery ribs with leaves, chopped**
- **1 can (6 ounces) tomato paste**
- **1/4 cup dried lentils, rinsed**
- **1 tablespoon sugar**
- **1 tablespoon Worcestershire sauce**
- **2 teaspoons dried parsley flakes**
- **1 teaspoon dried marjoram**

In a 3-qt. slow cooker, combine all the ingredients. Cover and cook on low for 6-8 hours or until the vegetables are tender.

southwestern chicken soup

PREP: 10 min. • **COOK:** 25 min. • **YIELD:** 4 servings.

Seasoned with zippy Southwestern flavor, this hearty soup is a tempting bowlful of chicken, corn, black beans and diced tomatoes. Mexican corn bread makes a delicious accompaniment. terri stevens // ardmore, oklahoma

- **1/2 pound boneless skinless chicken breast, cut into 1/2-inch cubes**
- **1/4 cup finely chopped onion**
- **2 tablespoons olive oil**
- **2 garlic cloves, minced**
- **1 can (15-1/4 ounces) whole kernel corn, drained**
- **1 can (15 ounces) black beans, rinsed and drained**
- **1 can (14-1/2 ounces) chicken broth**
- **1 can (10 ounces) diced tomatoes and green chilies, undrained**
- **1 teaspoon ground cumin**
- **1/2 teaspoon salt**
- **1/2 teaspoon chili powder**
- **1/8 teaspoon cayenne pepper**
- **Plain yogurt and minced fresh cilantro**

In a large skillet over medium heat, cook chicken and onion in oil until chicken is no longer pink. Add garlic; cook 1 minute longer.

Stir in the corn, beans, broth, tomatoes, cumin, salt, chili powder and cayenne. Bring to a boil. Reduce heat; cover and simmer for 10-15 minutes. Garnish with the yogurt and cilantro.

sausage kale soup

PREP: 10 min. • **COOK:** 25 min. • **YIELD:** 7 servings.

The hearty sausage slices, white kidney beans and colorful kale in this soup will have your gang asking for seconds. Yum!

susan pursell // fountain valley, california

- **3/4 cup chopped onion**
- **1 tablespoon olive oil**
- **2 garlic cloves, minced**
- **4 cups reduced-sodium chicken broth**
- **2 medium potatoes, peeled and cubed**
- **1/4 teaspoon salt**
- **1/4 teaspoon pepper**
- **1 bunch kale, trimmed and chopped**
- **1 can (15 ounces) white kidney *or* cannellini beans, rinsed and drained**
- **1/2 pound reduced-fat fully cooked Polish sausage *or* turkey kielbasa, sliced**

In a large saucepan or Dutch oven, saute onion in oil until tender. Add garlic; cook 1 minute longer. Add the broth, potatoes, salt and pepper. Bring to a boil. Reduce heat; cover and simmer for 10-15 minutes or until potatoes are tender.

Using a potato masher, mash potatoes slightly. Add the kale, beans and sausage; cook over medium-low heat until kale is tender.

TRIMMING KALE

If the stems from kale leaves are thin and tender, you can easily snip and use them. If they're thick, however, you'll want to remove them completely. Place each leaf on a cutting board, fold the leaf in half lengthwise and use a knife to carefully slice away the stem. Then chop or slice the leaves as desired.

chicken soup with spaetzle

PREP: 20 min. + cooling • **COOK:** 2-1/2 hours + cooling • **YIELD:** 8-10 servings (2 1/2 quarts).

Here's a new and interesting twist to traditional chicken soup. Everyone who samples it can't resist the delicious soup paired with homemade spaetzle. elaine lange // grand rapids, michigan

- **1 broiler/fryer chicken (2 to 3 pounds), cut into pieces**
- **2 tablespoons canola oil**
- **8 cups chicken broth**
- **2 bay leaves**
- **1/2 teaspoon dried thyme**
- **1/4 teaspoon pepper**
- **1 cup sliced carrots**
- **1 cup sliced celery**
- **3/4 cup chopped onion**
- **1 garlic clove, minced**
- **1/3 cup medium pearl barley**
- **2 cups sliced fresh mushrooms**

SPAETZLE:

- **1-1/4 cups all-purpose flour**
- **1/8 teaspoon baking powder**
- **1/8 teaspoon salt**
- **1 egg, lightly beaten**
- **1/4 cup water**
- **1/4 cup 2% milk**

In a Dutch oven or large soup kettle, brown chicken pieces in oil. Add the broth, bay leaves, thyme and pepper. Slowly bring to a boil; skim foam. Reduce heat; cover and simmer for 45-60 minutes or until chicken is tender. Remove chicken and set aside until cool enough to handle. Remove meat from bones; discard bones and skin and cut chicken into bite-size pieces. Cool broth and skim off fat.

Return chicken to broth along with the carrots, celery, onion, garlic and barley. Bring to a boil. Reduce heat; cover and simmer for 35 minutes. Add mushrooms and simmer 8-10 minutes longer. Remove bay leaves.

In a small bowl, combine first three spaetzle ingredients. Stir in the egg, water and milk; blend well. Drop batter by 1/2 teaspoonfuls into simmering soup. Cook for 10 minutes.

brown rice turkey soup

PREP/TOTAL TIME: 30 min. • **YIELD:** 5 servings.

I don't recall where I got this recipe, but it's my all-time favorite turkey soup. Everyone who has tried it agrees. The sweet red pepper gives the soup a deliciously distinctive flavor. bobby langley // rocky mount, north carolina

- **1 cup diced sweet red pepper**
- **1/2 cup chopped onion**
- **1/2 cup sliced celery**
- **2 garlic cloves, minced**
- **2 tablespoons butter**
- **3 cans (14-1/2 ounces *each*) reduced-sodium chicken broth**
- **3/4 cup white wine *or* additional reduced-sodium chicken broth**
- **1 teaspoon dried thyme**
- **1/4 teaspoon pepper**
- **2 cups cubed cooked turkey breast**
- **1 cup instant brown rice**
- **1/4 cup sliced green onions**

In a Dutch oven, saute red pepper, onion, celery and garlic in butter for 5-7 minutes or until vegetables are tender. Add the broth, wine or additional broth, thyme and pepper. Bring to a boil.

Reduce heat; cover and simmer for 5 minutes. Stir in turkey and rice. Bring to a boil; simmer, uncovered, for 5 minutes or until rice is tender. Garnish with green onions.

egg drop soup

PREP/TOTAL TIME: 15 min. • **YIELD:** 4 servings.

We start many stir-fry meals with this easy first course, which cooks in minutes flat. There are many recipe variations, but we especially like the addition of cornstarch to thicken the broth. I got the recipe from my grandma's old cookbook.
amy corlew-sherlock // lapeer, michigan

3 cups chicken broth
1 tablespoon cornstarch
2 tablespoons cold water
1 egg, lightly beaten
1 green onion, sliced

In a large saucepan, bring broth to a boil over medium heat. Combine cornstarch and water until smooth; gradually stir into broth. Bring to a boil; cook and stir for 2 minutes or until thickened.

Reduce heat. Drizzle beaten egg into hot broth, stirring constantly. Remove from the heat; stir in onion.

after-thanksgiving turkey soup

PREP: 15 min.
COOK: 2-1/2 hours + cooling
YIELD: 16 servings (about 4 quarts).

As much as our family adores Thanksgiving, we look forward to this cream soup using leftover turkey even more. It makes a big batch that we can enjoy for days.
valorie walker // bradley, south carolina

1 leftover turkey carcass (from a 12- to 14-pound turkey)
3 medium onions, chopped
2 large carrots, diced
2 celery ribs, diced
1 cup butter, cubed
1 cup all-purpose flour
2 cups half-and-half cream
1 cup uncooked long grain rice
2 teaspoons salt
1 teaspoon chicken bouillon granules
3/4 teaspoon pepper

Place turkey carcass in a Dutch oven or soup kettle and cover with water. Slowly bring to a boil; skim foam. Reduce heat; cover and simmer for 1 hour. Remove the carcass; cool. Set aside 3 qt. broth. Remove turkey from bones and cut into bite-size pieces; set aside.

In a Dutch oven or soup kettle, saute the onions, carrots and celery in butter until tender. Reduce heat; stir in flour until blended. Gradually add 1 qt. of reserved broth. Bring to a boil; cook and stir for 2 minutes or until thickened.

Add cream, rice, salt, bouillon, pepper, remaining broth and reserved turkey. Reduce heat; cover pot and simmer for 30-35 minutes or until rice is tender.

comforting chicken noodle soup

PREP/TOTAL TIME: 25 min.
YIELD: 10-12 servings (about 2-1/2 quarts).

This rich, comforting soup is so simple to fix. I like to give a pot of it, along with the recipe, to new mothers so they don't have to worry about dinner. joanna sargent // sandy, utah

- **2 quarts water**
- **8 teaspoons chicken bouillon granules**
- **6-1/2 cups uncooked wide egg noodles**
- **2 cans (10-3/4 ounces *each*) condensed cream of chicken soup, undiluted**
- **3 cups cubed cooked chicken**
- **1 cup (8 ounces) sour cream**
- **Minced fresh parsley**

In a large saucepan, bring water and bouillon to a boil. Add the noodles; cook, uncovered, until tender, about 10 minutes. Do not drain. Add soup and chicken; heat through.

Remove from the heat; stir in the sour cream. Sprinkle with minced parsley.

turkey meatball soup

PREP: 30 min. • **COOK:** 20 min. • **YIELD:** 6 servings.

I developed this recipe myself to take advantage of the abundant fresh veggies available in our area. It's an economical yet hearty main dish that my husband and children love. lora rehm // endicott, new york

- **1/2 cup dry bread crumbs**
- **3 tablespoons milk**
- **1 egg, lightly beaten**
- **1/2 teaspoon salt**
- **1-1/4 pounds ground turkey**
- **2-1/2 cups water**
- **1 can (14-1/2 ounces) stewed tomatoes**
- **2 medium zucchini, halved and sliced**
- **2 small carrots, thinly sliced**
- **2/3 cup frozen corn**
- **1/2 cup cut fresh green beans *or* frozen cut green beans**
- **2 teaspoons chicken bouillon granules**
- **1 teaspoon dried basil**
- **1/4 teaspoon pepper**

In a large bowl, combine the bread crumbs, milk, egg and salt. Crumble turkey over mixture and mix well. Shape into 1/2-in. balls. In a nonstick skillet over medium heat, brown meatballs in batches; drain if necessary.

In a large saucepan, combine the remaining ingredients. Bring to a boil. Carefully add meatballs. Reduce heat; cover and simmer for 20-25 minutes or until vegetables are tender.

turkey soup with slickers

PREP: 20 min. • **COOK:** 3-1/4 hours + cooling • **YIELD:** 8-10 servings (2-1/2 quarts).

Our grandson calls this "bone soup" because I make it with holiday turkey bones! The recipe for slickers—a cross between dumplings and egg noodles—comes from my grandmother. christine fleeman // salem, oregon

- **1 leftover turkey carcass (from a 14-pound turkey)**
- **5 quarts water**
- **1/2 cup chopped onion**
- **1/2 cup chopped carrot**
- **1/2 cup chopped celery**
- **3 tablespoons dried parsley flakes**
- **2 teaspoons salt**
- **1/2 teaspoon pepper**
- **2 bay leaves**
- **1 egg**
- **2-1/2 to 3 cups all-purpose flour**
- **1/2 teaspoon dill weed**
- **1/2 teaspoon poultry seasoning**
- **1 cup frozen peas**

In a Dutch oven or soup kettle, add the first nine ingredients. Slowly bring to a boil; skim foam. Reduce heat; cover and simmer for 2 hours. Discard bay leaves. Remove carcass; set aside until cool enough to handle. Remove turkey from bones; discard bones. Cut turkey into bite-size pieces; set aside.

In a large bowl, beat 1 cup of the broth and egg. Stir in enough flour to form a stiff dough. Turn onto a floured surface; knead 8-10 times or until smooth. Divide dough in half; roll out each piece to 1/8-in. thickness. Cut into 2-in. x 1/4-in. strips.

Add dill and poultry seasoning to remaining broth; bring to a gentle boil. Drop slickers into broth; cover and cook for 30-35 minutes or until tender. Add peas and reserved turkey; heat through.

creamy chicken soup with veggies

PREP: 20 min. • **COOK:** 20 min. • **YIELD:** 7 cups.

With lots of beans, chicken and tons of vegetables, this quick soup is one everyone in the family will enjoy—and it tastes like it's been cooking all day! taste of home test kitchen

- **3/4 pound boneless skinless chicken breasts, cut into 1/2-inch cubes**
- **1/2 cup chopped onion**
- **2 teaspoons olive oil**
- **1-1/2 teaspoons minced garlic**
- **2 tablespoons all-purpose flour**
- **2 cans (14-1/2 ounces *each*) vegetable broth**
- **2 cans (15-1/2 ounces *each*) great northern beans, rinsed and drained**
- **1-1/2 cups frozen mixed vegetables, thawed**
- **1 cup frozen chopped broccoli, thawed**
- **1 can (4 ounces) chopped green chilies**
- **3/4 teaspoon Italian seasoning**
- **1/2 teaspoon ground cumin**
- **1/4 teaspoon pepper**
- **1/2 cup shredded part-skim mozzarella cheese**

In a Dutch oven, saute chicken and onion in oil until chicken is no longer pink. Add garlic; cook 1 minute longer. Stir in flour until blended; gradually add broth. Bring to a boil; cook and stir for 2 minutes or until thickened.

Reduce heat; stir in the beans, vegetables and seasonings. Cook, stirring occasionally, for 8-10 minutes or until vegetables are tender. Garnish with cheese.

MAKE YOUR OWN ITALIAN SEASONING

Italian seasoning can be found in the spice aisle of most grocery stores. A basic blend might contain marjoram, thyme, rosemary, savory, sage, oregano and basil. You can easily mix up your own. If you don't have all the ingredients, you can blend just a few of them with good results. Try substituting 1/4 teaspoon each of basil, thyme, rosemary and oregano for each teaspoon of Italian seasoning called for in a recipe.

spicy chicken rice soup

PREP/TOTAL TIME: 25 min. **YIELD:** 8 servings.

Since we live in a rice-producing state, rice is a staple in my recipes. It's a key ingredient in my tongue-tingling spicy soup.

mary shaver // jonesboro, arkansas

- **2 cans (14-1/2 ounces *each*) chicken broth**
- **3 cups cooked rice**
- **2 cups cubed cooked chicken**
- **1 can (15-1/4 ounces) whole kernel corn, undrained**
- **1 can (11-1/2 ounces) V8 juice**
- **1 cup salsa**
- **1 can (4 ounces) chopped green chilies, drained**
- **1/2 cup chopped green onions**
- **2 tablespoons minced fresh cilantro**
- **1/2 cup shredded Monterey Jack cheese, optional**

In a large saucepan, combine the first nine ingredients. Bring to a boil. Reduce heat; cover and simmer for 15 minutes or until heated through. Sprinkle with cheese if desired.

granny's spicy soup

PREP: 10 min. • **COOK:** 3-1/4 hours
YIELD: 12 servings (about 3 quarts).

My mother makes the best soups around, and others have started calling her "The Soup Lady." When my kids ask me to make Granny's soup, I'm happy to oblige.

r. rose // akron, ohio

- **1 broiler/fryer chicken (3-1/2 to 4 pounds), cut up**
- **8 cups water**
- **4 to 5 celery ribs with leaves, diced**
- **2 medium carrots, diced**
- **1 large onion, diced**
- **1 to 1-1/2 teaspoons pickling spices**
- **1-1/2 teaspoons salt, optional**
- **4 chicken bouillon cubes**
- **1/4 teaspoon pepper**
- **1 cup uncooked noodles**

Place chicken and water in a large stockpot. Cover and slowly bring to a boil; skim fat. Reduce heat; cover and simmer for 2 hours or until chicken falls off bone.

Strain broth; return to kettle. Allow chicken to cool; debone and cut into chunks. Skim fat from broth. Return chicken to broth along with celery, carrots and onion.

Place pickling spices in a tea ball or cheesecloth bag; add to soup. Bring to a boil. Reduce heat; cover and simmer for 1 hour. Remove spices; add salt if desired, bouillon, pepper and noodles. Cook for 10-15 minutes or until noodles are tender.

EDITOR'S NOTE: The soup gets its name from the pickling spices, not from being hot.

PICKLING SPICES TIP

I love pickling spices in all sorts of soups and stews. I fill a tea ball with pickling spices and hang it in the kettle while the mixture is simmering. The deliciously different flavor keeps people wondering what my secret ingredient is. sherry t. // didsbury, alberta

oodles of noodles soup

PREP: 15 min. • **COOK:** 30 min. • **YIELD:** 6 servings.

When my goddaughter was young, I often gave her a children's cookbook for birthdays and other special occasions. We'd plan an entire menu from the books, prepare the meal together and serve it to her family. This soup recipe was one of her favorites. lorri reinhardt // big bend, wisconsin

3/4 pound boneless skinless chicken breasts, cubed
2 medium carrots, sliced
1 small onion, chopped
2 celery ribs, sliced
1 garlic clove, minced
5 cups water
1/4 teaspoon pepper
2 packages (3 ounces *each*) chicken ramen noodles

In a large saucepan coated with cooking spray, saute the chicken, carrots, onion, celery and garlic until chicken is no longer pink. Add water, pepper and contents of seasoning packets from the noodles. Bring to a boil. Reduce heat; cover and simmer for 15-20 minutes or until carrots are tender.

Break the noodles into pieces and add to soup; cover and cook for 3 minutes or until tender.

wild rice turkey soup

PREP: 1 hour • **COOK:** 15 min.
YIELD: 9 servings (3-1/2 quarts).

This creamy, comforting soup really chases away the chill on cold fall or winter nights. Turn to this recipe when you need to use up leftover turkey from a holiday meal.
val lefebvre // rosetown, saskatchewan

6 cups chicken broth, *divided*
2 cups sliced fresh mushrooms
2 medium onions, chopped
2 medium carrots, shredded
1/2 cup uncooked wild rice
4 garlic cloves, minced
6 tablespoons butter, cubed
1/2 cup all-purpose flour
1 teaspoon salt
1/2 teaspoon pepper
4 cups milk
2 cups cubed cooked turkey
2 to 3 teaspoons Worcestershire sauce
1/4 cup minced fresh parsley

In a Dutch oven, combine 3 cups broth, mushrooms, onions, carrots, rice and garlic; bring to a boil. Reduce heat; cover and simmer for 50-55 minutes or until rice is tender.

In a large saucepan, melt butter over medium heat. Whisk in the flour, salt and pepper until smooth. Gradually whisk in milk and the remaining broth. Bring to a boil. Cook and stir for 2 minutes or until thickened. Add to rice mixture. Add turkey and Worcestershire sauce; heat through. Garnish with parsley.

creamy chicken vegetable soup

PREP/TOTAL TIME: 30 min. • **YIELD:** 5 servings.

It's easy to entice kids of all ages to eat their vegetables when they show up in a velvety chicken soup. Brie cheese adds a delightfully mild yet rich flavor. taste of home test kitchen

1 small onion, finely chopped
1 celery rib, chopped
1 medium carrot, chopped
1 garlic clove, minced
1 tablespoon butter
2 cans (14-1/2 ounces *each*) chicken broth
1/2 teaspoon salt
1/2 teaspoon pepper
3 tablespoons all-purpose flour
1-1/2 cups half-and-half cream
2 cups cubed cooked chicken breast
1 package (10 ounces) frozen chopped spinach, thawed and squeezed dry
1 round (8 ounces) Brie cheese, rind removed and chopped

In a Dutch oven, saute the onion, celery and carrot until crisp-tender. Add garlic; saute for 1 minute more. Stir in the broth, salt and pepper. Bring to a boil. Reduce heat; simmer, uncovered, for 10 minutes.

Combine flour and cream until smooth; gradually stir into soup. Bring to a boil; cook and stir for 2 minutes. Stir in the chicken, spinach and cheese. Cook and stir for 5 minutes or until cheese is melted.

DRAINING SPINACH

Thaw frozen spinach in a colander in the sink or over a bowl or plate. With clean hands, press the water out of the spinach. You can use the same method to get excess water out of spinach that has been cooked. Pour it into a colander. Allow to cool before pressing out the water with your hands.

quick turkey-bean soup

PREP/TOTAL TIME: 30 min.
YIELD: 14-16 servings (4 quarts).

Since this recipe calls for canned beans, cooking time is minimal. I make the soup mild and let guests add as much "heat" as they want with hot pepper sauce.
deborah schermerhorn
colorado springs, colorado

- **1 pound ground turkey**
- **2 garlic cloves, minced**
- **1 medium onion, chopped**
- **1 tablespoon canola oil**
- **1-1/2 cups chopped celery**
- **1 medium green pepper, chopped**
- **1 medium sweet red pepper, chopped**
- **2 cans (14-1/2 ounces *each*) beef broth**
- **1 can (28 ounces) stewed tomatoes**
- **3 tablespoons tomato paste**
- **1/2 teaspoon cayenne pepper**
- **1/4 teaspoon dried basil**
- **1/4 teaspoon dried oregano**
- **2 cans (16 ounces *each*) kidney beans, rinsed and drained**
- **1 can (15 ounces) black beans, rinsed and drained**
- **1 can (15 ounces) pinto beans, rinsed and drained**
- **1 can (15-1/4 ounces) whole kernel corn, drained**

In a Dutch oven or soup kettle over medium heat, brown turkey, garlic and onion in oil; drain. Add the celery and peppers; cook and stir for 2 minutes.

Add broth, tomatoes, tomato paste, cayenne, basil and oregano. Bring to a boil. Add beans and corn. Reduce heat; cover and simmer for 15 minutes.

curly noodle chicken soup

PREP: 10 min. • **COOK:** 1 hour 25 min.
YIELD: 9 servings (about 2 quarts).

Diners will ladle out praise all around the table when you serve this flavorful soup. My husband and three sons can't get enough of it. I created the recipe for a dinner I hosted for a group of friends. The main course was Italian, and I needed a good soup, so I converted a favorite tortilla soup recipe by substituting pasta and adding different seasonings. maxine pierson // san ramon, california

- **1 pound boneless skinless chicken breasts, cut into 1/2-inch pieces**
- **1 large onion, chopped**
- **4 celery ribs, sliced**
- **2 medium carrots, sliced**
- **4 garlic cloves, minced**
- **2 tablespoons butter**
- **2 tablespoons olive oil**
- **1 teaspoon dried basil**
- **1/2 teaspoon dried oregano**
- **1/8 teaspoon pepper**
- **3 cans (14-1/2 ounces *each*) chicken broth, *divided***
- **1 can (14-1/2 ounces) diced tomatoes, undrained**
- **6 ounces uncooked tricolor spiral pasta**
- **1/4 cup all-purpose flour**

In a large saucepan, saute the chicken, onion, celery, carrots and garlic in butter and oil for 5 minutes. Stir in the basil, oregano and pepper until blended.

Set aside 1 cup broth. Gradually add remaining broth to the pan. Stir in tomatoes. Bring to a boil. Reduce heat; cover and simmer for 45-60 minutes.

Return to a boil; stir in the pasta. Reduce heat; simmer, uncovered, for 10-13 minutes or until pasta is almost tender. Combine flour and reserved broth until smooth. Stir into pan. Bring to a boil; cook and stir for 2 minutes or until thickened.

meatball noodle soup

PREP: 25 min. • **COOK:** 30 min. • **YIELD:** 5 servings.

Since you don't need to cook the tender homemade meatballs and boil the egg noodles separately, you can easily stir up this savory soup in no time. I usually double the recipe for our family of seven. carol losier // baldwinsville, new york

- **2 cans (14-1/2 ounces *each*) chicken broth**
- **1 celery rib with leaves, thinly sliced**
- **1 medium carrot, thinly sliced**
- **1/4 cup chopped onion**
- **1 tablespoon butter**
- **1 egg, lightly beaten**
- **1/2 cup dry bread crumbs**
- **2 tablespoons dried parsley flakes**
- **1 tablespoon Worcestershire sauce**
- **1/4 teaspoon pepper**
- **1/2 pound lean ground turkey**
- **1 cup uncooked egg noodles**

In a large saucepan, bring the broth, celery and carrot to a boil. Reduce heat; cover and simmer for 10 minutes.

Meanwhile, in a small skillet, saute onion in butter until tender. Transfer to a large bowl. Add the egg, bread crumbs, parsley, Worcestershire sauce and pepper. Crumble turkey over mixture and mix well. Shape into 1-in. balls.

Add meatballs to the simmering broth. Bring to a boil. Reduce heat; cover and simmer for 15 minutes or until no meat is longer pink. Add noodles. Cover and simmer for 5 minutes or until noodles are tender.

cider turkey soup

PREP: 15 min. • **COOK:** 2-1/2 hours • **YIELD:** 15 servings (3-3/4 quarts).

Use the turkey carcass from your Thanksgiving dinner to make this super soup the next day! Apple cider gives the broth a delightful hint of sweetness. taste of home test kitchen

- 1 leftover turkey carcass (from a 12-pound turkey)
- 3-1/2 quarts water
- 4 cups apple cider *or* juice
- 2 celery ribs, cut into 2-inch pieces
- 1 large onion, cut into wedges
- 1 large apple, cut into wedges
- 1 large carrot, cut into 2-inch pieces
- 8 sprigs fresh thyme
- 2 sprigs fresh sage

SOUP:

- 3 cups shredded cooked turkey breast
- 2 cups cooked long grain and wild rice
- 2 large carrots, shredded
- 1 large onion, chopped
- 1 cup chopped celery
- 1 teaspoon salt
- 1/2 teaspoon dried thyme
- 1/4 teaspoon pepper

Place the first nine ingredients in a stockpot. Slowly bring to a boil over low heat; skim foam. Cover and simmer for 1-1/2 hours.

Discard the carcass. Strain broth through a cheesecloth-lined colander; discard the vegetables and herbs. If using immediately, skim fat. Or cool, then refrigerate for 8 hours or overnight.

Remove fat from surface before using. Broth may be refrigerated for up to 3 days or frozen for 4-6 months.

Place the soup ingredients in a stockpot; add broth. Bring to a boil. Reduce heat; cover and simmer for 30 minutes or until vegetables are tender. Serve immediately or cool and transfer to freezer containers. May be frozen for up to 3 months.

TO USE FROZEN SOUP: Thaw soup in the refrigerator overnight. Transfer to a saucepan. Cover and cook over medium heat until heated through.

HOW TO SHRED COOKED MEAT

Place cooked meat or poultry in a shallow pan or on a plate. Using two forks, pull meat into thin shreds. Return shredded meat to the pan to warm or use as recipe directs.

tex-mex chicken soup

PREP: 10 min. • **COOK:** 45 min. • **YIELD:** 12 servings (3 quarts).

We keep busy here on our ranch, so I'm always looking for dishes that can be prepared in a hurry but are still filling and tasty. This soup is a real winner! maydell spiess // industry, texas

- **1/2 cup chopped onion**
- **1 tablespoon canola oil**
- **2 garlic cloves, minced**
- **4 cups chicken broth**
- **3 cups cubed cooked chicken**
- **3 medium zucchini, sliced**
- **1 can (14-1/2 ounces) diced tomatoes, undrained**
- **1 can (11 ounces) whole kernel corn, drained**
- **1 can (8 ounces) tomato sauce**
- **1/2 cup salsa**
- **2 teaspoons ground cumin**
- **1 teaspoon salt, optional**
- **3/4 teaspoon pepper**
- **1/2 teaspoon dried oregano**
- **Shredded cheddar cheese, optional**
- **Tortilla chips, optional**

In a large stockpot, saute onion in oil until tender. Add garlic; cook 1 minute longer. Add the next 11 ingredients; bring to a boil. Reduce heat; cover and simmer for 30 minutes. Serve with cheese and tortilla chips.

CANOLA OR VEGETABLE OIL?

When a recipe calls for canola oil or vegetable oil, you can use either one in equal amounts. There should be no difference in the final product.

chunky chicken soup

PREP: 15 min. • **COOK:** 70 min. • **YIELD:** 8 servings (2 quarts).

Here's a satisfying soup that you'll find yourself serving year-round. Every spoonful is loaded with the fantastic flavor of chicken, celery, carrots and peas.

kathy both // rocky mountain house, alberta

- **1 pound boneless skinless chicken thighs, cut into 1-inch pieces**
- **1 cup sliced celery**
- **1/2 cup chopped onion**
- **2 tablespoons canola oil**
- **6 cups chicken broth**
- **1-1/2 cups sliced carrots**
- **1 teaspoon dried thyme**
- **1/2 teaspoon salt, optional**
- **1/4 teaspoon pepper**
- **1/2 cup uncooked macaroni**
- **1-1/2 cups frozen peas**

In a large saucepan, cook the chicken, celery and onion in oil until chicken is no longer pink.

Add the broth, carrots, thyme, salt if desired and pepper; bring to a boil. Reduce heat; cover and simmer for 45 minutes or until vegetables are tender.

Stir in macaroni and peas. Cover and simmer for 15 minutes or until the macaroni is tender.

quick chicken tortilla soup

PREP/TOTAL TIME: 25 min.
YIELD: 7 servings.

This soup is as good as (if not better than) any I've had in a restaurant. I get so many compliments on it. I know you will, too!

laura johnson // largo, florida

- **1 large onion, chopped**
- **2 tablespoons olive oil**
- **1 can (4 ounces) chopped green chilies**
- **2 garlic cloves, minced**
- **1 jalapeno pepper, seeded and chopped**
- **1 teaspoon ground cumin**
- **5 cups chicken broth**
- **1 can (15 ounces) tomato sauce**
- **1 can (14-1/2 ounces) diced tomatoes with garlic and onion, undrained**
- **3 cans (5 ounces *each*) white chicken, drained**
- **1/4 cup minced fresh cilantro**
- **2 teaspoons lime juice**
- **Salt and pepper to taste**
- **Crushed tortilla chips**
- **Shredded Monterey Jack cheese *or* cheddar cheese**

In a large saucepan, saute onion in oil; add the chilies, garlic, jalapeno and cumin. Stir in the broth, tomato sauce and tomatoes. Bring to a boil. Reduce heat; stir in chicken. Simmer, uncovered, for 10 minutes. Add the cilantro, lime juice, salt and pepper. Top with chips and cheese.

EDITOR'S NOTE: Wear disposable gloves when cutting hot peppers; the oils can burn your skin. Avoid touching your face.

texas turkey soup

PREP: 20 min. • **COOK:** 40 min.
YIELD: 10-12 servings (3 quarts).

I'm not really fond of soup, so I was a little hesitant to try this recipe. But after some adjustments over the years, I've come to love this one-of-a-kind turkey soup. It's so soothing on a chilly day.

betty bakas // lakehills, texas

- **8 cups chicken broth**
- **4 cups cubed cooked turkey**
- **2 large white onions, halved**
- **2 celery ribs, sliced**
- **3 medium carrots, sliced**
- **1 cup *each* frozen corn, cut green beans and peas**
- **2 bay leaves**
- **1/2 to 1 teaspoon dried tarragon**
- **3/4 teaspoon garlic powder**
- **1/4 to 1/2 teaspoon hot pepper sauce**
- **Salt and pepper to taste**
- **1-1/2 cups uncooked noodles**
- **1 tablespoon cornstarch**
- **1 tablespoon water**

In a Dutch oven or soup kettle, combine the broth, turkey, vegetables and seasonings; bring to a boil. Reduce heat; cover and simmer for 20-30 minutes or until vegetables are tender.

Return to a boil; add noodles. Reduce heat; cover and simmer for 15-20 minutes or until noodles are tender.

Combine cornstarch and water until smooth; add to soup. Bring to a boil; boil for 2 minutes, stirring constantly. Discard bay leaves.

chunky turkey vegetable soup

PREP/TOTAL TIME: 25 min. • **YIELD:** 2 servings.

It's been more than 25 years since I cut this recipe out of a newspaper, and I've made it countless times since then. We like it so well that I always boil the leftover turkey bones and freeze the broth with turkey meat in quart containers so it's available whenever I want to make soup.

suzanne fawkes // cameron, missouri

- **3 cups chicken broth**
- **1/2 cup frozen baby lima beans, thawed**
- **1/3 cup cubed peeled potato**
- **1/3 cup sliced carrot**
- **1/3 cup sliced celery**
- **2 tablespoons chopped onion**
- **3/4 cup cubed cooked turkey *or* chicken**
- **1/2 cup cooked spiral pasta**
- **1 tablespoon minced fresh parsley**

In a large saucepan, combine the broth, lima beans, potato, carrot, celery and onion. Bring to a boil. Reduce heat; cover and cook for 15 minutes or until vegetables are tender. Add turkey and pasta; cook until heated through. Stir in parsley.

pasta sausage soup

PREP: 10 min. • **COOK:** 30 min.
YIELD: 10 servings (2-1/2 quarts).

Our family looks forward to a pot of soup every Saturday. This one ranks high at our house because the flavor is so good! The wonderful aroma of simmering Italian seasonings always brings folks to the table. The soup's nicely spiced, and the turkey sausage makes it a little lighter.

janet eggers // pound, wisconsin

1-1/2 pounds turkey Italian sausage links
1 medium green pepper, cut into 1-inch strips
1/2 cup chopped onion
1 garlic clove, minced
6 cups water
1 can (28 ounces) diced tomatoes, undrained
1 tablespoon sugar
1 tablespoon Worcestershire sauce
2 teaspoons chicken bouillon granules
1 teaspoon salt
1 teaspoon dried basil
1 teaspoon dried thyme
2-1/2 cups uncooked bow tie pasta

Remove casings from sausage; cut links into 1/2-in. pieces. In a Dutch oven or soup kettle, cook sausage over medium heat for 5-7 minutes or until no longer pink. Remove with a slotted spoon; drain, reserving 2 tablespoons drippings.

In the drippings, saute green pepper, onion and garlic for 4-5 minutes or until tender.

Add the water, tomatoes, sugar, Worcestershire sauce, bouillon, salt, basil, thyme and sausage. Bring to a boil; add pasta. Reduce heat; simmer, uncovered, for 18-22 minutes or until pasta is tender.

meatball alphabet soup

PREP: 20 min. • **COOK:** 35 min. • **YIELD:** 9 servings.

Bite-size meatballs made from ground turkey perk up this fun alphabet soup. A variety of vegetables accents the rich tomato broth, which is nicely seasoned with herbs.

taste of home test kitchen

1 egg, lightly beaten
2 tablespoons quick-cooking oats

2 tablespoons grated Parmesan cheese
1/4 teaspoon garlic powder
1/4 teaspoon Italian seasoning
1/2 pound lean ground turkey
1 cup chopped onion
1 cup chopped celery
1 cup chopped carrots
1 cup diced peeled potatoes
1 tablespoon olive oil
2 garlic cloves, minced
4 cans (14-1/2 ounces *each*) reduced-sodium chicken broth
1 can (28 ounces) diced tomatoes, undrained
1 can (6 ounces) tomato paste
1/4 cup minced fresh parsley
1 teaspoon dried basil
1 teaspoon dried thyme
3/4 cup uncooked alphabet pasta

In a bowl, combine the first five ingredients. Crumble turkey over mixture and mix well. Shape into 1/2-in. balls. In a nonstick skillet, brown meatballs in small batches over medium heat until no longer pink. Remove from the heat; set aside.

In a large saucepan or Dutch oven, saute the onion, celery, carrots and potatoes in oil for 5 minutes or until crisp-tender. Add garlic; saute for 1 minute longer. Add the broth, tomatoes, tomato paste, parsley, basil and thyme; bring to a boil. Add pasta; cook for 5-6 minutes. Reduce heat; add meatballs. Simmer, uncovered, for 15-20 minutes or until vegetables are tender.

BASQUE VEGETABLE SOUP, PG. 130

SOUPS

pork, ham & sausage

ZUCCHINI SAUSAGE SOUP, PG. 127

EASY BAKED POTATO SOUP, PG. 133

MAC 'N' CHEESE SOUP, PG. 156

split pea sausage soup

PREP: 15 min.
COOK: 1-1/2 hours
YIELD: 8 servings (2 quarts).

When my husband and I eat out and enjoy a dish, I go home and try to duplicate it. That's how I came up with this recipe. While it's good at any time, we especially enjoy this thick, hearty soup in the winter months.
donna mae young
menomonie, wisconsin

- **1 pound smoked kielbasa**
- **1 pound dried split peas**
- **6 cups water**
- **1 cup chopped carrots**
- **1 cup chopped onion**
- **1 cup chopped celery**
- **1 tablespoon minced fresh parsley**
- **1 teaspoon salt**
- **1/2 teaspoon coarse black pepper**
- **2 bay leaves**

Cut sausage in half lengthwise; cut into 1/4-in. pieces. Place in a Dutch oven or soup kettle; add remaining ingredients. Bring to a boil. Reduce heat; cover and simmer for 1-1/4 to 1-1/2 hours or until peas are tender. Discard bay leaves.

hearty ham borscht

PREP: 10 min. • **COOK:** 2-1/2 hours + cooling
YIELD: 12-14 servings (3-1/2 quarts).

I like to keep a big pot of this borscht simmering on the stove during busy times on the farm. That way, folks can dip into the soup when they have a chance to sit down for a quick meal. joanne kukurudz // river hills, manitoba

- **1 meaty ham bone *or* 2 smoked ham hocks**
- **6 cups water**
- **2 cups cubed fully cooked ham**
- **3 cups chopped cooked beets**
- **1 can (14 ounces) pork and beans**
- **1 can (10-3/4 ounces) condensed tomato soup, undiluted**
- **1 cup frozen peas**
- **1 cup chopped carrots**
- **1 cup frozen cut green beans**
- **1 medium onion, chopped**
- **2 to 3 tablespoons snipped fresh dill *or* 1 tablespoon dill weed**

Sour cream, optional

Place ham bone and water in a Dutch oven or soup kettle; bring to a boil. Reduce heat; cover and simmer for 1-1/2 hours. Remove ham bone; allow to cool.

Remove meat from bone and cut into bite-size pieces; discard bone. Return meat to pot. Add ham, beets, pork and beans, soup, peas, carrots, beans, onion and dill. Cover and simmer for 45 minutes or until vegetables are tender. Garnish with sour cream if desired.

HAM OR HOCKS

Instead of using ham hocks in soups, beans and other dishes, I buy a fully cooked ham and ask the butcher to cut it into large chunks. I package them individually in large, heavy-duty resealable plastic bags and freeze until I need them. They require less trimming and provide a lot more meat than the ham hocks.
thela o. // roscommon, michigan

zucchini sausage soup

PREP/TOTAL TIME: 30 min. • **YIELD:** 11 servings (2-3/4 quarts).

Nothing beats a warm bowl of soup on cool day. This recipe is simple to make and leaves you feeling satisfied. Plus, it makes enough so you can enjoy leftovers later in the week. janelle moore // federal way, washington

- **1 pound bulk Italian sausage**
- **2/3 cup chopped onion**
- **5 cups water**
- **2 medium zucchini, sliced**
- **1 can (14-1/2 ounces) diced tomatoes, undrained**
- **1 jar (14 ounces) pizza sauce**
- **3/4 cup uncooked orzo pasta**
- **1 envelope au jus gravy mix**
- **1 tablespoon dried basil**
- **2 teaspoons dried oregano**

In a Dutch oven, cook sausage and onion over medium heat until meat is no longer pink; drain. Stir in the remaining ingredients. Bring to a boil. Reduce heat; cover and simmer for 10-15 minutes or until pasta is tender.

green bean soup

PREP: 15 min. • **COOK:** 30 min. • **YIELD:** 6 servings.

Since this recipe started with my great-grandmother, it has certainly proven to be a family favorite! I make it often, especially when I can use homegrown beans, carrots, onions and potatoes. elvira beckenhauer // omaha, nebraska

- **4 cups water**
- **2 cups fresh green beans, cut into 2-inch pieces**
- **1-1/2 cups cubed peeled potatoes**
- **1 cup cubed fully cooked ham**
- **1/2 cup thinly sliced carrot**
- **1 medium onion, diced**
- **1 bay leaf**
- **1 sprig fresh parsley**
- **1 sprig fresh savory *or* 1/4 teaspoon dried savory**
- **1 teaspoon beef bouillon granules**
- **1/4 teaspoon pepper**
- **1/2 teaspoon salt, optional**

In a large saucepan or soup kettle, combine all the ingredients. Bring to a boil. Reduce heat; cover and simmer for 20 minutes or until vegetables are tender. Before serving, discard bay leaf and parsley and savory sprigs.

hearty pasta tomato soup

PREP: 15 min. • **COOK:** 3-1/2 hours
YIELD: 14 servings (about 3-1/2 quarts).

I adapted the original recipe for this flavorful soup so I could make it in the slow cooker. It's ideal for staff luncheons at the school where I work, since we don't have easy access to a stove or oven. lydia kroese // plymouth, minnesota

1 pound bulk Italian sausage
6 cups beef broth
1 can (28 ounces) stewed tomatoes
1 can (15 ounces) tomato sauce
2 cups sliced zucchini
1 large onion, chopped
1 cup sliced carrots
1 cup sliced fresh mushrooms
1 medium green pepper, chopped
1/4 cup minced fresh parsley
2 teaspoons sugar
1 teaspoon dried oregano
1 teaspoon dried basil
1 garlic clove, minced
2 cups frozen cheese tortellini
Grated Parmesan cheese, optional

In a skillet, cook the sausage over medium heat until no longer pink; drain. Transfer to a 5-qt. slow cooker; add the next 13 ingredients. Cover and cook on high for 3-4 hours or until the vegetables are tender.

Cook tortellini according to package directions; drain. Stir into slow cooker; cover and cook 30 minutes longer. Serve with Parmesan cheese if desired.

EASY MINCED PARSLEY

Here's a tip that saves on cleanup. Don't use a knife and a cutting board to mince fresh parsley! Simply place parsley in a small glass container and snip sprigs with kitchen shears until completely minced.

bean and vegetable soup

PREP/TOTAL TIME: 25 min.
YIELD: 6-8 servings (2 quarts).

If you rustle up this soup, you can expect a fast feast for the eyes as well as the stomach.
janet frieman // kenosha, wisconsin

1 pound bulk Italian sausage
1 medium onion, sliced
1-1/2 cups water
1 can (15 ounces) garbanzo beans *or* chickpeas, rinsed and drained
1 can (14-1/2 ounces) diced tomatoes, undrained
1 can (14-1/2 ounces) beef broth
2 medium zucchini, cut into 1/4-inch slices
1/2 teaspoon dried basil
Grated Parmesan cheese

In a large saucepan, cook the sausage and onion over medium heat until meat is no longer pink; drain. Stir in the water, beans, tomatoes, broth, zucchini and basil.

Bring to a boil. Reduce heat and simmer for 5 minutes or until the zucchini is tender. Garnish with cheese.

basque vegetable soup

PREP: 25 min. • **COOK:** 2-1/4 hours + cooling • **YIELD:** 10-12 servings (3 quarts).

This is a hearty soup widely served here, especially at the many restaurants specializing in Basque cuisine. It's a nice way to use the abundant vegetables that are available this time of year. Give it a try this harvest season.

norman chegwyn // richmond, california

- **1 broiler/fryer chicken (2 to 3 pounds)**
- **8 cups water**
- **2 medium leeks, sliced**
- **2 medium carrots, sliced**
- **1 large turnip, peeled and cubed**
- **1 large onion, chopped**
- **1 large potato, peeled and cubed**
- **1 garlic clove, minced**
- **1-1/2 teaspoons salt**
- **1/2 teaspoon pepper**
- **1 tablespoon snipped fresh parsley**
- **1 teaspoon dried thyme**
- **3/4 pound fresh Polish sausage links**
- **2 cups navy beans, rinsed and drained**
- **1 cup shredded cabbage**
- **1 can (15 ounces) tomato sauce**

In Dutch oven, slowly bring chicken and water to a boil; skim foam. Reduce heat; cover and simmer for 45-60 minutes or until tender. Remove chicken; set aside until cool enough to handle.

Strain broth and skim fat. Return broth to Dutch oven. Add the leeks, carrots, turnip, onion, potato, garlic, salt, pepper, parsley and thyme. Bring to a boil. Reduce heat; cover and simmer for 30 minutes.

In a large skillet, cook sausage over medium heat until no longer pink. Drain on paper towels; set aside.

Meanwhile, remove chicken from the bones; discard bones and skin. Cut chicken into bite-size pieces; add to the Dutch oven. Add the beans, cabbage and cooked sausage. Simmer, uncovered, for 30 minutes or until vegetables are tender. Stir in tomato sauce; heat through.

LEARNING ABOUT LEEKS

A member of the onion family, leeks resemble oversize green onions with wide green leaves, a fat white stalk and roots at the bulb end. But the flavor of leeks is very subtle. Buy leeks with crisp, brightly colored leaves and an unblemished white stalk. Leeks that are larger than 1-1/2 inches in diameter will be less tender. Refrigerate leeks in a plastic bag for up to 5 days. Before using, cut off the roots. Trim the tough leaf ends. Slit the leek from end to end and wash thoroughly under cold water to remove dirt trapped between the leaf layers. Chop or slice the white portion to use in a variety of recipes.

easy baked potato soup

PREP/TOTAL TIME: 30 min. • **YIELD:** 10 servings (2-1/2 quarts).

I came up with this comforting soup when I was crunched for time and wanted to use up leftover baked potatoes. Since then, it has become a mealtime staple. Its wonderful aroma always gets cheers from my husband when he arrives home from work.
julie smithouser // colorado springs, colorado

- **3 to 4 medium baking potatoes, baked**
- **5 bacon strips, diced**
- **2 cans (10-3/4 ounces *each*) condensed cream of potato soup, undiluted**
- **1 can (10-3/4 ounces) condensed cheddar cheese soup, undiluted**
- **3-1/2 cups 2% milk**
- **2 teaspoons garlic powder**
- **2 teaspoons Worcestershire sauce**
- **1/2 teaspoon onion powder**
- **1/4 teaspoon pepper**
- **Dash Liquid Smoke, optional**
- **1 cup (8 ounces) sour cream**
- **Shredded cheddar cheese**

Peel and dice the baked potatoes; set aside. In a Dutch oven or soup kettle, cook the bacon over medium heat until crisp. Using a slotted spoon, remove to paper towels. Drain, reserving 1-1/2 teaspoons drippings.

Add the soups, milk, garlic powder, Worcestershire sauce, onion powder, pepper, Liquid Smoke if desired and reserved potatoes to the drippings.

Cook, uncovered, for 10 minutes or until heated through, stirring occasionally. Stir in sour cream; cook for 1-2 minutes or until heated through (do not boil). Garnish with cheddar cheese and bacon.

EXTRA BAKED POTATOES

When making a dish that needs to bake for more than an hour, I place a few potatoes in the oven to bake at the same time. I keep the baked potatoes in the refrigerator for quick meals or to add to soups and other recipes.
donna w. // goshen, indiana

hearty minestrone soup

PREP: 25 min. • **COOK:** 30 min.
YIELD: 9 servings.

Packed with tasty sausage and healthy veggies, this soup is not only nutritious, it's also a great way to get rid of your garden bounty.
donna smith // fairport, new york

- **1 pound bulk Italian sausage**
- **2 cups sliced celery**
- **1 cup chopped onion**
- **6 cups chopped zucchini**
- **1 can (28 ounces) diced tomatoes, undrained**
- **1-1/2 cups chopped green pepper**
- **1-1/2 teaspoons Italian seasoning**
- **1-1/2 teaspoons salt**
- **1 teaspoon dried oregano**
- **1 teaspoon sugar**
- **1/2 teaspoon dried basil**
- **1/4 teaspoon garlic powder**

In a large saucepan, cook the sausage until no longer pink. Remove with a slotted spoon to paper towel to drain, reserving 1 tablespoon of drippings. Saute celery and onion in drippings for 5 minutes. Add sausage and remaining ingredients; bring to a boil. Reduce heat; cover and simmer for 20-30 minutes or until the vegetables are tender.

garden vegetable soup

PREP: 5 min. • **COOK:** 50 min. • **YIELD:** 16 servings (1 gallon).

To get energy to face the day, try this mild-tasting soup for lunch or dinner. The recipe makes a whole gallon, but don't worry about leftovers—it's great reheated!
kelly rettinger // emporia, kansas

- **1-1/2 cups chopped onions**
- **1 cup chopped leeks**
- **1 garlic clove, minced**
- **1 tablespoon canola oil**
- **8 cups chicken broth**
- **8 cups cubed peeled potatoes**
- **4 carrots, sliced**
- **2 cups diced turnips**
- **2 cups sliced mushrooms**
- **6 ounces spinach, cut into thin strips**
- **1 pound smoked Polish sausage, thinly sliced and browned**
- **1 package (8 ounces) pasta wheels, cooked and drained**
- **1/2 teaspoon salt**
- **1/4 teaspoon pepper**
- **Grated Parmesan cheese, optional**

In a Dutch oven or large soup kettle, cook onions, leeks and garlic in oil until tender, about 5 minutes. Add chicken broth, potatoes, carrots, turnips and mushrooms. Cover and cook over low heat until vegetables are tender, about 30-40 minutes. Add spinach and sausage; cook for 10 minutes. Add pasta, salt and pepper; heat through. Serve with Parmesan cheese if desired.

TURNIP TIPS

When shopping for turnips, select those that are smooth-skinned, unblemished, heavy, firm and not spongy. Look for turnips no larger than 2 inches in diameter. Keep unwashed turnips in a plastic bag in your refrigerator's crisper drawer for up to 1 week. Just before using, wash, trim ends and peel.

curried pumpkin soup

PREP/TOTAL TIME: 20 min. • **YIELD:** 3 cups.

For special flavor, you'd can't beat this rich, creamy pumpkin soup. As a bonus, it's also really quick and easy to make. I serve it with banana bread or muffins and often double the recipe just to have leftovers. sarah perry // camarillo, california

- **2 green onions, sliced**
- **3/4 teaspoon curry powder**
- **2 tablespoons butter**
- **2 tablespoons all-purpose flour**
- **1 cup chicken broth**
- **3/4 cup canned pumpkin**
- **1 cup buttermilk**
- **1/2 cup cubed fully cooked ham**

In a small saucepan, saute onions with curry powder in butter until tender. Stir in flour. Gradually add broth and pumpkin. Bring to a boil over medium heat, stirring constantly; cook for 1-2 minutes or until thickened.

Reduce heat. Stir in buttermilk and ham; heat through.

savory sausage soup

PREP/TOTAL TIME: 30 min. • **YIELD:** 10 servings (3 quarts).

This is definitely a meal on its own. It smells so good while cooking. The men are always glad to walk in the door after work and see this on the stove. joan oakland // troy, montana

- **5 Italian sausage links (4 ounces *each*), sliced**
- **1 large onion, halved and sliced**
- **6 cups water**
- **1 can (28 ounces) crushed tomatoes, undrained**
- **2 small zucchini, quartered and sliced**
- **1/2 cup chopped green pepper**
- **1 tablespoon beef bouillon granules**
- **1/2 teaspoon dried basil**
- **1/2 teaspoon dried oregano**
- **1/4 teaspoon pepper**
- **3 ounces uncooked linguine, broken into 2-inch pieces**
- **3 tablespoons grated Parmesan cheese**

In a Dutch oven, cook sausage and onion over medium heat until sausage is no longer pink; drain.

Stir in the water, tomatoes, zucchini, green pepper, bouillon, basil, oregano and pepper. Bring to a boil. Stir in linguine. Cover and simmer for 10-15 minutes or until linguine is tender. Sprinkle with cheese.

pork garden bean soup

PREP: 10 min. • **COOK:** 30 min. • **YIELD:** 2 servings.

For a great way to start a meal, try this creamy soup.

florence schneidewend // neenah, wisconsin

- **1-3/4 cups water**
- **1 bone-in pork loin chop (about 1/2 pound)**
- **3/4 cup cut fresh green beans**
- **3/4 cup cubed peeled potatoes**
- **1 medium carrot, thinly sliced**
- **1/2 teaspoon salt**
- **1/4 teaspoon pepper**
- **1/3 cup half-and-half cream**

Place water and pork chop in a saucepan. Bring to a boil. Reduce heat; cover and simmer 15 minutes, just until pork is tender. Remove from water. Cool; cut into cubes.

Add the beans, potatoes, carrot, salt and pepper to cooking liquid. Return to a boil. Reduce heat; cover and simmer for 12 minutes or until vegetables are tender. Return pork to pan; stir in cream and heat through (do not boil).

grandma's harvest soup

PREP: 20 min. • **COOK:** 2-1/2 hours
YIELD: 16-18 servings (4-1/4 quarts).

I have fond memories of eating Grandma's soup when I was a child. Now I give my wife a break in the kitchen by making this soup every once in a while. It tastes just like home!

ronald desjardins // st. andrews west, ontario

- **1 smoked ham shank *or* ham hocks (1-1/2 pounds)**
- **3 quarts water**
- **1 tablespoon beef bouillon granules**
- **6 medium potatoes, peeled and chopped**
- **6 medium carrots, sliced**
- **2 medium onions, chopped**
- **1/2 medium head cabbage, chopped**
- **1 small turnip, diced**
- **1-1/2 teaspoons salt**
- **1/4 teaspoon pepper**

Place ham shank, water and bouillon in a Dutch oven or soup kettle; bring to a boil. Reduce heat; cover and simmer for 1-1/2 hours. Remove shank; allow to cool.

Add potatoes, carrots, onions, cabbage and turnip to broth; cover and simmer for 1 hour or until vegetables are tender. Using a potato masher, coarsely mash vegetables.

Remove meat from shank; cut into bite-size pieces and add to soup. Stir in salt and pepper; heat through.

ham and vegetable soup

PREP: 15 min. • **COOK:** 4 hours
YIELD: 14-16 servings (4 quarts).

The basis for this soup's broth conveniently comes from canned bean soup. Everyone who tries this comments on how nicely the smoky flavor of ham blends with the vegetables.

helen peterson // rives junction, michigan

- **2 pounds smoked ham shanks**
- **4 medium carrots, sliced**
- **1 cup thinly sliced celery**
- **1 medium onion, chopped**
- **8 cups water**
- **2-1/2 cups diced unpeeled red potatoes**
- **1 cup *each* frozen corn, peas and cut green beans**
- **1 can (11-1/2 ounces) condensed bean and bacon soup, undiluted**
- **1/4 teaspoon pepper**

Place ham shanks, carrots, celery, onion and water in a Dutch oven or soup kettle; bring to a boil. Reduce heat; cover and simmer for 2-1/2 hours or until meat starts to fall off the bones.

Add potatoes and vegetables; bring to a boil. Reduce heat; cover and simmer for 1 hour. Remove shanks; allow to cool. Remove meat from bones and cut into bite-size pieces; discard bones. Return meat to pan. Stir in bean and bacon soup and pepper; heat through.

kielbasa bean soup

PREP: 10 min. • **COOK:** 1-1/4 hours • **YIELD:** 12 servings (about 3 quarts).

I usually make a double batch of this meaty vegetable soup and freeze some in serving-size containers. It makes a nice meal for busy days.

emily chaney // blue hill, maine

- **4-1/2 cups water**
- **2 cans (14-1/2 ounces *each*) diced tomatoes, undrained**
- **1 can (16 ounces) kidney beans, rinsed and drained**
- **1 can (15-1/2 ounces) great northern beans, rinsed and drained**
- **1 can (15 ounces) garbanzo beans *or* chickpeas, rinsed and drained**
- **2 medium green peppers, chopped**
- **2 medium onions, chopped**
- **2 celery ribs, chopped**
- **1 medium zucchini, sliced**
- **2 teaspoons chicken bouillon granules**
- **2 garlic cloves, minced**
- **2-1/2 teaspoons chili powder**
- **2 teaspoons dried basil**
- **1-1/2 teaspoons salt**
- **1/2 teaspoon pepper**
- **2 bay leaves**
- **3/4 pound smoked kielbasa *or* smoked Polish sausage, halved lengthwise and sliced**

In a Dutch oven or soup kettle, combine all ingredients except the sausage. Bring to a boil. Reduce heat; cover. Simmer for 1 hour. Add sausage; heat through. Discard bay leaves.

potato and cabbage soup

PREP: 10 min. • **COOK:** 30 min.
YIELD: 12-14 servings (about 3-1/2 quarts).

I can trace this recipe back to my great-grandmother, whose parents were potato farmers in Ireland. Here's a delicious way to use that crop.

pat rimmel // ford city, pennsylvania

- **1 large onion, chopped**
- **2 tablespoons butter**
- **10 cups water**
- **6 cups chopped cabbage**
- **4 cups diced peeled potatoes**
- **3 tablespoons chicken bouillon granules**
- **1/2 teaspoon coarsely ground pepper**
- **1/2 teaspoon dried minced garlic**
- **4 cups cubed fully cooked ham**

In a large saucepan or Dutch oven, saute onion in butter until tender. Add the water, cabbage, potatoes, bouillon, pepper and garlic. Cover and simmer for 20-25 minutes or until potatoes are tender. Stir in ham; heat through.

parmesan potato soup

PREP: 45 min. + cooling • **COOK:** 20 min. • **YIELD:** 10-12 servings.

Even my husband, who's not much of a soup eater, likes this. Our two boys do too. With homemade bread and a salad, it's a satisfying meal. tami walters // kingsport, tennessee

- **4 medium baking potatoes (about 2 pounds)**
- **3/4 cup chopped onion**
- **1/2 cup butter**
- **1/2 cup all-purpose flour**
- **1/2 teaspoon dried basil**
- **1/2 teaspoon seasoned salt**
- **1/4 teaspoon celery salt**
- **1/4 teaspoon garlic powder**
- **1/4 teaspoon onion salt**
- **1/4 teaspoon pepper**
- **1/4 teaspoon rubbed sage**
- **1/4 teaspoon dried thyme**
- **4-1/2 cups chicken broth**
- **6 cups milk**
- **3/4 to 1 cup grated Parmesan cheese**
- **10 bacon strips, cooked and crumbled**

Pierce potatoes with a fork; bake at 375° for 40-60 minutes until tender. Cool, peel and cube; set aside.

In a large Dutch oven or soup kettle, saute onion in butter until tender. Stir in flour and seasonings until blended. Gradually add broth, stirring constantly. Bring to a boil; cook and stir for 2 minutes or until thickened. Add potatoes; return to a boil. Reduce heat; cover and simmer for 10 minutes.

Add milk and cheese; heat through. Stir in bacon.

GREAT GARNISHES

Aside from cooked, crumbled bacon, you can dress up a soup by adding a garnish like a sprinkling of nuts, chopped fresh herbs, sliced green onions, slivers of fresh vegetables, croutons or shredded cheese.

wisconsin split pea soup

PREP: 10 min. + cooling • **COOK:** 3 hours + cooling
YIELD: 12 servings (3 quarts).

Field peas that have been dried (split peas) have been a staple soup ingredient for country cooks for years. Marjoram, garlic, potatoes and carrots blend nicely with peas in this hearty and economical soup. linda rock // stratford, wisconsin

- **1 pound dried green split peas**
- **2-1/2 quarts water**
- **1 meaty ham bone *or* 2 smoked ham hocks**
- **1-1/2 cups chopped onion**
- **1 cup *each* diced celery, carrots and potatoes**
- **1 teaspoon dried parsley flakes**
- **1/2 teaspoon pepper**
- **1/4 teaspoon garlic salt**
- **1/4 teaspoon dried marjoram**
- **Salt to taste**

In a Dutch oven, add peas, water and ham bone; bring to a boil. Reduce heat; cover and simmer for 2 hours, stirring occasionally.

Stir in the remaining ingredients. Bring to a boil. Reduce heat; cover and simmer for 30 minutes or until vegetables are tender.

Set aside ham bone until cool enough to handle. Remove meat from bone; discard bone. Cut ham into bite-size pieces. Return to the soup and heat through.

best-ever potato soup

PREP/TOTAL TIME: 30 min.
YIELD: 8 servings (2 quarts).

You'll be surprised at the taste of this rich, cheesy concoction—it's not a typical potato soup. I came up with the recipe after enjoying baked potato soup at one of my favorite restaurants. I added bacon, and I think that makes it even better.
coleen morrissey // sweet valley, pennsylvania

- **6 bacon strips, diced**
- **3 cups cubed peeled potatoes**
- **1 can (14-1/2 ounces) chicken broth**
- **1 small carrot, grated**
- **1/2 cup chopped onion**
- **1 tablespoon dried parsley flakes**
- **1/2 teaspoon *each* celery seed, salt and pepper**
- **3 tablespoons all-purpose flour**
- **3 cups 2% milk**
- **8 ounces process cheese (Velveeta), cubed**
- **2 green onions, thinly sliced, optional**

In a large saucepan, cook bacon until crisp; drain. Add potatoes, broth, carrot, onion, parsley, celery seed, salt and pepper. Cover and simmer until potatoes are tender, about 15 minutes.

Combine flour and milk until smooth; stir into soup. Bring to a boil; boil and stir for 2 minutes. Add cheese; stir until cheese is melted and the soup is heated through. Garnish with green onions if desired.

sauerkraut soup

PREP: 10 min. • **COOK:** 70 min. • **YIELD:** 8-10 servings (2-1/2 quarts).

The medley of tomato, sauerkraut and smoked sausage gives this savory soup old-world flavor. It's enjoyable to make and serve, especially during the colder months. The tangy taste and aroma really warm you up!

jean marie cornelius // whitesville, new york

- **1 pound smoked Polish sausage, cut into 1/2- inch pieces**
- **5 medium potatoes, peeled and cubed**
- **2 medium onions, chopped**
- **2 carrots, cut into 1/4-inch slices**
- **3 cans (14-1/2 ounces *each*) chicken broth**
- **1 can (32 ounces) sauerkraut, rinsed and drained**
- **1 can (6 ounces) tomato paste**

In a large saucepan or Dutch oven, combine sausage, potatoes, onions, carrots and chicken broth; bring to a boil. Reduce heat; cover and simmer for 30 minutes or until potatoes are tender.

Add the sauerkraut and tomato paste; mix well. Return to a boil. Reduce heat; cover and simmer 30 minutes longer. If a thinner soup is desired, add additional water or chicken broth.

split pea soup with meatballs

PREP: 20 min. • **COOK:** 2 hours • **YIELD:** 10-14 servings (3-1/2 quarts).

The addition of tender meatballs in this recipe adds a flavorful twist to ordinary split pea soup. Whenever I prepare this for our church soup suppers, I come home with an empty kettle! donna smith // grey cliff, montana

- 1 pound dry green split peas
- 3 medium carrots, cut into 1/2-inch pieces
- 3/4 cup diced celery
- 1 medium onion, diced
- 8 cups water
- 3 medium potatoes, cut into 1/2-inch cubes
- 2-1/2 teaspoons salt
- 1/4 teaspoon pepper

MEATBALLS:

- 3/4 cup finely chopped celery
- 1 medium onion, finely chopped
- 4 tablespoons canola oil, *divided*
- 1-1/2 cups soft bread crumbs
- 2 tablespoons water
- 1 teaspoon salt
- 1/2 teaspoon dried sage, crushed
- 1 egg
- 1 pound ground pork

In a Dutch oven or soup kettle, combine peas, carrots, celery, onion and water; bring to a boil over medium heat. Reduce heat; cover and simmer for 1 hour.

Add potatoes, salt and pepper; cover and simmer for 30 minutes.

Meanwhile, in a large skillet, saute celery and onion in 2 tablespoons oil until tender; transfer to a large bowl. Add bread crumbs, water, salt, sage and egg; crumble pork over mixture and mix well. Form into 3/4-in. balls.

In the same skillet, brown meatballs in remaining oil until no longer pink inside. Add to soup; cover and simmer for 15 minutes.

SOFT BREAD CRUMBS

Some recipes call for soft bread crumbs. However, soft bread crumbs cannot be purchased since they're made from fresh bread. The easiest method is to tear 1-2 slices of bread into 1-inch pieces and process in a blender or a food processor until the desired crumb size is reached.

pork and veggie soup

PREP: 20 min. • **COOK:** 7 hours
YIELD: 9 servings.

Looking for a change from typical vegetable soup? Try this hearty combination. A tasty broth has tender chunks of pork and a bounty of veggies, including carrots, green beans, diced tomatoes and corn.

jennifer honeycutt
nashville, tennessee

- 2 pounds boneless pork, cubed
- 2 tablespoons canola oil
- 2 cups water
- 4 medium carrots, cut into 1-inch pieces
- 1 can (14-1/2 ounces) diced tomatoes, undrained
- 1-1/2 cups frozen corn
- 1-1/2 cups frozen cut green beans
- 1 large onion, chopped
- 1 cup salsa
- 1 can (4 ounces) chopped green chilies
- 1 tablespoon minced fresh parsley
- 2 garlic cloves, minced
- 2 teaspoons beef bouillon granules
- 2 teaspoons ground cumin
- 1/2 teaspoon salt
- 1/2 teaspoon pepper

In a large skillet, brown pork in oil over medium heat; drain. Transfer to a 5-qt. slow cooker. Stir in the remaining ingredients. Cover and cook on low for 7-8 hours or until meat juices run clear and vegetables are tender.

ham and bean soup

PREP/TOTAL TIME: 30 min. **YIELD:** 7 servings.

If you like ham and bean soup but don't want to spend hours in the kitchen, this tasty and speedy version will leave you with a satisfied smile.

taste of home test kitchen

- 2 medium carrots, sliced
- 2 celery ribs, chopped
- 1/2 cup chopped onion
- 2 tablespoons butter
- 4 cans (15-1/2 ounces *each*) great northern beans, rinsed and drained
- 4 cups chicken broth
- 2 cups cubed fully cooked ham
- 1 teaspoon chili powder
- 1/2 teaspoon minced garlic
- 1/4 teaspoon pepper
- 1 bay leaf

In a large saucepan, saute the carrots, celery and onion in butter until tender. Stir in the remaining ingredients. Bring to a boil. Reduce the heat; cook for 15 minutes or until heated through. Discard bay leaf.

speedy minestrone

PREP/TOTAL TIME: 25 min. • **YIELD:** 6 servings.

I maximize the potential of convenience products to create a hearty soup for cold winter nights. This full-bodied dish contains lots of beans, veggies and sausage, and the pasta mix ties everything together. dona hoffman // addison, illinois

- **2 cans (14-1/2 ounces each) beef broth**
- **1 package (24 ounces) frozen vegetable and pasta medley in garlic sauce**
- **1 pound smoked sausage, cut into 1/2-inch slices**
- **1 can (16 ounces) kidney beans, rinsed and drained**
- **1/4 cup chopped onion**
- **1 teaspoon dried basil**
- **1 teaspoon dried parsley flakes**

Shredded Parmesan cheese

In a large saucepan, combine the first seven ingredients. Bring to a boil. Reduce the heat; simmer, uncovered, for 10-15 minutes or until heated through. Sprinkle with Parmesan cheese.

italian peasant soup

PREP/TOTAL TIME: 25 min.
YIELD: 11 servings (2-3/4 quarts).

My father shared this recipe with me, and I use it when I need a hearty meal. It's my sons' favorite. Loaded with sausage, chicken, beans and spinach, the quick soup is nice for special occasions, too. kim knight // hamburg, pennsylvania

- **1 pound Italian sausage links, casings removed and cut into 1-inch slices**
- **2 medium onions, chopped**
- **6 garlic cloves, chopped**
- **1 pound boneless skinless chicken breasts, cut into 1-inch cubes**
- **2 cans (15 ounces *each*) white kidney *or* cannellini beans, rinsed and drained**
- **2 cans (14-1/2 ounces *each*) chicken broth**
- **2 cans (14-1/2 ounces *each*) diced tomatoes**
- **1 teaspoon dried basil**
- **1 teaspoon dried oregano**
- **6 cups fresh spinach leaves, chopped**

Shredded Parmesan cheese, optional

In a Dutch oven, cook sausage and onions over medium heat until sausage is no longer pink. Add garlic; cook 1 minute longer. Drain. Add chicken; cook and stir until chicken is no longer pink.

Stir in the beans, broth, tomatoes, basil and oregano. Bring to a boil. Reduce the heat; simmer, uncovered, for 10 minutes. Add the spinach and heat just until wilted. Serve with cheese if desired.

cheesy ham 'n' potato soup

PREP/TOTAL TIME: 30 min. • **YIELD:** 7 servings.

When I'm in the mood for comfort food, I prepare a pot of this soup. It's always a warming treat on a cold day.
melissa sherlock // omaha, nebraska

- **2 cups cubed potatoes**
- **1-1/2 cups water**
- **1-1/2 cups cubed fully cooked ham**
- **1 large onion, chopped**
- **3 tablespoons butter**
- **3 tablespoons all-purpose flour**
- **1/4 teaspoon pepper**
- **3 cups milk**
- **1-1/2 cups (6 ounces) finely shredded cheddar cheese**
- **1 cup frozen broccoli florets, thawed and chopped**

In a saucepan, bring potatoes and water to a boil. Cover and cook for 10-15 minutes or until tender. Drain, reserving 1 cup cooking liquid; set potatoes and liquid aside.

In a large saucepan, saute ham and onion in butter until onion is tender. Stir in the flour and pepper until smooth; gradually add milk and reserved cooking liquid. Bring to a boil; cook and stir for 2 minutes or until thickened. Reduce heat to low. Add the cheese, broccoli and reserved potatoes; cook and stir until cheese is melted and soup is heated through.

HANDY CHICKEN

When preparing boneless chicken breasts for the freezer, I first wrap them individually in plastic wrap. Then I put several in a resealable plastic freezer bag. Later, if I want only a couple pieces, they come out easily since they're not frozen together.
jennifer r. // redondo beach, california

spaghetti soup

PREP/TOTAL TIME: 30 min.
YIELD: 12-14 servings (3 quarts).

With tomato sauce, noodles and Italian seasonings, this soup tastes like spaghetti! It's so easy, even our preteen daughter can make it by herself. laura braun // appleton, wisconsin

2 pounds bulk Italian sausage
1 cup chopped onion
1 garlic clove, minced
2 cans (14-1/2 ounces *each*) beef broth
1 jar (30 ounces) spaghetti sauce
1 can (15 ounces) sliced carrots, drained
1 can (14-1/2 ounces) Italian flat beans, drained
1 cup water
1 teaspoon Italian seasoning
1 teaspoon dried basil
3-1/2 cups cooked macaroni
Grated Parmesan *or* shredded mozzarella cheese, optional

In a large saucepan or Dutch oven over medium heat, brown the sausage, onion and garlic; drain. Add broth, spaghetti sauce, carrots, beans, water, Italian seasoning and basil; bring to a boil. Reduce heat; cover and simmer for 10-15 minutes. Just before serving, add the macaroni and heat through. Garnish with cheese if desired.

posole

PREP: 15 min. + standing • **COOK:** 65 min.
YIELD: 8 servings (2-1/2 quarts).

This spicy stew-like soup is traditionally served in New Mexico at holiday time to celebrate life's blessings, but it's good any time of the year. taste of home test kitchen

4 dried ancho chilies
4 dried guajillo *or* pasilla chilies
2 tablespoons canola oil, *divided*
1-1/2 cups boiling water
2 pounds boneless pork, cut into 1-inch cubes
1/2 cup chopped onion
4 garlic cloves, minced
3 cups chicken broth
2 cans (29 ounces *each*) hominy, rinsed and drained
1-1/2 teaspoons dried Mexican oregano
1 teaspoon salt
Optional toppings: lime wedges, sliced radishes, diced avocado and chopped onion

In a Dutch oven, saute chilies in 1 tablespoon oil for 1-2 minutes or until heated through, pressing with a spatula (do not brown). Transfer chilies to a bowl; add boiling water. Soak for 20 minutes or until softened; remove stems and seeds. Reserve water.

In the Dutch oven, brown pork in remaining oil in batches. Saute onion and garlic with the last batch of pork. Add broth; bring to a boil. Reduce heat; cover and simmer for 30 minutes or until meat is tender.

Transfer chilies and soaking liquid to a blender; cover and process until smooth. Strain through a fine strainer, reserving pulp and discarding skins. Add pulp to pork mixture. Stir in the hominy, oregano and salt. Cover and simmer for 20 minutes. Serve with toppings of your choice.

EDITOR'S NOTE: When handling chilies, disposable gloves are recommended. Avoid touching your face.

cabbage sausage soup

PREP: 5 min. • **COOK:** 45 min.
YIELD: 16 servings (4 quarts).

We grow cabbage and like to use it often in our own recipes. Cabbage makes a nice addition to this hearty, savory tomato-based soup.

bill brim // tiffin, georgia

1 pound bulk Italian sausage
1 large onion, chopped
2 garlic cloves, minced
7 cups chopped cabbage (about 1-1/2 pounds)
4 cans (28 ounces *each*) diced tomatoes, undrained
2 teaspoons dried basil
2 teaspoons brown sugar
1 teaspoon dried oregano
1 bay leaf
3/4 teaspoon minced fresh rosemary *or* 1/4 teaspoon dried rosemary, crushed
1/2 teaspoon salt
1/8 teaspoon pepper

In a Dutch oven or soup kettle, cook sausage, onion and garlic over medium heat until meat is browned. Add the cabbage; cook and stir for 3-5 minutes or until cabbage is crisp-tender.

Stir in the remaining ingredients. Bring to a boil. Reduce heat; cover and simmer for 30-35 minutes or until cabbage is tender. Discard bay leaf.

mock minestrone

PREP/TOTAL TIME: 30 min. • **YIELD:** 20-22 servings (5-1/2 quarts).

Don't let the number of ingredients in this recipe fool you. The bulk of the items are combined all at once and simmered, making this a no-fuss favorite.

jorja hutton // sturgeon bay, wisconsin

2 pounds bulk Italian sausage
1 large onion, chopped
1 garlic clove, minced
6 cups water
1 jar (30 ounces) chunky spaghetti sauce
2 cans (10-3/4 ounces *each*) condensed beef broth, undiluted
1 can (15 ounces) garbanzo beans *or* 15 ounces garbanzo beans, rinsed and drained
1 package (10 ounces) frozen chopped spinach, thawed and squeezed dry
1 cup diced zucchini
1 cup thinly sliced carrots
1-1/2 teaspoons dried basil
1/2 teaspoon pepper
4 cups cooked pasta
Grated Parmesan cheese, optional

In a Dutch oven or soup kettle, cook sausage, onion and garlic until sausage is browned and onion is tender; drain. Stir in all remaining ingredients except the pasta and cheese. Simmer for 20 minutes. Add pasta and heat through. Garnish with cheese if desired.

ANOTHER USE FOR BULK ITALIAN SAUSAGE

When I make meat loaf, I replace some of the ground beef with bulk Italian sausage and substitute seasoned bread crumbs for regular dry bread crumbs. It gives the meat loaf slices a deliciously different flavor.

lotte w. // sebring, florida

spicy zucchini soup

PREP: 20 min. • **COOK:** 1-1/2 hours • **YIELD:** 14-16 servings (4 quarts).

My files are overflowing with recipes I keep meaning to try, so when I encountered a bumper crop of zucchini, I finally had the chance to simmer up this soup. Now, I look forward to it every summer. catherine johnston // stafford, new york

- **1 pound bulk Italian sausage**
- **3 cans (28 ounces *each*) diced tomatoes, undrained**
- **3 cans (14-1/2 ounces *each*) beef broth**
- **2 pounds zucchini, diced**
- **2 medium green peppers, diced**
- **2 cups thinly sliced celery**
- **1 cup chopped onion**
- **2 teaspoons Italian seasoning**
- **1 teaspoon dried basil**
- **1 teaspoon dried oregano**
- **1 teaspoon salt**
- **1/2 teaspoon sugar**
- **1/4 teaspoon pepper**
- **1/4 teaspoon garlic powder**
- **3 cups cooked macaroni**

In a Dutch oven or soup kettle, brown and crumble sausage; drain. Add tomatoes, broth, zucchini, green peppers, celery, onion and seasonings; bring to a boil. Reduce heat; cover and simmer for 1-1/4 to 1-1/2 hours or until vegetables are tender. Add macaroni; heat through.

pizza soup

PREP: 5 min. • **COOK:** 40 min. • **YIELD:** 10 servings (about 2-1/2 quarts).

My family regularly requests this robust soup, and it's also a big hit with my canasta group. I top each bowl with a slice of toasted bread and cheese, but you can have fun incorporating other pizza toppings like cooked sausage.

jackie brossard // kitchener, ontario

- **2 cans (14-1/2 ounces *each*) diced tomatoes**
- **2 cans (10-3/4 ounces *each*) condensed tomato soup, undiluted**
- **2-1/2 cups water**
- **1 package (3-1/2 ounces) sliced pepperoni, quartered**
- **1 medium sweet red pepper, chopped**
- **1 medium green pepper, chopped**
- **1 cup sliced fresh mushrooms**
- **2 garlic cloves, minced**
- **1/2 teaspoon rubbed sage**
- **1/2 teaspoon dried basil**
- **1/2 teaspoon dried oregano**
- **Salt and pepper to taste**
- **10 slices French bread, toasted**
- **1-1/2 cups (6 ounces) shredded part-skim mozzarella cheese**

In a Dutch oven, bring the tomatoes, soup and water to a boil. Reduce heat; cover and simmer for 15 minutes. Mash with a potato masher. Add the pepperoni, red and green peppers, mushrooms, garlic, sage, basil, oregano, salt and pepper. Cover and simmer for 10 minutes or until vegetables are tender.

Ladle into ovenproof bowls. Top each with a slice of bread and sprinkle with cheese. Broil 4 in. from the heat until cheese is melted and bubbly.

SIMPLE MUSHROOM SLICING

My husband and I love fresh mushrooms in lots of different recipes, but slicing them takes a lot of time. I discovered how quick and easy the job is when I use an egg slicer. jennifer i. //brookhaven, pennsylvania

sunday gumbo

PREP: 10 min. • **COOK:** 50 min.
YIELD: 16 servings (about 4 quarts).

With sausage, chicken and shrimp, plus rice, a medley of vegetables and the heat of cayenne pepper, this warming soup is a great addition to Sunday meals.

debbie burchette // summitville, indiana

- **1 pound Italian sausage links, cut into 1/4-inch pieces**
- **1 pound boneless skinless chicken breasts, cubed**
- **3 tablespoons canola oil**
- **1 medium sweet red pepper, chopped**
- **1 medium onion, chopped**
- **3 celery ribs, chopped**
- **1 teaspoon dried marjoram**
- **1 teaspoon dried thyme**
- **1/2 teaspoon garlic powder**
- **1/2 teaspoon cayenne pepper**
- **3 cans (14-1/2 ounces *each*) chicken broth**
- **2/3 cup uncooked brown rice**
- **1 can (14-1/2 ounces) diced tomatoes, undrained**
- **1 pound uncooked medium shrimp, peeled and deveined**
- **2 cups frozen sliced okra**

In a Dutch oven, brown sausage and chicken in oil. Remove with a slotted spoon and keep warm. In the drippings, saute red pepper, onion and celery until tender. Stir in the seasonings; cook for 5 minutes. Stir in the broth, rice and sausage mixture; bring to a boil. Reduce heat; cover and simmer for 20-25 minutes or until rice is tender.

Stir in tomatoes, shrimp and okra; cook for 10 minutes or until shrimp turn pink, stirring occasionally.

cauliflower pork soup

PREP/TOTAL TIME: 30 min.
YIELD: 6-8 servings (2 quarts).

I picked up this delicious recipe several years ago from a friend. Everyone enjoys it, even my husband, who typically doesn't care for cauliflower.

loretta wohlenhaus // cumberland, iowa

- **1 pound ground pork**
- **1 small head cauliflower, broken into florets**
- **2 cups water**
- **1/2 cup chopped onion**
- **2 cups milk, *divided***
- **1/4 cup all-purpose flour**
- **2 cups (8 ounces) shredded sharp cheddar cheese**
- **1/2 teaspoon salt**
- **1/8 teaspoon pepper**
- **Chopped chives, optional**

In a large skillet, cook the pork until no longer pink; drain and set aside.

In a Dutch oven or large soup kettle, cook cauliflower in water for 10 minutes or until tender. Do not drain. Add pork, onion and 1-1/4 cups milk to cauliflower.

In a small bowl, combine flour and remaining milk until smooth; stir into cauliflower mixture. Bring to a boil; boil and stir for 2 minutes. Remove from the heat; add cheese, salt and pepper, stirring until cheese melts. Garnish with chives if desired.

creamy kale soup

PREP: 35 min. • **COOK:** 20 min. • **YIELD:** 8 servings (2 quarts).

To me, the spicier the seasoning in the sausage, the better the soup—that's why I use spicy sausage in this recipe. Kale is also great here since, when heated, it keeps its texture better than spinach. nancy dyer // grover, oklahoma

- **1 pound uncooked Italian sausage links**
- **3/4 cup chopped onion**
- **1 bacon strip, diced**
- **2 garlic cloves, minced**
- **2 cups water**
- **1 can (14-1/2 ounces) chicken broth**
- **2 cups diced potatoes**
- **2 cups thinly sliced fresh kale**
- **1/3 cup heavy whipping cream**

Place the sausages in a ungreased 15-in. x 10-in. x 1-in. baking pan; pierce casings. Bake at 325° for 15-20 minutes or until fully cooked. Drain; set aside to cool.

Meanwhile, in a saucepan, saute onion and bacon for 3 minutes or until onion is tender. Add garlic; saute for 1 minute. Add water, broth and potatoes; bring to a boil. Reduce heat; cover and simmer for 20 minutes or until potatoes are tender.

Cut sausages in half lengthwise, then into 1/4-in. slices. Add kale, cream and sausage to soup; heat through (do not boil).

ham and chicken gumbo

PREP: 10 min. • **COOK:** 30 min.
YIELD: 4 servings.

I've always enjoyed spending time in the kitchen and worked as a home economist for a utility company in the 1940s. With two kinds of meat, this gumbo makes a hearty supper.
jean leonard // houston, texas

- **6 bacon strips, cut into 1/2-inch pieces**
- **3/4 cup chopped onion**
- **2 garlic cloves, minced**
- **1 cup cubed fully cooked ham**
- **1/2 cup cubed cooked chicken**
- **2 cups frozen sliced okra**
- **1 can (14-1/2 ounces) diced tomatoes, undrained**
- **2 cups chicken broth**
- **1 teaspoon Worcestershire sauce**
- **1/4 teaspoon salt**
- **8 drops hot pepper sauce**
- **Hot cooked rice**

In a large skillet, cook bacon over medium heat just until crisp. Add onion and cook, stirring constantly, until the onion is soft. Add the garlic, ham and chicken; cook for 2 minutes, stirring constantly. Stir in the okra, tomatoes and broth; bring to a boil. Reduce heat; cover and simmer for 30 minutes. Add Worcestershire sauce, salt and hot pepper sauce. Serve over rice.

mac 'n' cheese soup

PREP/TOTAL TIME: 30 min. • **YIELD:** 8 servings (2 quarts).

I came across this unique recipe a few years ago and made some changes to suit our tastes. Because it starts with packaged macaroni and cheese, the creamy soup is ready in a jiffy. nancy daugherty // cortland, ohio

- **1 package (14 ounces) deluxe macaroni and cheese dinner mix**
- **9 cups water, *divided***
- **1 cup fresh broccoli florets**
- **2 tablespoons finely chopped onion**
- **1 can (10-3/4 ounces) condensed cheddar cheese soup, undiluted**
- **2-1/2 cups 2% milk**
- **1 cup chopped fully cooked ham**

Set aside cheese sauce packet from macaroni and cheese mix. In a large saucepan, bring 8 cups water to a boil. Add macaroni; cook for 8-10 minutes or until tender.

Meanwhile, in another large saucepan, bring remaining water to a boil. Add broccoli and onion; cook, uncovered, for 3 minutes. Stir in the soup, milk, ham and contents of cheese sauce packet; heat through. Drain macaroni; stir into soup.

pork 'n' bean soup

PREP/TOTAL TIME: 30 min. • **YIELD:** 6 servings.

I like to make this comforting soup at least once a month. It simmers on its own while you prepare the rest of the meal. Try adding cooked elbow noodles or cubed cooked chicken.

kelly olson // moab, utah

- 2 cans (11 ounces *each*) pork and beans
- 1 can (15-1/2 ounces) great northern beans, rinsed and drained
- 1 package (16 ounces) frozen corn, thawed
- 4 cups chicken broth
- 3 pickled jalapeno peppers, seeded and chopped
- 1 teaspoon garlic salt

In a large saucepan, combine the beans, corn, broth, peppers and garlic salt. Bring to a boil. Reduce heat; simmer, uncovered, for 20 minutes or until heated through.

EDITOR'S NOTE: We recommend wearing disposable gloves when cutting hot peppers. Avoid touching your face.

canadian bacon potato soup

PREP: 20 min. • **COOK:** 30 min.
YIELD: 7 servings.

Canadian bacon adds a hint of smoky flavor to this hearty soup that my husband loves. It doesn't have the typical butter and heavy cream you'll find in many potato soups, but it's still rich-tasting and satisfying.

cheryl morgan // dover, minnesota

- 2 medium onions, chopped
- 4 medium potatoes, peeled and quartered
- 2 cups chicken broth
- 1 can (12 ounces) fat-free evaporated milk
- 5 slices (3 ounces) Canadian bacon, chopped
- 1 package butter-flavored granules
- 1/4 teaspoon salt
- 1/8 teaspoon pepper
- 7 tablespoons fat-free sour cream
- 1/3 cup minced chives

In a large saucepan or Dutch oven coated with cooking spray, saute onions until tender. Add potatoes and broth; bring to a boil. Reduce heat; cover and simmer for 20-25 minutes or until potatoes are very tender. Set aside 1 cup potato mixture.

Puree remaining mixture in batches in a blender or food processor; return to the pan. Stir in the milk, Canadian bacon, butter-flavored granules, salt, pepper and reserved potato mixture. Heat through (do not boil). Garnish each serving with 1 tablespoon sour cream; sprinkle with chives.

EDITOR'S NOTE: This recipe was tested with Butter Buds butter-flavored mix. Look for it in the spice aisle.

ROASTED TOMATO SOUP WITH FRESH BASIL, PG. 162

SOUPS

fish & meatless

CARROT SOUP, PG. 164
CARROT ZUCCHINI SOUP, PG. 169
HEARTY MEATLESS MINESTRONE, PG. 176

chilled squash and carrot soup

PREP: 30 min. + chilling
YIELD: 4 servings.

This smooth soup is colorful as well as nutritious and filling. Served chilled, it makes an elegant first course when entertaining. But it's also good warm. elaine sabacky // litchfield, minnesota

- **1-1/2 pounds butternut squash, peeled, seeded and cubed (about 3 cups)**
- **1 can (14-1/2 ounces) chicken *or* vegetable broth**
- **2 medium carrots, sliced**
- **1 medium onion, chopped**
- **1/4 teaspoon salt**
- **1/2 cup fat-free evaporated milk**
- **3 tablespoons reduced-fat sour cream**

In a large saucepan, combine the squash, broth, carrots, onion and salt. Bring to a boil. Reduce heat; cover and simmer for 15-20 minutes or until the vegetables are very tender. Remove from the heat; cool.

In a blender or food processor, puree squash mixture in batches. Transfer to a bowl, stir in milk. Cover and chill until serving. Garnish with sour cream.

southern okra bean stew

PREP/TOTAL TIME: 30 min. • **YIELD:** 11 servings.

When this spicy stew is simmering on the stove, my family has a hard time waiting for dinner. It's like a thick tomato-based soup with a hearty mix of okra, brown rice and beans. Everyone leaves the table feeling satisfied—and eager to have it again soon. beverly mcdowell // athens, georgia

- **4 cups water**
- **1 can (28 ounces) diced tomatoes, undrained**
- **1-1/2 cups chopped green peppers**
- **1 large onion, chopped**
- **3 garlic cloves, minced**
- **1 teaspoon Italian seasoning**
- **1 teaspoon chili powder**
- **1/2 to 1 teaspoon hot pepper sauce**
- **3/4 teaspoon salt**
- **1 bay leaf**
- **4 cups cooked brown rice**
- **2 cans (16 ounces *each*) kidney beans, rinsed and drained**
- **3 cans (8 ounces *each*) tomato sauce**
- **1 package (16 ounces) frozen sliced okra**

In a large Dutch oven or soup kettle, combine the water, tomatoes, green peppers, onion, garlic, Italian seasoning, chili powder, hot pepper sauce, salt and bay leaf. Bring to a boil. Reduce heat; simmer, uncovered, for 5 minutes.

Add the rice, beans, tomato sauce and okra. Simmer, uncovered, for 8-10 minutes or until the vegetables are tender. Discard bay leaf.

EASY GREAT GRAINS

When I have time, I cook several batches of brown rice, barley or wild rice at one time, divide them into 1/2-cup and 1-cup portions. I place the portions in small freezer bags and freeze. I can easily defrost a bag when I need it and add it to casseroles or soups. It's a quick way to add healthy whole grains to our diet anytime.

amy m. // elizabethtown, kentucky

hearty fish soup

PREP: 15 min. • **COOK:** 20 min. • **YIELD:** 4 cups.

I stay away from recipes that require a lot of preparation, so this chunky soup recipe is perfect for me. Its simple ingredient list calls for frozen vegetables and already seasoned canned tomatoes. deborah groff // live oak, texas

- **2 small shallots, chopped**
- **1 small garlic clove, minced**
- **1 can (14-1/2 ounces) diced tomatoes with basil, oregano and garlic, undrained**
- **1-1/2 cups chicken broth**
- **3/4 cup frozen mixed vegetables**
- **1/2 cup frozen cubed hash brown potatoes**
- **1 teaspoon seafood seasoning**
- **1/4 teaspoon sugar**
- **1/4 teaspoon ground allspice**
- **Dash cayenne pepper**
- **2 bay leaves**
- **1 halibut fillet (6 ounces), cut into bite-size pieces**

In a large saucepan coated with cooking spray, saute shallots and garlic until tender. Add the tomatoes, broth, mixed vegetables, hash browns, seafood seasoning, sugar, allspice, cayenne and bay leaves. Bring to a boil. Reduce heat; simmer, uncovered, for 5 minutes or until vegetables are tender.

Add halibut; simmer 2-3 minutes longer or until fish turns opaque. Discard bay leaves.

roasted tomato soup with fresh basil

PREP: 40 min. • **COOK:** 5 min. • **YIELD:** 6 servings.

Roasting really brings out the flavor of the tomatoes in this wonderful soup. It has a slightly chunky texture that indicates it's fresh and homemade. marie forte // raritan, new jersey

- **3-1/2 pounds tomatoes (about 11 medium), halved**
- **1 small onion, quartered**
- **2 garlic cloves, peeled and halved**
- **2 tablespoons olive oil**
- **2 tablespoons fresh thyme leaves**
- **1 teaspoon salt**
- **1/4 teaspoon pepper**
- **12 fresh basil leaves**
- **Salad croutons and additional fresh basil leaves, optional**

Place the tomatoes, onion and garlic in a greased 15-in. x 10-in. x 1-in. baking pan; drizzle with oil. Sprinkle with thyme, salt and pepper; toss to coat. Bake at 400° for 25-30 minutes or until tender, stirring once. Cool slightly.

In a blender, process tomato mixture and basil in batches until blended. Transfer to a large saucepan and heat through. Garnish each serving with croutons and additional basil if desired.

herbed fish chowder

PREP: 15 min. • **COOK:** 30 min. • **YIELD:** 7 servings (about 2 quarts).

My husband loves fish prepared in a variety of ways, so it's no surprise this soup has become one of his most requested meals. I think you'll also enjoy the soup's comforting flavor. geraldine de lure // calgary, alberta

- **2 bacon strips, diced, optional**
- **1 cup chopped carrots**
- **1 cup sliced fresh mushrooms**
- **1 medium onion, sliced**
- **1 garlic clove, minced**
- **2 tablespoons canola oil**
- **1/2 cup all-purpose flour**
- **1/4 teaspoon dried thyme**
- **1/4 teaspoon dill weed**
- **Dash pepper**
- **4 cups chicken broth**
- **1 bay leaf**
- **1 pound cod *or* haddock, cut into 3/4-inch pieces**
- **1-1/2 cups frozen cut green beans**

In a large saucepan, cook bacon over medium heat until crisp. Using a slotted spoon, remove to paper towels to drain. Carefully discard drippings.

In the same pan, saute the carrots, mushrooms, onion and garlic in oil until onion is tender. Stir in the flour, thyme, dill and pepper until smooth. Stir in broth; bring to a boil. Add bay leaf. Reduce heat; cover and simmer for 12-15 minutes or until carrots and mushrooms are tender.

Add fish and beans. Simmer, uncovered, for 5 minutes or until fish flakes easily with a fork. Remove bay leaf. Garnish individual servings with bacon.

HOW MUCH IS A "DASH"?

Traditionally, a dash is a very small amount of seasoning added with a quick downward stroke of the hand. A pinch is thought to be the amount of a dry ingredient that can be held between your thumb and forefinger. To measure a pinch or a dash of an ingredient, use somewhere between 1/16 and a scant 1/8 teaspoon.

italian vegetable soup

PREP/TOTAL TIME: 30 min.
YIELD: 6 servings.

When my husband and I needed a quick supper, I threw together this satisfying soup using only what we had on hand. Now it's a family favorite, and it's good for us, too!
margaret glassic
easton, pennsylvania

- **2 cans (14-1/2 ounces *each*) reduced-sodium chicken *or* vegetable broth**
- **1 medium potato, peeled and cubed**
- **1 medium onion, chopped**
- **1 medium carrot, chopped**
- **1 celery rib, chopped**
- **1/2 cup frozen peas**
- **1 bay leaf**
- **1 teaspoon Italian seasoning**
- **1/8 teaspoon pepper**
- **1/2 cup small shell pasta, cooked and drained**
- **1 can (14-1/2 ounces) diced tomatoes, undrained**

In a large saucepan, combine the first nine ingredients. Bring to a boil. Reduce heat; cover and simmer for 15-20 minutes or until vegetables are crisp-tender.

Add the pasta and tomatoes; heat through. Discard bay leaf.

carrot soup

PREP: 20 min. • **COOK:** 35 min. • **YIELD:** 6 servings.

Using fat-free half-and-half gives this colorful dish a velvety texture. It is especially satisfying on cold days.

barbara richard // houston, ohio

- **3/4 cup finely chopped onion**
- **3 garlic cloves, minced**
- **2 teaspoons olive oil**
- **3 cans (14-1/2 ounces *each*) reduced-sodium chicken broth *or* vegetable broth**
- **6 cups sliced carrots (about 2-1/2 pounds)**
- **3/4 cup cubed peeled potatoes**
- **1 teaspoon salt**
- **1 teaspoon dried thyme**
- **1/4 teaspoon pepper**
- **1 bay leaf**
- **1 cup fat-free half-and-half**

In a large saucepan, saute onion and garlic in oil until tender. Add the broth, carrots, potatoes, salt, thyme, pepper and bay leaf. Bring to a boil. Reduce heat; cover and simmer for 20-30 minutes or until vegetables are very tender.

Remove from the heat; cool slightly. Discard bay leaf. In a blender, puree carrot mixture in batches. Return to the pan. Stir in half-and-half; heat through (do not boil).

BOUILLON OR BROTH?

When a recipe calls for broth, you can substitute prepared bouillon if you desire. One bouillon cube or 1 teaspoon of bouillon granules dissolved in 1 cup of boiling water may be substituted for 1 cup of broth in any recipe.

taco twist soup

PREP/TOTAL TIME: 20 min. • **YIELD:** 6 servings.

I lightened up this soup recipe by substituting black beans for the ground beef originally called for...and by topping off bowlfuls with reduced-fat sour cream and cheese. Spiral pasta adds a fun twist. colleen zertler // menomonie, wisconsin

- **1 medium onion, chopped**
- **2 garlic cloves, minced**
- **2 teaspoons olive oil**
- **3 cups vegetable broth *or* reduced-sodium beef broth**
- **1 can (15 ounces) black beans, rinsed and drained**
- **1 can (14-1/2 ounces) diced tomatoes**
- **1-1/2 cups picante sauce**
- **1 cup uncooked spiral pasta**
- **1 small green pepper, chopped**
- **2 teaspoons chili powder**
- **1 teaspoon ground cumin**
- **1/2 cup shredded reduced-fat cheddar cheese**
- **3 tablespoons reduced-fat sour cream**

In a large saucepan, saute onion and garlic in oil until tender. Add the broth, beans, tomatoes, picante sauce, pasta, green pepper and seasonings. Bring to a boil, stirring frequently. Reduce heat; cover and simmer for 10-12 minutes or until pasta is tender, stirring occasionally. Serve with cheese and sour cream.

curry pumpkin mushroom soup

PREP/TOTAL TIME: 20 min. • **YIELD:** 7 servings.

I whipped up this satisfying dish last Thanksgiving for my family, and everyone was crazy about it! Even my brother, who is one of the pickiest eaters I know, asked for seconds. kimberly knepper // euless, texas

- **1/2 pound fresh mushrooms, sliced**
- **1/2 cup chopped onion**
- **2 tablespoons butter**
- **2 tablespoons all-purpose flour**
- **1/2 to 1 teaspoon curry powder**
- **3 cups vegetable broth**
- **1 can (15 ounces) solid-pack pumpkin**
- **1 can (12 ounces) evaporated milk**
- **1 tablespoon honey**
- **1/2 teaspoon salt**
- **1/4 teaspoon pepper**
- **1/4 teaspoon ground nutmeg**
- **Minced chives, optional**

In a large saucepan, saute the mushrooms and onion in butter until tender. Stir in the flour and curry powder until blended. Gradually add the broth. Bring to a boil; cook and stir for 2 minutes or until thickened. Add the pumpkin, milk, honey, salt, pepper and nutmeg; heat through. Garnish with chives if desired.

pesto minestrone

PREP/TOTAL TIME: 30 min.
YIELD: 4 servings.

I rely on store-bought pesto to provide mild flavor to my chunky tortellini and vegetable soup. It's a hit in my house. If you don't like zucchini, use another vegetable.
natalie cataldo // des moines, iowa

- **1/2 cup chopped onion**
- **2 teaspoons olive oil**
- **1 teaspoon minced garlic**
- **2-1/4 cups water**
- **2 cups frozen mixed vegetables**
- **1 can (14-1/2 ounces) vegetable broth**
- **3/4 teaspoon dried oregano**
- **1/2 teaspoon salt**
- **1/2 teaspoon pepper**
- **1 package (9 ounces) refrigerated cheese tortellini**
- **2 cups diced zucchini**
- **2 tablespoons prepared pesto**

In a large saucepan, saute onion in oil until tender. Add garlic; cook 1 minute longer. Stir in water, mixed vegetables, broth, oregano, salt and pepper. Bring to a boil. Reduce heat; cover and simmer for 3 minutes.

Add tortellini, zucchini and pesto. Simmer, uncovered, 7-9 minutes longer or until pasta and vegetables are tender.

herbed potato soup

PREP/TOTAL TIME: 30 min.
YIELD: 5 servings.

Making this potato soup is almost as easy as opening a can of the store-bought stuff—and it tastes so much better. The rosemary and thyme add just the right amount of seasoning.

jo crouch // east alton, illinois

- **3 medium potatoes, peeled and diced**
- **2 cups water**
- **1 large onion, chopped**
- **1/4 cup butter, cubed**
- **1/4 cup all-purpose flour**
- **1 teaspoon salt**
- **1/2 teaspoon dried thyme**
- **1/4 teaspoon dried rosemary, crushed**
- **1/4 teaspoon pepper**
- **1-1/2 cups 2% milk**

Place potatoes and water in a large saucepan. Bring to a boil. Reduce heat; cover and simmer for 15-20 minutes or until tender.

Meanwhile, in another large saucepan, saute the onion in butter until tender. Stir in the flour, salt, thyme, rosemary and pepper until blended. Gradually add the milk. Bring to a boil; cook and stir for 2 minutes or until thickened. Add potatoes with the cooking liquid; heat through.

corn and pepper chowder

PREP/TOTAL TIME: 30 min. • **YIELD:** 6 servings.

Chunks of potato, kernels of corn and flecks of red pepper punctuate the creamy broth of this hearty chowder. Cilantro and cumin lend a Southwestern flavor. I got this recipe from someone I work with. It's quick and tasty.

donna hackman // bedford, virginia

- **1 large onion, chopped**
- **1 medium sweet red pepper, chopped**
- **1 teaspoon canola oil**
- **3 tablespoons all-purpose flour**
- **1/2 teaspoon ground cumin**
- **2 cups water**
- **1-1/3 cups cubed potatoes**
- **1 teaspoon chicken bouillon granules**
- **3/4 teaspoon salt**
- **1/4 teaspoon white pepper**
- **2 cups frozen corn**
- **1 can (12 ounces) fat-free evaporated milk**
- **1/4 cup minced fresh cilantro**

In a saucepan, saute onion and red pepper in oil until tender. Stir in flour and cumin until blended. Gradually stir in water. Bring to a boil; cook and stir for 2 minutes or until thickened.

Reduce heat; add the potatoes, bouillon, salt and pepper. Cover and cook for 10 minutes or until potatoes are tender.

Add corn and milk. Cook, uncovered, 5 minutes longer or until heated through. Garnish with cilantro.

FRESH CILANTRO

To easily trim cilantro (or flat-leaf parsley) from its stems so you can chop or mince the leaves, hold the bunch, then angle the blade of a chef's knife almost parallel with the stems. With short, downward strokes, shave off the leaves where they meet the stems.

carrot zucchini soup

PREP: 30 min. • **COOK:** 30 min. • **YIELD:** 2-4 servings.

Here's an easy way to get kids to eat their vegetables. Carrots were never my family's favorite, but with this delicious soup, they hardly know that's what they're eating. joanne novellino // bayville, new jersey

- **2 small onions**
- **2 cups water**
- **1/2 pound carrots, cut into 1-inch pieces**
- **1/8 teaspoon celery salt**
- **1/8 teaspoon pepper**
- **2 cups diced zucchini (3 to 4 medium)**
- **1-1/2 teaspoons olive oil**
- **1-1/2 teaspoons butter**
- **1/2 cup chopped seeded tomatoes**
- **2/3 cup evaporated milk**
- **2 tablespoons minced fresh parsley**

Chop one onion; set aside. Quarter the other onion and place in a large saucepan. Add the water, carrots, celery salt and pepper; bring to a boil. Reduce heat; cover and simmer for 20 minutes or until carrots are tender. Cool slightly. Transfer to a blender; cover and process until pureed. Return to the pan.

In a large skillet, saute zucchini and chopped onion in oil and butter until tender; add to carrot mixture. Stir in tomatoes. Cover and simmer for 10 minutes or until tomatoes are tender. Stir in milk and parsley; heat through.

southwestern broccoli cheese soup

PREP/TOTAL TIME: 25 min.
YIELD: 9 servings (about 2 quarts).

A friend gave me the recipe for this chunky vegetable soup, which I've been making for years. Recently, I changed the ingredients to give it a Southwestern flavor—and my husband liked it even better. peggy hendrix // richardson, texas

- **4 cups water**
- **4 teaspoons reduced-sodium chicken bouillon granules *or* 2 vegetable bouillon cubes**
- **4 cups fresh broccoli florets**
- **3 cups frozen cubed hash brown potatoes**
- **1 cup chopped carrots**
- **1 cup chopped celery**
- **1/2 teaspoon salt**
- **1/2 teaspoon pepper**
- **3 tablespoons all-purpose flour**
- **2 cups fat-free milk**
- **6 ounces reduced-fat process cheese (Velveeta), cubed**
- **1 cup chunky salsa**

In a large saucepan, combine the water, bouillon, vegetables, salt and pepper. Bring to a boil. Reduce heat; cover and simmer for 8-10 minutes or until the vegetables are tender.

Combine the flour and milk until smooth; gradually stir into the soup. Bring to a boil; cook and stir for 2 minutes or until thickened. Reduce heat to low. Add the cheese; cook and stir until cheese is melted. Add the salsa; cook and stir until heated through.

vegetarian black bean soup

PREP: 20 min. • **COOK:** 25 min. • **YIELD:** 6 servings.

This soup is chock-full of hearty ingredients like black beans and potatoes. The tasty vegetable broth is a nice change from chicken or beef. heather baldry // knoxville, tennessee

- **1 cup chopped onion**
- **2 garlic cloves, minced**
- **1 can (14-1/2 ounces) vegetable broth, *divided***
- **2 cans (15 ounces *each*) black beans, rinsed and drained**
- **1 cup diced peeled potato**
- **1/2 teaspoon dried thyme**
- **1/2 teaspoon ground cumin**
- **1 can (14-1/2 ounces) diced tomatoes, undrained**
- **1/4 to 1/2 teaspoon hot pepper sauce**
- **2 green onions, sliced**

In a large saucepan, bring the onion, garlic and 1/4 cup broth to a boil. Reduce heat; cover and simmer for 6-8 minutes or until onion is tender. Stir in the beans, potato, thyme, cumin and remaining broth; return to a boil. Reduce heat; cover and simmer for 20-25 minutes or until potatoes are tender.

Stir in tomatoes and hot pepper sauce; heat through. Sprinkle with green onions.

spicy tomato soup

PREP/TOTAL TIME: 20 min. • **YIELD:** 8-10 servings.

When you'd rather be playing than cooking, you might want to give my tomato soup a try. With canned corn and black beans, it goes together fast and is a great accompaniment to any sandwich.

jaime hampton // richmond, virginia

- **8 ounces uncooked elbow macaroni**
- **1 can (46 ounces) tomato juice**
- **1 can (15-1/4 ounces) whole kernel corn, drained**
- **1 can (15 ounces) black beans, rinsed and drained**
- **1/4 cup salsa**
- **3 teaspoons dried oregano**
- **1-1/2 teaspoons garlic powder**
- **1 teaspoon dried basil**
- **1 teaspoon ground cumin**
- **1/2 to 1 teaspoon crushed red pepper flakes, optional**
- **Shredded cheddar *or* Monterey Jack cheese, optional**

Cook the macaroni according to package directions. In a large saucepan, combine the tomato juice, corn, beans, salsa, oregano, garlic powder, basil, cumin and pepper flakes if desired; bring to a boil. Reduce heat; cover and simmer for 8-10 minutes.

Drain macaroni; stir into the soup. Garnish with cheese if desired.

creole fish soup

PREP: 5 min. • **COOK:** 30 min.
YIELD: 8 servings (2 quarts).

You can make a pot of this soup and serve it in under an hour! The recipe calls for using frozen mixed veggies, so there's not a lot of peeling and chopping.

ruby williams // bogalusa, louisiana

- **1 can (28 ounces) diced tomatoes, undrained**
- **1 can (15 ounces) tomato sauce**
- **1/2 cup chopped onion**
- **1/2 teaspoon garlic powder**
- **1/2 teaspoon celery salt**
- **1/4 teaspoon dried thyme**
- **1/8 to 1/4 teaspoon cayenne pepper**
- **2 bay leaves**
- **1 package (16 ounces) frozen mixed vegetables**
- **1 pound cod, cut into 3/4-inch pieces**

In a Dutch oven, combine the first eight ingredients; cover and simmer for 10 minutes. Add vegetables; cover and simmer for 10 more minutes.

Add fish; cover and simmer for 8-10 minutes or until the fish flakes easily with a fork. Discard bay leaves.

curried sweet potato soup

PREP: 30 min. • **COOK:** 45 min. • **YIELD:** 8 servings.

This lovely cream soup makes a fabulous first course at special sit-down dinners. I often double the recipe because family and friends can't stop eating it! paula marchesi // lenhartsville, pennsylvania

- 1 medium onion, chopped
- 2 tablespoons butter
- 2 teaspoons curry powder
- 2 teaspoons minced fresh gingerroot
- 1/2 teaspoon salt
- 2 pounds sweet potatoes, peeled and cubed
- 1 can (14-1/2 ounces) vegetable broth
- 1-1/4 cups water
- 1 can (13.66 ounces) coconut milk
- 3/4 cup half-and-half cream
- 1/3 cup minced fresh cilantro
- Optional garnishes: minced fresh cilantro, toasted flaked coconut and toasted chopped pecans

In a large saucepan, saute onion in butter until tender. Stir in the curry, gingerroot and salt; cook 1 minute longer. Stir in the potatoes, broth and water. Bring to a boil. Reduce heat; cover and simmer for 15-20 minutes or until sweet potatoes are tender. Cool slightly.

In a blender, process soup in batches until smooth. Return all to the pan. Stir in the coconut milk, cream and cilantro; heat through. Garnish with cilantro, coconut and pecans if desired.

HANDY FRESH GINGER

One of the best ways I've found to jazz up a recipe is to use fresh ginger instead of the dried powdered spice. The difference in the flavor of my dishes, especially stir-fry meals, is unbelievable. Store the unpeeled gingerroot in the freezer. When needed, simply peel and use a vegetable grater to grate the ginger into your recipe.
sheila m. // mesa, arizona

cheesy potato soup

PREP/TOTAL TIME: 30 min.
YIELD: 8 servings.

My home state is famous for cheese, which I use in many recipes, such as this delightful soup. Cheddar gives it a sunny color and tantalizing taste. A good meal starter, it's also a great choice for a light lunch or supper.
mark trinklein // cedarburg, wisconsin

1/3 cup chopped onion
1/3 cup chopped celery
2 tablespoons butter
4 cups diced peeled potatoes
3 cups chicken *or* vegetable broth
2 cups (8 ounces) shredded cheddar cheese
2 cups 2% milk
1/4 teaspoon pepper
Dash paprika
Seasoned croutons and minced fresh parsley

In a saucepan, saute onion and celery in butter. Add potatoes and broth; bring to a boil. Reduce heat; cover and simmer for 10-15 minutes or until potatoes are tender. Cool slightly.

Puree in small batches in a blender until smooth; return to the pan. Stir in cheese, milk, pepper and paprika. Cook and stir over low heat until the cheese is melted. Garnish with the croutons and parsley.

french onion soup

PREP: 55 min. • **BAKE:** 10 min. • **YIELD:** 2 servings.

I adapted a basic recipe to copy the onion soup served at my favorite restaurant. No matter what my entree, I always ordered the soup there. Now I can make it at home. It's a meal in itself or an impressive beginning to a full-course meal.
barbara brunner // steelton, pennsylvania

2 medium onions, chopped
1 teaspoon sugar
6 tablespoons butter, *divided*
1 tablespoon all-purpose flour
1/8 teaspoon pepper
Dash ground nutmeg
2-1/2 cups beef *or* vegetable broth
2 tablespoons grated Parmesan cheese
2 slices French bread (1 inch thick)
4 slices provolone cheese

In a large saucepan, saute onions and sugar in 3 tablespoons of butter until golden brown. Stir in the flour, pepper and nutmeg until blended. Gradually stir in broth. Bring to a boil; cook and stir for 2 minutes. Reduce heat; cover and simmer for 30 minutes. Stir in the Parmesan cheese.

Meanwhile, in a large skillet, melt remaining butter; add bread. Cook until golden brown on both sides. Ladle soup into two oven-proof bowls. Place a slice of cheese in each bowl; top with bread and remaining cheese. Bake at 375° for 10 minutes or until the cheese is bubbly.

zippy corn chowder

PREP: 30 min. • **COOK:** 15 min.
YIELD: 8 servings (2 quarts).

My thick, colorful chowder was so well received the first time I made it that some of us had to go without seconds. Now I make this hearty soup often.

kera bredin // vancouver, british columbia

- **1 medium onion, chopped**
- **1 medium green pepper, chopped**
- **2 tablespoons butter**
- **1 can (14-1/2 ounces) chicken *or* vegetable broth**
- **2 large red potatoes, cubed**
- **1 jalapeno pepper, chopped**
- **2 teaspoons Dijon mustard**
- **1 teaspoon salt**
- **1/2 teaspoon paprika**
- **1/4 to 1/2 teaspoon crushed red pepper flakes**
- **3 cups frozen corn**
- **4 green onions, chopped**
- **3 cups milk, *divided***
- **1/4 cup all-purpose flour**

In a large saucepan, saute onion and green pepper in butter until tender. Add broth and potatoes. Bring to a boil. Reduce heat; cover and simmer for 15 minutes or until potatoes are almost tender. Stir in jalapeno, mustard, salt, paprika and red pepper flakes. Add corn, green onions and 2-1/2 cups milk. Bring to a boil.

Combine flour and remaining milk until smooth; gradually add to soup. Bring to a boil. Cook and stir for 2 minutes or until thickened and bubbly.

EDITOR'S NOTE: We recommend wearing disposable gloves when cutting hot peppers. Avoid touching your face.

southwestern bean soup

PREP/TOTAL TIME: 25 min.
YIELD: 12 servings (3 quarts).

When a friend needs a night off from cooking, I throw together this one-pot meal. I deliver it with tortilla chips, shredded cheese and sour cream for garnish. The pepper sauce can be adjusted to suit individual tastes, and the broth can be eliminated for a thicker batch. jackie hacker // seville, ohio

- **1 large onion, chopped**
- **1 teaspoon canola oil**
- **2 cans (15 ounces *each*) black beans, rinsed and drained**
- **2 cans (14-1/2 ounces *each*) diced tomatoes with garlic and onion**
- **2 cans (14-1/2 ounces *each*) chicken *or* vegetable broth**
- **1 can (16 ounces) kidney beans, rinsed and drained**
- **1 can (15 ounces) cannellini *or* white kidney beans, rinsed and drained**
- **1-1/2 cups fresh *or* frozen corn**
- **4 garlic cloves, minced**
- **1-1/2 teaspoons ground cumin**
- **1-1/2 teaspoons chili powder**
- **1/8 to 1/4 teaspoon hot pepper sauce**

In a Dutch oven, saute the onion in oil until tender. Stir in the remaining ingredients; bring to a boil. Reduce heat; simmer, uncovered, for 5 minutes or until heated through.

hearty meatless minestrone

PREP: 30 min. • **COOK:** 40 min. • **YIELD:** 8 servings (3 quarts).

A friend gave me this quick, healthy recipe, and it's so tasty! It makes a big batch and is great for leftovers. To enhance the flavor, add a pound or two of sweet Italian sausage. mickey turner // grants pass, oregon

1 large onion, chopped
3 tablespoons olive oil
2 celery ribs, chopped
2 medium carrots, chopped
1 cup chopped cabbage
1 medium green pepper, chopped
1 medium zucchini, chopped
6 garlic cloves, minced
3-1/2 cups water
2 cans (14-1/2 ounces *each*) diced tomatoes, undrained
1 can (15 ounces) garbanzo beans *or* chickpeas, rinsed and drained
1 can (15 ounces) tomato puree
1 can (8 ounces) tomato sauce
3 tablespoons dried parsley flakes
2 teaspoons dried basil
2 teaspoons dried oregano
1 teaspoon salt
1/2 teaspoon pepper
1/4 teaspoon cayenne pepper
1/2 cup small pasta shells
Fresh basil leaves and shaved Parmesan cheese, optional

In a Dutch oven, saute onion in oil for 2 minutes. Add the celery, carrots, cabbage, green pepper, zucchini and garlic; saute 3 minutes longer. Stir in the water, tomatoes, beans, tomato puree, tomato sauce and seasonings. Bring to a boil. Reduce heat; cover and simmer for 15 minutes.

Stir in pasta; cook 12-15 minutes longer or until tender. Garnish each serving with basil and cheese if desired.

MINCED GARLIC

Minced garlic that you can buy in a jar, fresh garlic that's been finely chopped by hand, and garlic that's been put through a garlic press can all be used interchangeably in recipes. Choose whichever form is the easiest and most convenient for you.

cheesy broccoli soup

PREP/TOTAL TIME: 30 min. • **YIELD:** 4 servings.

This creamy and flavorful soup goes together in a flash because it uses frozen chopped broccoli and process American cheese. Plus, it's easy to warm up for people who are late for dinner. jo maasberg // farson, wyoming

- **2 cups water**
- **1 teaspoon chicken bouillon *or* 1/2 vegetable bouillon cube**
- **1 package (16 ounces) frozen chopped broccoli, thawed**
- **1 medium onion, chopped**
- **1/4 cup butter, cubed**
- **3 tablespoons all-purpose flour**
- **1 cup 2% milk**
- **1 pound process cheese (Velveeta), cubed**

In a large saucepan, bring water and bouillon to a boil. Add broccoli. Reduce heat; cover and simmer for 3-4 minutes or until crisp-tender. Drain, reserving 3/4 cup liquid.

In another large saucepan, saute onion in butter until tender. Whisk in flour until blended. Add the milk and cheese. Cook over medium-low heat until thickened and cheese is melted, stirring frequently. Stir in broccoli and reserved cooking liquid.

seafood soup

PREP: 20 min. • **COOK:** 50 min. • **YIELD:** 6 servings.

This tomato-based soup is loaded with shrimp, chopped veggies and tender chunks of salmon. Simply seasoned with basil, oregano and garlic, it makes a filling meal in a bowl. valerie bradley // beaverton, oregon

- **1/2 cup chopped onion**
- **1/2 cup chopped green pepper**
- **3 tablespoons minced fresh parsley**
- **1 tablespoon olive oil**
- **1 cup chopped carrots**
- **1 garlic clove, minced**
- **1 can (15 ounces) tomato sauce**
- **1 can (14-1/2 ounces) diced tomatoes**
- **3/4 cup white wine *or* chicken broth**
- **1 bay leaf**
- **1/2 teaspoon dried oregano**
- **1/4 teaspoon dried basil**
- **1/4 teaspoon pepper**
- **3/4 pound salmon fillets, skinned and cut into 3/4-inch cubes**
- **1/2 pound uncooked medium shrimp, peeled and deveined**

In a large saucepan, saute the onion, green pepper and parsley in oil until tender. Add carrots and garlic; cook and stir for 3 minutes. Stir in the tomato sauce, tomatoes, wine or broth and seasonings.

Bring to a boil. Reduce heat; cover and simmer for 30 minutes. Stir in salmon and shrimp. Cover and cook 7-10 minutes longer or until fish flakes easily with a fork and shrimp turn pink. Discard bay leaf.

mushroom bisque

PREP/TOTAL TIME: 25 min.
YIELD: 4 servings.

This is a lovely dish to make when you have an abundance of fresh mushrooms on hand. Sauteeing them slowly with the onion brings out the onion's sweetness. No one will ever guess this soup is so easy to make. emily chaney // blue hill, maine

- **1/2 pound fresh mushrooms, sliced**
- **1 medium onion, sliced**
- **1 cup minced fresh parsley**
- **1/4 cup butter, cubed**
- **1 tablespoon all-purpose flour**
- **1 can (14-1/2 ounces) beef broth**
- **1 cup (8 ounces) sour cream**

In a large saucepan, saute mushrooms, onion and parsley in butter until tender. Stir in the flour until blended; gradually add broth. Bring to a boil; cook and stir for 2 minutes or until soup is thickened. Cool slightly.

Transfer to a blender; cover and process until pureed. Return all to pan. Stir in the sour cream; heat through, stirring occasionally (do not boil).

asparagus brie soup

PREP/TOTAL TIME: 30 min.
YIELD: 4 servings.

My rich soup is wonderful when fresh asparagus is in season. It's an elegant dish to serve company.
melissa petrek-myer // austin, texas

- **1/2 pound fresh asparagus, cut into 2-inch pieces**
- **1/2 cup butter, cubed**
- **1/4 cup all-purpose flour**
- **3 cups chicken *or* vegetable broth**
- **1 cup heavy whipping cream**
- **1/2 cup white wine**
- **4 to 6 ounces Brie cheese, rind removed**

In a large saucepan, saute asparagus in butter until tender. Stir in flour until blended. Cook and stir for 2 minutes or until golden brown. Gradually add broth, cream and wine. Bring to a boil. Reduce heat; simmer for 10-15 minutes. Cool slightly.

In a blender; cover and process soup in batches until smooth. Return to the pan. Cube Brie and add to soup. Simmer, uncovered, for 5 minutes or until cheese is melted.

tomato green bean soup

PREP: 10 min. • **COOK:** 35 min. • **YIELD:** 9 servings.

This colorful soup is delicious any time of year. When I can't get homegrown tomatoes and green beans, I've found that frozen beans and canned tomatoes (or even stewed tomatoes) work just fine. Served with warm breadsticks, this is a complete meal. My husband and I enjoy it as a meatless dish, but you could also add diced chicken or ham. bernice nolan // granite city, illinois

- **1 cup chopped onion**
- **1 cup chopped carrots**
- **2 teaspoons butter**
- **6 cups chicken *or* vegetable broth**
- **1 pound fresh green beans, cut into 1-inch pieces**
- **1 garlic clove, minced**
- **3 cups diced fresh tomatoes**
- **1/4 cup minced fresh basil *or* 1 tablespoon dried basil**
- **1/2 teaspoon salt**
- **1/4 teaspoon pepper**

In a large saucepan, saute onion and carrots in butter for 5 minutes. Stir in the broth, beans and garlic; bring to a boil. Reduce heat; cover and simmer for 20 minutes or until vegetables are tender.

Stir in the tomatoes, basil, salt and pepper. Cover and simmer 5 minutes longer.

apple squash soup

PREP: 10 min. • **COOK:** 35 min. + cooling
YIELD: 5 servings.

Here's a new twist on an old favorite—pumpkin soup. I add a little ginger and sage to apples and squash to make my version. My family loves it when autumn rolls around!
crystal ralph-haughn // bartlesville, oklahoma

- **1 large onion, chopped**
- **1/2 teaspoon rubbed sage**
- **2 tablespoons butter**
- **1 can (14-1/2 ounces) chicken *or* vegetable broth**
- **3/4 cup water**
- **2 medium tart apples, peeled and finely chopped**
- **1 package (12 ounces) frozen mashed squash, thawed**
- **1 teaspoon ground ginger**
- **1/2 teaspoon salt**
- **1/2 cup fat-free milk**

In a large saucepan, saute onion and sage in butter for 3 minutes or until tender. Add the broth, water and apples; bring to a boil. Reduce heat; cover and simmer for 12 minutes.

Add squash, ginger and salt; return to a boil. Reduce heat; simmer, uncovered, for 10 minutes. Cool slightly.

In a blender, process soup in batches until smooth; return to pan. Add milk; heat through. (Do not boil.)

cauliflower soup

PREP/TOTAL TIME: 30 min.
YIELD: 8 servings (about 2 quarts).

Cauliflower and carrots share the stage in this cheesy soup that's sure to warm you up on the chilliest nights. We like it with hot pepper sauce; however, it can be omitted with equally tasty results. debbie ohlhausen // chilliwack, british columbia

- **1 medium head cauliflower, broken into florets**
- **1 medium carrot, shredded**
- **1/4 cup chopped celery**
- **2-1/2 cups water**
- **2 teaspoons chicken *or* 1 vegetable bouillon cube**
- **3 tablespoons butter**
- **3 tablespoons all-purpose flour**
- **3/4 teaspoon salt**
- **1/8 teaspoon pepper**
- **2 cups 2% milk**
- **1 cup (4 ounces) shredded cheddar cheese**
- **1/2 to 1 teaspoon hot pepper sauce, optional**

In a large bowl, combine the cauliflower, carrot, celery, water and bouillon. Bring to a boil. Reduce heat; cover and simmer for 12-15 minutes or until vegetables are tender (do not drain).

In another large saucepan, melt butter. Stir in the flour, salt and pepper until smooth. Gradually add milk. Bring to a boil over medium heat; cook and stir for 2 minutes or until thickened. Reduce heat. Add cheese; stir until melted. Add hot pepper sauce if desired. Stir into the cauliflower mixture.

SOUTHWEST BLACK BEAN SOUP, PG. 193

SOUPS

beans & lentils

SPINACH BEAN SOUP, PG. 185

LIMA BEAN SOUP, PG. 195

SPICY BLACK BEAN SOUP, PG. 211

bean and pasta soup

PREP: 10 min. • **COOK:** 30 min.
YIELD: 5 servings.

Packed with veggies and leftover ham, this recipe really dresses up canned soup. Who would believe that such a hearty meal could be ready in so little time? julia cox // chesapeake, virginia

- **1 cup cubed fully cooked ham**
- **1 small onion, chopped**
- **1 celery rib, chopped**
- **1 garlic clove, minced**
- **1 tablespoon canola oil**
- **1 can (18.8 ounces) ready-to-serve chunky savory vegetable soup**
- **1 can (16 ounces) kidney beans, rinsed and drained**
- **1-3/4 cups water**
- **2 teaspoons minced fresh thyme *or* 1/2 teaspoon dried thyme**
- **1 bay leaf**
- **1/8 teaspoon pepper**
- **1/2 cup uncooked medium pasta shells**

In a large saucepan, saute ham, onion, celery and garlic in oil for 3-4 minutes or until vegetables are tender. Stir in the soup, beans, water, thyme, bay leaf and pepper. Bring to a boil. Stir in pasta. Reduce heat; simmer, uncovered, for 20-25 minutes or until pasta is tender. Discard bay leaf.

old-world bean soup

PREP: 35 min. + soaking • **COOK:** 3 hours + cooling
YIELD: 7 servings.

Looking for a thick, hearty tomato-based soup loaded with veggies and perfectly seasoned with herbs? Then this one is for you! Cayenne pepper gives it some zip. I usually make up soup recipes as I go along. My husband, who doesn't usually care much for soup, really likes this one. erin lembke // bothell, washington

- **3/4 cup dried navy beans**
- **1-1/2 pounds smoked ham shank**
- **6 cups water**
- **4 celery ribs, sliced**
- **4 carrots, halved and sliced**
- **1 large onion, chopped**
- **1 cup fresh green beans, cut into 1-inch pieces**
- **1 can (14-1/2 ounces) diced tomatoes**
- **1-1/2 teaspoons garlic powder**
- **1-1/2 teaspoons dried basil**
- **1 teaspoon salt**
- **1 teaspoon paprika**
- **1/2 teaspoon dried oregano**
- **1/4 teaspoon *each* dried thyme, white pepper and Liquid Smoke**
- **1/8 teaspoon cayenne pepper**
- **2 cups chopped cabbage**

Sort beans and rinse with cold water. Place beans in a Dutch over or soup kettle; add water to cover by 2 in. Bring to a boil; boil for 2 minutes. Remove from the heat; cover and let stand for 1 to 4 hours or until beans are softened. Drain and rinse beans, discarding liquid.

In a Dutch oven or soup kettle, place ham shank and water. Cover and bring to a boil. Reduce heat; simmer for 1 hour. Add beans; simmer 1 hour longer or until meat and beans are tender. Remove from heat. Cool slightly. Remove ham shank. Cover and refrigerate ham shank and soup.

Remove meat from ham bone; discard bone. Set meat aside. Remove fat from broth. Add the beans and meat to pan with broth. Add the celery, carrots, onion and green beans. Bring to a boil over medium heat. Reduce heat; simmer, uncovered, for 10 minutes. Add tomatoes and seasonings; cook for 10 minutes. Add cabbage; cook 35 minutes longer or until vegetables are tender.

spinach bean soup

PREP: 20 min. • **COOK:** 6-1/4 hours • **YIELD:** 8 servings (2 quarts).

This meatless soup is great for a busy weeknight supper after I get home from my job as a college nursing professor. The soup provides plenty of nutrients to keep me healthy. brenda jeffers // ottumwa, iowa

- **3 cans (14-1/2 ounces *each*) vegetable broth**
- **1 can (15-1/2 ounces) great northern beans, rinsed and drained**
- **1 can (15 ounces) tomato puree**
- **1/2 cup finely chopped onion**
- **1/2 cup uncooked converted long grain rice**
- **2 garlic cloves, minced**
- **1 teaspoon dried basil**
- **1/2 teaspoon salt**
- **1/4 teaspoon pepper**
- **1 package (6 ounces) fresh baby spinach, coarsely chopped**
- **1/4 cup shredded Parmesan cheese**

In a 4-qt. slow cooker, combine the first nine ingredients. Cover and cook on low for 6-7 hours or until heated through. Stir in spinach. Cover and cook for 15 minutes or until spinach is wilted. Sprinkle with cheese.

SLOW COOKER SAVVY

Unless the recipe instructs you to stir in or add ingredients, refrain from lifting the lid while the slow cooker is cooking. Every time you lift the lid, steam is lost and you add 15 to 30 minutes of cooking time. Be sure the lid is sealed properly, not tilted or askew. The steam creates a seal.

texas black bean soup

PREP: 5 min. • **COOK:** 4 hours • **YIELD:** 8 -10 servings (about 2-1/2 quarts).

Why not try this hearty stew-like soup made with convenient canned items? It's easy and perfect for spicing up a family gathering on a cool day. It tastes great and requires so little time and attention. pamela scott // garland, texas

- **2 cans (15 ounces *each*) black beans, rinsed and drained**
- **1 can (14-1/2 ounces) stewed tomatoes *or* Mexican stewed tomatoes, cut up**
- **1 can (14-1/2 ounces) diced tomatoes *or* diced tomatoes with green chilies**
- **1 can (14-1/2 ounces) chicken broth**
- **1 can (11 ounces) Mexicorn, drained**
- **2 cans (4 ounces *each*) chopped green chilies**
- **4 green onions, thinly sliced**
- **2 to 3 tablespoons chili powder**
- **1 teaspoon ground cumin**
- **1/2 teaspoon dried minced garlic**

In a 3-qt. slow cooker, combine all ingredients. Cover and cook on high for 4-6 hours or until heated through.

TO DRAIN OR NOT TO DRAIN

The reason for draining canned beans is to remove the excess salt used in the canning process. You may use the liquid, but be sure to adjust the salt level in your recipe.

bean soup with dumplings

PREP: 15 min. • **COOK:** 1-1/4 hours • **YIELD:** 8 servings (2-1/4 quarts).

I often rely on my slow cooker to simmer this nicely spiced, bean-filled broth while I'm busy or running errands. It's a treat to come home and just have to drop in the dumplings. jane mullins // livonia, missouri

- 3 cups water
- 1 can (15-1/2 ounces) kidney beans, rinsed and drained
- 1 can (15 ounces) black beans, rinsed and drained
- 1 can (14-1/2 ounces) Mexican stewed tomatoes
- 1 can (4 ounces) chopped green chilies
- 2 cups frozen corn, thawed
- 1 cup chopped onion
- 1 cup chopped carrots
- 3 beef bouillon cubes
- 3 garlic cloves, minced
- 1 teaspoon chili powder
- 1/2 teaspoon salt
- 1/4 teaspoon pepper

DUMPLINGS:

- 1/2 cup all-purpose flour
- 1/4 cup yellow cornmeal
- 1 teaspoon baking powder
- Dash *each* salt and pepper
- 1 egg white, beaten
- 3 tablespoons milk
- 1 tablespoon canola oil

In a large saucepan over medium heat, combine the first 13 ingredients; bring to a boil. Reduce heat; cover and simmer for 1 hour or until vegetables are tender.

For dumplings, combine flour, cornmeal, baking powder, salt and pepper. Combine egg white, milk and oil; stir into dry ingredients. Drop into eight mounds onto boiling soup. Reduce heat; cover and simmer for 15-20 minutes (do not lift the cover).

butter bean veggie soup

PREP/TOTAL TIME: 30 min.
YIELD: 8 servings (about 2 quarts).

I know you'll like this hearty basil-seasoned soup that's chock-full of five different vegetables. I like to serve big bowls of it with corn bread.
dorothy bertrand // sellersburg, indiana

- 3 celery ribs, chopped
- 3 medium carrots, chopped
- 1 small onion, chopped
- 2 tablespoons olive oil
- 3 tablespoons all-purpose flour
- 2 cans (14-1/2 ounces *each*) chicken broth
- 2 cans (15 ounces *each*) butter beans, rinsed and drained
- 1 can (14-1/2 ounces) stewed tomatoes, cut up
- 1 teaspoon dried basil
- 1/2 teaspoon salt
- 1/2 teaspoon dried parsley flakes
- 1/4 teaspoon pepper

In a large saucepan, saute celery, carrots and onion in oil until tender. Stir in flour until blended. Gradually add the broth.

Stir in all the remaining ingredients. Bring to a boil. Reduce heat; simmer, uncovered, for 10 minutes or until soup is heated through.

beef barley lentil soup

PREP: 5 min. • **COOK:** 8 hours • **YIELD:** 10 servings.

I serve this soup often to family and friends on cold nights since it's so hearty and satisfying. For variety, you can substitute jicama for the potatoes. judy metzentine // the dalles, oregon

- **1 pound lean ground beef (90% lean)**
- **1 medium onion, chopped**
- **2 cups cubed red potatoes (1/4-inch pieces)**
- **1 cup chopped celery**
- **1 cup chopped carrot**
- **1 cup dried lentils, rinsed**
- **1/2 cup medium pearl barley**
- **8 cups water**
- **2 teaspoons beef bouillon granules**
- **1 teaspoon salt**
- **1/2 teaspoon lemon-pepper seasoning**
- **2 cans (14-1/2 ounces *each*) stewed tomatoes**

In a nonstick skillet, cook beef and onion over medium heat until meat is no longer pink; drain.

Transfer to a 5-qt. slow cooker. Layer with the potatoes, celery, carrot, lentils and barley. Combine the water, bouillon, salt and lemon pepper; pour over vegetables. Cover and cook on low for 6 hours or until vegetables and barley are tender.

Add the tomatoes; cook 2 hours longer.

HEALTHY SOUP STARTER

To make a large batch of healthy soup, I start by simmering a low-sodium broth and any combination of barley, dried beans, peas or rice. Then I add several vegetables and seasonings. I keep this homemade soup starter in a sealed container in the refrigerator. To serve, I add some cubed cooked chicken breast to a portion and heat it up. It's a quick and easy way to serve a meal on busy days...and it helps us eat lighter. mary ann d. // minneapolis, minnesota

hearty italian vegetable soup

PREP: 10 min. • **COOK:** 50 min. • **YIELD:** 6-8 servings.

With macaroni, kidney beans, tomatoes, zucchini and lots of other veggies, this flavorful soup is hearty enough for dinner with corn bread or hot rolls. It really hits the spot on a cold day. phyllis schmalz // kansas city, kansas

- 2 medium carrots, diced
- 1 small onion, chopped
- 1 tablespoon olive oil
- 2 garlic cloves, minced
- 2 cans (14-1/2 ounces each) beef broth
- 1 can (14-1/2 ounces) diced tomatoes, undrained
- 2 cups water
- 1 small zucchini, diced
- 1 teaspoon dried basil
- 1 teaspoon salt
- 1/2 teaspoon dried oregano
- 1/4 teaspoon pepper
- 2 to 3 drops hot pepper sauce
- 1 can (16 ounces) kidney beans, rinsed and drained
- 1 cup chopped fresh spinach
- 3/4 cup uncooked elbow macaroni
- 2 tablespoons minced fresh parsley
- 1/2 cup shredded Parmesan cheese

In a Dutch oven, saute carrots and onion in oil until tender. Add garlic; cook 1 minute longer. Stir in the broth, tomatoes, water, zucchini, basil, salt, oregano, pepper and hot pepper sauce. Bring to a boil. Reduce heat; cover and simmer for 15 minutes.

Stir in the kidney beans, spinach, macaroni and parsley. Cover and cook 15 minutes longer or until macaroni is tender. Garnish with cheese.

bean counter chowder

PREP/TOTAL TIME: 30 min.
YIELD: 8 servings (2 quarts).

Wonderfully seasoned Bean Counter Chowder is easy to make and also inexpensive to serve.

vivian haen
menomonee falls, wisconsin

- **1/2 cup chopped onion**
- **1 tablespoon canola oil**
- **2 garlic cloves, minced**
- **1 medium tomato, chopped**
- **2 cans (14-1/2 ounces *each*) chicken *or* vegetable broth**
- **1-3/4 cups water**
- **1/2 teaspoon *each* dried basil, oregano and celery flakes**
- **1/4 teaspoon pepper**
- **3 cans (15-1/2 ounces *each*) great northern beans, rinsed and drained**
- **1 cup uncooked elbow macaroni**
- **1 tablespoon minced parsley**

In a large saucepan, saute onion in oil until tender; Add garlic; cook 1 minute longer. Add the tomato; simmer for 5 minutes. Add the broth, water and seasonings. Bring to a boil; cook for 5 minutes. Add beans and macaroni; return to a boil.

Reduce heat; simmer, uncovered, for 15 minutes or until macaroni is tender. Sprinkle with parsley.

black bean chipotle soup

PREP: 15 min. • **COOK:** 30 min. • **YIELD:** 8 servings (2 quarts, 1 cup sauce).

I am a vegetarian, but the rest of my family is not. Even they prefer this soup to a traditional meaty version because it's packed with so much flavor!
janice schneider // parkville, missouri

- **1 large onion, chopped**
- **3 garlic cloves, minced**
- **1 teaspoon canola oil**
- **2 cans (15 ounces *each*) black beans, rinsed and drained**
- **2 cans (14-1/2 ounces *each*) vegetable broth**
- **1 can (28 ounces) crushed tomatoes**
- **1 tablespoon chopped chipotle pepper in adobo sauce**
- **2 bay leaves**
- **1 tablespoon minced fresh cilantro**
- **2 teaspoons ground cumin**
- **1 teaspoon ground coriander**
- **1/8 teaspoon salt**
- **1/8 teaspoon pepper**

SAUCE:

- **1 cup (8 ounces) reduced-fat sour cream**
- **2 green onion tops, chopped**
- **1 garlic clove, peeled**
- **1/8 teaspoon salt**
- **1/8 teaspoon adobo sauce**
- **1 tablespoon minced fresh cilantro**

In a large saucepan coated with cooking spray, saute onion and garlic in oil until tender. Add the beans, broth, tomatoes, chipotle pepper, bay leaves and seasonings. Bring to a boil. Reduce heat; cover and simmer for 20 minutes.

Meanwhile, in a blender, combine the sour cream, green onion tops, garlic, salt and adobo sauce; cover and process until blended.

Discard bay leaves from the soup. Top each serving with sauce and sprinkle with cilantro.

EDITOR'S NOTE: We recommend wearing disposable gloves when cutting hot peppers. Avoid touching your face.

southwest black bean soup

PREP: 15 min. • **COOK:** 35 min. **YIELD:** 6 servings.

A friend brought this recipe to a gathering, and it has been a hit with my family ever since! I prefer to use brown rice for more fiber and whole-grain goodness. jill heatwole // pittsville, maryland

- **1 medium sweet red pepper, chopped**
- **2 celery ribs, chopped**
- **1 small onion, chopped**
- **1 tablespoon canola oil**
- **2 cans (15 ounces *each*) black beans, rinsed and drained**
- **1 can (14-1/2 ounces) reduced-sodium chicken broth**
- **1 can (14-1/2 ounces) diced tomatoes, undrained**
- **1 can (4 ounces) chopped green chilies**
- **3/4 teaspoon ground cumin**
- **1-1/2 cups cooked instant brown rice**
- **6 tablespoons reduced-fat sour cream**

In a large nonstick saucepan, saute the pepper, celery and onion in oil until tender. Add the beans, broth, tomatoes, chilies and cumin. Bring to a boil. Reduce heat; simmer, uncovered, for 30 minutes or until thickened.

Divide rice among six soup bowls; top with soup and sour cream.

lima bean soup

PREP: 20 min. + standing • **COOK:** 2 hours 50 min. • **YIELD:** 14 servings (3-1/2 quarts).

For a deliciously different twist on lunch or a dinner's first course, try this colorful soup. It has a golden broth dotted with tender vegetables and lima beans. betty korcek // bridgman, michigan

- 1 pound dried lima beans
- 1 large meaty ham bone *or* 2 ham hocks
- 2-1/2 quarts water
- 5 celery ribs, cut into chunks
- 5 medium carrots, cut into chunks
- 1 garlic clove, minced
- 2 tablespoons butter
- 2 tablespoons all-purpose flour
- 2 teaspoons salt
- 1/2 teaspoon pepper
- Pinch paprika
- 1 cup cold water
- 1 can (14-1/2 ounces) stewed tomatoes

Place the beans in a Dutch oven; add water to cover by 2 in. Bring to a boil; boil for 2 minutes. Remove from the heat; cover and let stand for 1 to 4 hours or until beans are softened. Drain and discard liquid; return beans to pan.

Add ham bone and the 2-1/2-qt. of water; bring to a boil. Reduce heat; cover and simmer for 1-1/2 hours.

Debone ham and cut into chunks; return to pan. Add celery and carrots. Cover and simmer for 1 hour or until beans are tender.

In a small skillet, saute garlic in butter for 1 minute. Stir in the flour, salt, pepper and paprika. Add cold water; bring to a boil. Reduce heat; cook and stir for 2 minutes or until thickened. Add to the soup with the tomatoes; simmer for 10 minutes or until heated through.

BEST BET FOR BEANS

When cooking dried lima or navy beans in a recipe with tomatoes, the acidity of the tomatoes slows down the cooking of dry beans. So tomato or tomato products should be added after the beans are nearly tender. Salt can also inhibit the cooking and should be added toward the end as well.

mexican bean soup

PREP: 20 min. • **COOK:** 45 min.
YIELD: 14-16 servings (4 quarts).

For our family's fall birthday bash, I make a big pot of this soup and serve it with plenty of oven-fresh corn bread.
vivian christian // stephenville, texas

- **2 pounds ground beef**
- **1 medium onion, chopped**
- **4 cups water**
- **3 cans (14-1/2 ounces *each*) diced tomatoes, undrained**
- **2 cans (15-1/2 ounces *each*) hominy, drained**
- **2 cans (15 ounces *each*) Ranch Style beans (pinto beans in seasoned tomato sauce)**
- **1 can (16 ounces) kidney beans, rinsed and drained**
- **1 can (4 ounces) chopped green chilies**
- **2 envelopes taco seasoning**
- **1 envelope (1 ounce) original ranch dressing mix**
- **2 tablespoons brown sugar**
- **1/4 teaspoon cayenne pepper**
- **Shredded cheddar cheese and sour cream, optional**

In a Dutch oven, cook beef and onion over medium heat until meat is no longer pink; drain. Add the next 10 ingredients; bring to a boil. Reduce heat; cover and simmer for 30 minutes. Garnish with cheese and sour cream if desired.

three-bean soup

PREP/TOTAL TIME: 30 min. • **YIELD:** 8 servings.

For a dish that's delicious and low in fat, try this chili-like soup. Salsa, cumin and chili powder gave it plenty of flavor while several canned items make it fast to throw together on busy nights. joni voit // champlin, minnesota

- **1 large onion, chopped**
- **1 medium green pepper, chopped**
- **2 teaspoons olive oil**
- **4 garlic cloves, minced**
- **1 can (16 ounces) kidney beans, rinsed and drained**
- **1 can (16 ounces) fat-free refried beans**
- **1 can (15 ounces) black beans, rinsed and drained**
- **1 can (14-1/2 ounces) reduced-sodium chicken broth**
- **1 can (14-1/2 ounces) stewed tomatoes, cut up**
- **3/4 cup salsa**
- **2 teaspoons chili powder**
- **1/2 teaspoon pepper**
- **1/4 teaspoon ground cumin**

In a large saucepan, saute onion and green pepper in oil until tender. Add the garlic; cook 1 minute longer. Add the remaining ingredients. Bring to a boil. Reduce heat; cover and simmer for 10 minutes.

lemon lentil soup

PREP: 10 min. • **COOK:** 1-1/4 hours • **YIELD:** 6 servings.

Loaded with protein-rich lentils, this hearty soup is rooted in the old-fashioned goodness of leeks, parsnips, celery and carrots. The addition of lemon juice transforms what might otherwise be an everyday soup into something wonderfully out of the ordinary. jean rawlings // saskatoon, saskatchewan

- **1 cup chopped leeks (white portion only)**
- **2 tablespoons canola oil**
- **1 can (15 ounces) tomato puree**
- **1 cup chopped celery**
- **1 cup chopped carrots**
- **1/4 cup chopped peeled parsnips**
- **2 tablespoons dried basil**
- **8 cups water**
- **1-1/2 cups dried lentils, rinsed**
- **2 bay leaves**
- **1 tablespoon grated lemon peel**
- **1-1/2 teaspoons salt**
- **1 teaspoon dill weed**
- **1/2 teaspoon pepper**
- **2 to 3 tablespoons lemon juice**

In a large saucepan, saute leeks in oil until tender. Add the tomato puree, celery, carrots, parsnips and basil; cook for 3-4 minutes. Add water; bring to a boil. Add lentils and bay leaves. Reduce heat; cover and simmer for 30 minutes.

Stir in lemon peel, salt, dill and pepper; simmer 30 minutes longer or until lentils are tender. Discard bay leaves. Stir in lemon juice.

FREEZE LEMON JUICE

I like to keep fresh lemon juice on hand because it's such an easy way to add refreshing flavor to many recipes. After juicing the lemons, I freeze the juice in ice cube trays. Then I simply defrost them and use in soups, poultry recipes, lemon desserts, iced or hot teas and many other dishes. **judy m. // south bend, indiana**

ham and black bean soup

PREP: 25 min. • **COOK:** 4 hours
YIELD: 8 servings (about 2 quarts).

I originally made this slightly spicy soup for my husband, who enjoys black beans. But I ended up loving it, too! Even more compliments came from our neighbors who stopped by and stayed for supper.
laura meurer // green bay, wisconsin

- **3 cans (15 ounces *each*) black beans, rinsed and drained**
- **2 cans (14-1/2 ounces *each*) beef broth**
- **1 can (14-1/2 ounces) diced tomatoes, undrained**
- **1-1/2 cups cubed fully cooked ham**
- **1 can (4 ounces) chopped green chilies**
- **1/4 cup red wine vinegar**
- **1 large onion, chopped**
- **3 garlic cloves, minced**
- **1 teaspoon dried oregano**
- **1 teaspoon dried thyme**
- **1 teaspoon pepper**

In a 3-qt. slow cooker, combine all ingredients. Cover and cook on high for 4-5 hours or until onion is tender.

pinto bean chicken soup

PREP/TOTAL TIME: 20 min. • **YIELD:** 8 servings.

Mexican Velveeta and chopped green chilies add a kick to this satisfying and different soup that I just adore. The recipe calls for a number of canned goods, so it's simple to stir up, simmer and serve. sybil brown // highland, california

- **1/3 cup all-purpose flour**
- **2 cans (14-1/2 ounces *each*) chicken broth**
- **1 can (15-1/4 ounces) whole kernel corn, drained**
- **1 can (15 ounces) pinto beans, rinsed and drained**
- **1 can (14-1/2 ounces) stewed tomatoes, cut up**
- **1 can (4 ounces) chopped green chilies**
- **1 can (10 ounces) chunk white chicken**
- **8 ounces Mexican process cheese (Velveeta), cubed**

In a large saucepan, combine flour and broth until smooth. Stir in the corn, beans, tomatoes and chilies. Bring to a boil; cook and stir for 2 minutes or until thickened. Reduce heat. Add the chicken and cheese; stir until cheese is melted.

tortilla soup

PREP/TOTAL TIME: 10 min. • **YIELD:** 5 servings.

Tasty toppings jazz up this no-fuss soup that has Mexican flair. The recipe for this sure-to-please soup was given to me by a friend. I make it often for company, and everyone asks for the recipe. You can substitute pinto beans in red chili sauce for the regular pinto beans and cumin called for in the recipe. michelle larson // greentown, indiana

- **1 can (10-1/2 ounces) condensed chicken with rice soup, undiluted**
- **1-1/3 cups water**
- **1 cup salsa**
- **1 cup canned pinto beans, rinsed and drained**
- **1 cup canned black beans, rinsed and drained**
- **1 cup frozen corn**
- **1 cup frozen diced cooked chicken**
- **1 teaspoon ground cumin**
- **Crushed tortilla chips, shredded cheddar cheese and sour cream**

In a large saucepan, combine the first eight ingredients. Cook over medium-high heat for 5-7 minutes or until heated through. Serve with tortilla chips, cheese and sour cream.

navy bean soup

PREP: 20 min. + standing • **COOK:** 1 hour 20 min.
YIELD: 8-10 servings.

We've been serving this soup for over 25 years. Everyone tells us they love its flavor. A clear chicken broth makes it different from other bean soups.
robert doumas // gaylord, michigan

- **1 pound dried navy beans**
- **2 quarts chicken broth**
- **2 tablespoons minced fresh parsley**
- **2 bay leaves**
- **1/4 teaspoon pepper**
- **1 medium onion, chopped**
- **1 medium carrot, chopped**
- **1 celery rib, chopped**
- **6 bacon strips, cooked and crumbled**

Place beans in a Dutch oven or soup kettle; add water to cover by 2 in. Bring to a boil; boil for 2 minutes. Remove from the heat; cover and let stand for 1 to 4 hours or until beans are softened. Drain and rinse beans, discard liquid.

In a large saucepan, combine the broth, beans, parsley, bay leaves and pepper. Bring to a boil. Reduce heat; cover and simmer for 1 hour. Add the onion, carrot and celery. Cover and simmer for 20-25 minutes or until vegetables and beans are tender. Stir in bacon. Discard the bay leaves.

hot dog bean soup

PREP/TOTAL TIME: 10 min. • **YIELD:** 4 servings.

My husband fixed this soup for our three kids years ago. They always loved it and now prepare it for their own kids. It's a real favorite on family camping trips. mary ann kime // sturgis, michigan

- **3 hot dogs, halved lengthwise and cut into 1/4-inch pieces**
- **1 teaspoon canola oil**
- **1 can (16 ounces) kidney beans, rinsed and drained**
- **1 can (11-1/2 ounces) condensed bean and bacon soup, undiluted**
- **1-1/4 cups water**
- **1 teaspoon dried minced onion**
- **1/4 teaspoon pepper**

In a large skillet, cook the hot dogs in oil over medium heat for 3-4 minutes or until browned.

Meanwhile, in a 2-qt. microwave-safe bowl, combine the remaining ingredients. Cover and microwave on high for 2-3 minutes or until heated through, stirring once. Stir in the hot dogs.

EDITOR'S NOTE: This recipe was tested in a 1,100-watt microwave.

black bean soup with fruit salsa

PREP: 20 min. • **COOK:** 20 min. • **YIELD:** 3 cups.

Flavorful and filling, this hearty black bean soup with bacon and peppers has a hint of lime and a zesty Southwest flair. It's really a meal in itself. Fresh fruit salsa makes an unexpected but perfect topping for each serving!

michaela rosenthal // woodland hills, california

- **1/4 cup diced seeded peeled cucumber**
- **1/4 cup diced peeled mango**
- **1/4 cup diced fresh pineapple**
- **2 tablespoons chopped sweet onion**
- **4-1/2 teaspoons lime juice**
- **1-1/2 teaspoons grated lime peel**
- **1-1/2 teaspoons minced fresh cilantro**
- **1/4 teaspoon chopped seeded jalapeno pepper**

SOUP:

- **3 bacon strips, diced**
- **3/4 cup chopped red onion**
- **1 Anaheim pepper, seeded and chopped**
- **2 garlic cloves, minced**
- **2 cups reduced-sodium chicken broth**
- **1 can (15 ounces) black beans, rinsed and drained**
- **4 teaspoons lime juice**
- **1 teaspoon ground cumin**
- **1/2 teaspoon lemon-pepper seasoning**
- **1/2 teaspoon ground coriander**

For salsa, combine the first eight ingredients in a small bowl; set aside. In large a saucepan, saute bacon and onion until bacon is crisp and onion is tender. Add Anaheim pepper and garlic; cook 1 minute longer.

Stir in the remaining ingredients. Bring to a boil. Reduce heat; simmer, uncovered, for 10 minutes. Cool slightly.

Puree half of the soup in a blender; return to the pan. Bring to a boil. Reduce heat; simmer for 5 minutes. Serve with fruit salsa.

EDITOR'S NOTE: We recommend wearing disposable gloves when cutting hot peppers. Avoid touching your face.

CITRUS JUICE AT THE READY

Whenever limes and lemons are on sale, I throw a bag of each in the freezer. Later, when a recipe calls for fresh lime or lemon juice, I just defrost a single lemon or lime in the microwave and juice it. This ensures I have fresh citrus juice available whenever I need it. joan f. // turah, montana

lucky bean soup

PREP: 30 min. + standing • **COOK:** 2 hours
YIELD: 14 servings (3-1/2 quarts).

This recipe is from a bean soup gift pack I developed as a fund-raiser for our church. We provide it along with the beans and a packet containing all the spices. The recipient just adds water and a can of tomatoes for a delicious pot of savory soup.
doris cox // south orange, new jersey

- **1/4 cup *each* dried yellow split peas, lentils, black beans, great northern beans, pinto beans, baby lima beans and kidney beans**
- **1/2 cup *each* dried green split peas, black-eyed peas and navy beans**
- **8 cups water**
- **1/3 cup dried minced onion**
- **1 tablespoon salt**
- **1 teaspoon dried thyme**
- **1 teaspoon dried rosemary, crushed**
- **1 teaspoon garlic powder**
- **1/2 teaspoon celery seed**
- **1/2 teaspoon dried basil**
- **1/4 to 1/2 teaspoon crushed red pepper flakes**
- **2 bay leaves**
- **1 can (28 ounces) crushed tomatoes**

Sort beans and rinse with cold water. Place the peas, lentils and beans in a Dutch oven; add water to cover by 2 in. Bring to a boil; boil for 2 minutes. Remove from the heat; cover and let stand for 1 to 4 hours or until beans are softened. Drain and rinse beans, discarding liquid.

Add water and seasonings; bring to a boil. Reduce heat; cover and simmer for 1-1/2 to 2 hours or until beans are tender. Stir in tomatoes; increase heat to medium. Cook, uncovered, for 15-30 minutes. Discard bay leaves.

two-bean soup

PREP: 10 min. + standing • **COOK:** 1-1/2 hours
YIELD: 7 servings.

My husband, David, and I volunteer at our American Legion post, cooking dinner on Friday nights. David, who loves beans, concocted this hearty soup that combines limas and great northerns with cubes of ham and chopped vegetables. I like to serve it with corn bread. lee hawk // san diego, california

- **1/2 pound dried baby lima beans**
- **1/2 pound dried great northern beans**
- **1 can (49-1/2 ounces) reduced-sodium chicken broth**
- **1-1/2 cups cubed fully cooked lean ham**
- **1 medium onion, chopped**
- **2 celery ribs with leaves, chopped**
- **2 medium carrots, sliced**
- **3 garlic cloves, minced**
- **1/8 teaspoon ground ginger**
- **2 green onions, sliced**

Place beans in a large saucepan or Dutch over; add water to cover by 2 in. Bring to a boil; boil for 2 minutes. Remove from the heat; cover and let stand for 1 to 4 hours or until beans are softened.

Drain and rinse beans, discarding liquid. Return beans to pan. Add broth and ham; bring to a boil. Reduce heat; cover and simmer for 1 hour. Add the onion, celery, carrots, garlic and ginger; return to a boil. Reduce heat; cover and simmer 30 minutes longer or until beans and vegetables are tender. Garnish with green onions.

neighborhood bean soup

PREP: 30 min. + standing • **COOK:** 3 hours • **YIELD:** 10 servings (2-3/4 quarts).

Even though I'm single, I make multiple servings of everything—as reflected in the name of my soup! Actually, that tendency has helped me get to know my neighbors. The local ladies have "adopted" me. They always volunteer to be my guinea pigs whenever I try out a new recipe or two. cheryl trowbridge // windsor, ontario

- **2 cups dried great northern beans**
- **5 cups chicken broth**
- **3 cups water**
- **1 meaty ham bone *or* 2 smoked ham hocks**
- **2 to 3 tablespoons chicken bouillon granules**
- **1 teaspoon dried thyme**
- **1/2 teaspoon dried marjoram**
- **1/2 teaspoon pepper**
- **1/4 teaspoon rubbed sage**
- **1/4 teaspoon dried savory**
- **2 medium onions, chopped**
- **3 medium carrots, chopped**
- **3 celery ribs, chopped**
- **1 tablespoon canola oil**

Place beans in a Dutch oven or soup kettle; add water to cover by 2 in. Bring to a boil; boil for 2 minutes. Remove from the heat; cover and let stand for 1 to 4 hours or until beans are softened. Drain and rinse beans, discarding liquid.

Add broth, water, ham bone, bouillon and seasonings; bring to a boil. Reduce heat; cover and simmer for 2 hours.

Meanwhile, saute the onions, carrots and celery in oil; add to soup. Cover and simmer 1 hour longer.

Debone ham and cut into chunks; return to soup. Skim fat.

lentil soup

PREP: 30 min. • **COOK:** 40 min. • **YIELD:** 8 servings (2 quarts).

If you love legumes, you can easily fill up on this substantial soup without expanding your waistline. Lentils lend great taste and nice texture to this mixture that also features barley. dorothy webb // estacada, oregon

- **2 cups sliced fresh carrots**
- **2 celery ribs, chopped**
- **1 large onion, chopped**
- **1 garlic clove, minced**
- **2 tablespoons butter**
- **7 cups reduced-sodium chicken broth *or* vegetable broth**
- **1-1/2 cups dried lentils, rinsed**
- **3 tablespoons medium pearl barley**
- **1-1/2 cups chopped fresh tomatoes**
- **2 tablespoons lemon juice**
- **4-1/2 teaspoons molasses**
- **1 tablespoon red wine vinegar**
- **1/2 teaspoon pepper**
- **Dash *each* dried thyme, basil and oregano**

In a Dutch oven, saute the carrots, celery, onion and garlic in butter until crisp-tender. Add the broth, lentils and barley; bring to a boil. Reduce heat; cover and simmer for 25-30 minutes or until lentils and barley are almost tender.

Stir in the remaining ingredients. Bring to a boil. Reduce heat; cover and simmer for 15 minutes or until lentils and barley are tender.

MEASURING MOLASSES

I like to wipe a bit of vegetable oil inside my measuring cup or spoon when I'm cooking with sticky ingredients like molasses or honey. This keeps the ingredients from clinging to the cup so I know I'm getting the full measure, and it makes cleanup a snap. lynn h. // st. john, new brunswick

white bean 'n' barley soup

PREP: 10 min. + standing • **COOK:** 1-1/4 hours
YIELD: 9 servings.

A friend gave me this recipe, and it's really delicious.
stephanie land // sudbury, ontario

- **1-1/2 cups dried great northern beans**
- **1 large onion, chopped**
- **2 garlic cloves, minced**
- **1 tablespoon olive oil**
- **4 cups chicken *or* vegetable broth**
- **4 cups water**
- **3 medium carrots, sliced**
- **2 medium sweet red peppers, chopped**
- **2 celery ribs, chopped**
- **1/2 cup medium pearl barley**
- **1/2 cup minced fresh parsley, *divided***
- **2 bay leaves**
- **1 teaspoon salt**
- **1/2 teaspoon dried thyme**
- **1/2 teaspoon pepper**
- **1 can (28 ounces) diced tomatoes, undrained**

Place beans in a Dutch oven or soup kettle; add enough water to cover beans by 2 in. Bring to a boil; boil for 2 minutes. Remove from the heat; cover and let stand for 1 to 4 hours or until beans are softened. Drain and rinse beans, discarding liquid.

In a Dutch oven, saute onion and garlic in oil. Add the broth, water, beans, carrots, red peppers, celery, barley, 1/4 cup parsley, bay leaves, salt, thyme and pepper. Bring to a boil. Reduce heat; cover and simmer for 1 hour or until beans are tender. Add tomatoes; heat through. Discard bay leaves. Sprinkle with remaining parsley.

navy bean squash soup

PREP: 10 min. + standing • **COOK:** 1-3/4 hours
YIELD: 12-14 servings (about 3 quarts).

On a chilly day, what could be more comforting than a pot of this homemade soup simmering on the stove? The mix of ham, beans and squash is such a hearty combination, you'll savor every steaming spoonful. linda eggers // albany, california

- **1 pound dried navy beans**
- **2 cans (14-1/2 ounces *each*) chicken broth**
- **2 cups water**
- **1 meaty ham bone**
- **2 to 2-1/2 pounds butternut squash, peeled, seeded and cubed (about 5 cups)**
- **1 large onion, chopped**
- **1/2 teaspoon salt**
- **1/2 teaspoon pepper**

Sort beans and rinse with cold water. Place the beans in a Dutch oven; add water to cover by 2 in. Bring to a boil; boil for 2 minutes. Remove from the heat; cover and let stand for 1 to 4 hours or until beans are softened.

Drain and discard liquid; return beans to pan. Add the broth, water, ham bone, squash, onion, salt and pepper. Bring to a boil. Reduce heat; cover and simmer for 1-1/2 to 1-3/4 hours or until beans are tender.

Remove ham bone. Mash the soup mixture, leaving some chunks if desired. Remove ham from bone; cut into chunks. Discard bone and fat. Return meat to the soup; heat through.

white bean and pasta soup

PREP: 10 min. + standing • **COOK:** 2 hours
YIELD: 12 servings (3 quarts).

My husband and I always enjoy big bowls of this hearty soup. With beans and pasta, it makes a real stick-to-your-ribs meal any day of the year. michelle harbour // lebanon, tennessee

- **1-1/2 cups dried great northern beans**
- **3/4 pound Italian sausage links, casings removed**
- **1 large onion, chopped**
- **1 large carrot, chopped**
- **3 garlic cloves, minced**
- **6 cups chicken broth**
- **3 cups hot water**
- **2 tablespoons dried currants**
- **1 teaspoon dried basil**
- **1 can (14-1/2 ounces) diced tomatoes, undrained**
- **1 cup uncooked small shell pasta**
- **Grated Parmesan cheese**

Sort beans and rinse with cold water. Place beans in a Dutch oven; add water to cover by 2 in. Bring to a boil; boil for 2 minutes. Remove from the heat; cover and let stand for 1 to 4 hours or until beans are softened. Drain and rinse beans, discarding liquid.

In the same pan, cook the sausage, onion, carrot and garlic over medium heat until the meat is no longer pink; drain. Add the broth, water, currants, basil and reserved beans. Bring to a boil. Reduce heat; cover and simmer for 1-1/2 to 2 hours or until the beans are tender, stirring occasionally.

Add tomatoes and pasta; bring to a boil. Reduce heat; cover and simmer for 15 minutes or until pasta is tender. Serve with cheese.

u.s. senate bean soup

PREP: 30 min. + standing • **COOK:** 3-3/4 hours + cooling
YIELD: 8-10 servings (2-1/2 quarts).

This soup recipe is a tempting classic that has stood the test of time. Freeze the bone from a holiday ham until you're ready to make soup. Plus, once prepared, it freezes well for a great make-ahead supper! rosemarie forcum // heathsville, virginia

- **1 pound dried great northern beans**
- **1 meaty ham bone *or* 2 smoked ham hocks**
- **3 quarts water**
- **3 medium onions, chopped**
- **3 garlic cloves, minced**
- **3 celery ribs, chopped**
- **1/4 cup minced fresh parsley**
- **1 cup mashed potatoes *or* 1/3 cup instant potato flakes**
- **Salt and pepper to taste**
- **Minced parsley *or* chives**

Rinse and sort beans. Place beans in a Dutch oven or soup kettle; add water to cover by 2 in. Bring to a boil; boil for 2 minutes. Remove from the heat; cover and let stand for 1 to 4 hours or until beans are softened.

Drain and rinse, discarding liquid. In a large Dutch oven or soup kettle, place the beans, ham bone or hocks and water. Bring to boil. Reduce heat; cover and simmer for 2 hours.

Skim fat if necessary. Add onions, garlic, celery, parsley, potatoes, salt and pepper; simmer 1 hour longer.

Set aside ham bones until cool enough to handle. Remove meat from bones; discard bones. Cut meat into bite-size pieces; return to Dutch oven. Heat through. Sprinkle with parsley or chives.

pasta bean soup

PREP/TOTAL TIME: 30 min.
YIELD: 2 servings.

My older relatives brought this recipe from Italy and made it often as I was growing up. It is truly a comfort food and a balanced meal.

barb swatz // davisburg, michigan

- **1/4 cup chopped onion**
- **1 garlic clove, minced**
- **1 tablespoon butter**
- **1 teaspoon olive oil**
- **3 cups chicken broth**
- **1/4 cup uncooked ditalini *or* other small pasta**
- **1/2 cup canned white kidney *or* cannellini beans**
- **1/2 cup canned diced tomatoes**
- **1/2 cup torn fresh spinach**
- **1/4 teaspoon salt**
- **Shredded Parmesan cheese**

In a saucepan, saute onion and garlic in butter and oil. Add broth; bring to a boil. Add pasta; reduce heat. Simmer, uncovered, for 10 minutes or until the pasta is tender. Add the beans, tomatoes, spinach and salt. Cook 5 minutes longer or until heated through. Serve with Parmesan cheese.

vegetable bean barley soup

PREP: 20 min. • **COOK:** 1 hour • **YIELD:** 6 servings.

This hearty soup is as filling as it is comforting. Full of zucchini, barley, tomatoes and carrots, it's one recipe that people always request.

tina dierking // skowhegan, maine

- **1 medium onion, chopped**
- **1/2 teaspoon dried basil**
- **1/2 teaspoon dill weed**
- **2 tablespoons canola oil**
- **1 garlic clove, minced**
- **2 cans (14-1/2 ounces *each*) reduced-sodium chicken broth**
- **1-3/4 cups water**
- **1 cup chopped carrots**
- **1/2 cup medium pearl barley**
- **1 can (15-3/4 ounces) pork and beans**
- **2 small zucchini, sliced**
- **1/2 teaspoon salt**
- **1/4 teaspoon pepper**
- **1 can (14-1/2 ounces) diced tomatoes, undrained**
- **1 teaspoon cider vinegar**

In a large saucepan, saute the onion, basil and dill in oil until onion is tender. Add garlic; cook 1 minute longer. Stir in the broth, water, carrots and barley. Bring to a boil. Reduce heat; cover and simmer for 30 minutes.

Add the pork and beans, zucchini, salt and pepper. Cover and simmer 10-15 minutes longer or until vegetables and barley are tender. Just before serving, stir in tomatoes and vinegar; heat through.

tomato bean soup

PREP: 15 min. + standing • **COOK:** 2 -1/4 hours
YIELD: 12-14 servings (3-1/2 quarts).

Here's a great recipe that starts with inexpensive dried beans and makes a tasty and filling soup. Chock-full of choice veggies and savory sausage, this dish will fit nicely into almost any event. It's a big hit at our house. My husband and our three children request it all year round.

diane antonioli // marmora, new jersey

- **1 pound dried great northern beans**
- **4 cups chicken broth**
- **2 cups water**
- **2 bay leaves**
- **7 bacon strips, diced**
- **3 cups thinly sliced onion**
- **2 cups thinly sliced celery**
- **2 large carrots, thinly sliced**
- **1/2 pound fully cooked smoked sausage, diced**
- **4 garlic cloves, minced**
- **2 teaspoons sugar**
- **2 cans (28 ounces *each*) diced tomatoes, drained**
- **1/2 teaspoon salt**
- **1/2 teaspoon pepper**
- **1/4 teaspoon hot pepper sauce**

Place beans in a Dutch over or soup kettle; add water to cover by 2 in. Bring to a boil; boil for 2 minutes. Remove from the heat; cover and let stand for 1 to 4 hours or until beans are softened.

Drain beans and discard liquid; return beans to Dutch oven. Add broth, water and bay leaves; bring to a boil. Reduce heat; cover and simmer for 1-1/4 hours or until the beans are tender.

Meanwhile, in a large skillet, cook bacon, onion, celery and carrots until vegetables are crisp-tender, about 12 minutes. Add sausage, garlic and sugar; cook for 5 minutes. Remove with a slotted spoon to Dutch oven. Stir in tomatoes; bring to a boil. Reduce heat; simmer, uncovered, for 45 minutes or until beans begin to break apart and soup thickens, stirring occasionally. Add salt, pepper and pepper sauce. Discard bay leaves.

italian meatball 'n' bean soup

PREP: 30 min. • **COOK:** 5 hours • **YIELD:** 6 servings.

Two kinds of beans plus savory homemade meatballs are an unexpected combination that taste so good together in this soup. With Italian seasoning, garlic and red pepper flakes, the broth is flavorful and a bit spicy. Give it a try!

amanda bowyer // caldwell, idaho

- **1 egg**
- **3 tablespoons 2% milk**
- **1/3 cup seasoned bread crumbs**
- **1 pound bulk Italian sausage**
- **1/2 pound ground turkey**
- **2 cans (14-1/2 ounces *each*) diced tomatoes**
- **1 can (15 ounces) white kidney *or* cannellini beans, rinsed and drained**
- **1 can (15 ounces) black beans, rinsed and drained**
- **1 can (8 ounces) tomato sauce**
- **1 cup water**
- **2 green onions, thinly sliced**
- **1 teaspoon Italian seasoning**
- **1 teaspoon dried minced garlic**
- **1/2 teaspoon crushed red pepper flakes**

In a large bowl, combine the egg, milk and bread crumbs. Crumble sausage and turkey over mixture and mix well. Shape into 1-in. balls. In a large skillet, brown meatballs in batches; drain.

Transfer meatballs to a 3-qt. slow cooker. Stir in the remaining ingredients. Cover and cook on low for 5-6 hours or until meat is no longer pink.

spicy black bean soup

PREP: 25 min. • **COOK:** 40 min. • **YIELD:** 12 servings (3/4 cup each).

A splash of sherry enhances this hearty, easy-to-make soup. For a milder flavor, remove the ribs and seeds from the jalapeno before dicing. tia musser // hudson, indiana

- 1 large red onion, chopped
- 1 medium sweet red pepper, chopped
- 1 jalapeno pepper, seeded and minced
- 2 tablespoons olive oil
- 3 garlic cloves, minced
- 3 cans (15 ounces *each*) black beans, rinsed and drained
- 3-1/2 cups vegetable broth
- 1 can (14-1/2 ounces) diced tomatoes with mild green chilies, undrained
- 1 can (4 ounces) chopped green chilies
- 1/3 cup sherry *or* additional vegetable broth
- 2 tablespoons minced fresh cilantro
- 1/2 cup fat-free sour cream
- 1/4 cup shredded cheddar cheese

In a Dutch oven, saute the onion and peppers in oil until tender. Add the garlic; cook 1 minute longer.

Stir in the beans, broth, tomatoes and chopped green chilies. Bring to a boil. Reduce heat; simmer, uncovered, for 25 minutes. Add sherry and cilantro; cook 5 minutes longer.

Remove from the heat; cool slightly. Place half of soup in a blender; cover and process until pureed. Return to the pan and heat through. Top each serving with 2 teaspoons sour cream and 1 teaspoon cheese.

EDITOR'S NOTE: We recommend wearing disposable gloves when cutting hot peppers. Avoid touching your face.

provencale bean soup

PREP: 30 min. + standing • **COOK:** 2-1/4 hours
YIELD: 16-18 servings (about 4-1/2 quarts).

We enjoy this soup's homegrown goodness so much I make an extra batch and freeze it. jan marto // algoma, wisconsin

- **1 pound dried navy beans**
- **3 medium leeks (white part only), chopped**
- **1 medium onion, chopped**
- **2 garlic cloves, minced**
- **1 tablespoon canola oil**
- **9 cups water**
- **1 smoked boneless ham *or* pork shoulder (about 2 pounds), cubed**
- **4 whole cloves**
- **2 bay leaves**
- **1 teaspoon dried thyme**
- **1 teaspoon salt**
- **1/2 teaspoon pepper**
- **5 medium carrots, thinly sliced**
- **2 medium turnips, peeled and cubed**
- **3 small potatoes, peeled and cubed**
- **2 cups shredded fresh kale**
- **1/2 cup minced fresh parsley**

Rinse and sort beans. Place beans in a Dutch oven or soup kettle; add water to cover by 2 in. Bring to a boil; boil for 2 minutes. Remove from the heat; cover and let stand for 1 to 4 hours or until beans are softened.

Drain and rinse, discarding liquid; set beans aside. In the same pan, saute the leeks, onion and garlic in oil until tender. Add the water, ham, cloves, bay leaves, thyme, salt, pepper and beans; bring to a boil. Reduce heat; cover and simmer for 1-1/4 hours or until the beans are almost tender.

Add carrots, turnips, potatoes, kale and parsley. Cover and simmer 25-35 minutes longer or until the beans and vegetables are tender. Discard bay leaves and cloves before serving.

EDITOR'S NOTE: 2 cups of shredded cabbage may be substituted for the kale.

satisfying lentil soup

PREP: 20 min. • **COOK:** 65 min.
YIELD: 10 servings (2-1/2 quarts).

Packed with a combination of flavorful ingredients, this heart-healthy soup packs 15 grams of fiber into each serving. I'm sure you'll go back for seconds! edna hoffman // hebron, indiana

- **4 medium carrots, chopped**
- **2 celery ribs, chopped**
- **1 large onion, chopped**
- **2 tablespoons olive oil**
- **1 tablespoon minced fresh gingerroot**
- **2 teaspoons curry powder**
- **2 garlic cloves, minced**
- **3/4 teaspoon ground cumin**
- **3/4 teaspoon ground coriander**
- **5 cups water**
- **2 cans (14-1/2 ounces *each*) reduced-sodium chicken broth *or* vegetable broth**
- **1 package (16 ounces) dried lentils, rinsed**
- **2 tablespoons minced fresh cilantro**
- **3/4 teaspoon salt**
- **Dash pepper**

In a Dutch oven, saute the carrots, celery and onion in oil until tender. Add the ginger, curry, garlic, cumin and coriander; cook and stir 1 minute longer.

Add the water, broth and lentils; bring to a boil. Reduce heat; cover and simmer for 50-55 minutes or until lentils are tender. Stir in the cilantro, salt and pepper.

three-bean vegetable soup

PREP: 10 min. • **COOK:** 40 min. • **YIELD:** 6 servings.

With lots of colorful vegetables and beans, this hearty soup is sure to fill up your hungry bunch on a chilly night. It is wonderfully easy to make and very tasty. In summer, use fresh produce from the garden or your local farmer's market. In winter, just use frozen or open some cans of veggies—it couldn't be simpler!

cathy seed // hudson, ohio

- **1 cup sliced carrots**
- **1 cup thinly sliced zucchini**
- **3/4 cup chopped onion**
- **1/2 cup chopped sweet red pepper**
- **1 tablespoon olive oil**
- **2 cans (14-1/2 ounces *each*) vegetable broth**
- **1 can (16 ounces) kidney beans, rinsed and drained**
- **1 can (16 ounces) chili beans, undrained**
- **1 can (15 ounces) garbanzo beans *or* chickpeas, rinsed and drained**
- **1 can (14-1/2 ounces) stewed tomatoes, cut up**
- **1 cup frozen white *or* frozen shoepeg corn**
- **4 teaspoons ground cumin**
- **1/4 teaspoon cayenne pepper**
- **2 tablespoons minced fresh cilantro**

In a large saucepan or Dutch oven, saute the carrots, zucchini, onion and red pepper in oil until crisp-tender. Add the broth, beans, tomatoes, corn, cumin and cayenne; bring to a boil.

Reduce heat; simmer, uncovered, for 30-35 minutes or until vegetables are tender, stirring occasionally. Stir in cilantro.

curried lentil soup

PREP: 15 min. • **COOK:** 8 hours
YIELD: 10 servings (2-1/2 quarts).

Curry gives a different taste twist to this chili-like soup. It's delicious with a dollop of sour cream. My family hurries to the table when they know it's on the menu.

christina till // south haven, michigan

- **4 cups hot water**
- **1 can (28 ounces) crushed tomatoes**
- **3 medium potatoes, peeled and diced**
- **3 medium carrots, thinly sliced**
- **1 large onion, chopped**
- **1 celery rib, chopped**
- **1 cup dried lentils, rinsed**
- **2 garlic cloves, minced**
- **2 bay leaves**
- **4 teaspoons curry powder**
- **1-1/2 teaspoons salt, optional**

In a 3-qt. slow cooker, combine all the ingredients. Cover and cook on low for 8 hours or until vegetables and lentils are tender. Discard bay leaves.

tangy bean soup

PREP: 15 min. • **COOK:** 4-1/2 hours • **YIELD:** 6 servings.

This soup has a great Southwestern flavor and is a real winner with my family. I love it because I can have the soup cooking in my crock pot, and when I get home from work, I can quickly make the dumplings and have dinner on the table in a snap.

joan hallford // north richland hills, texas

- **2 cans (14-1/2 ounces *each*) chicken broth**
- **1 package (16 ounces) frozen mixed vegetables**
- **1 can (15 ounces) black beans, rinsed and drained**
- **1 can (15 ounces) pinto beans, rinsed and drained**
- **1 can (14-1/2 ounces) diced tomatoes, undrained**
- **1 medium onion, chopped**
- **1 tablespoon chili powder**
- **1 tablespoon minced fresh cilantro**
- **4 garlic cloves, minced**
- **1/4 teaspoon pepper**

CORNMEAL DUMPLINGS:

- **1/2 cup all-purpose flour**
- **1/2 cup shredded cheddar cheese**
- **1/3 cup cornmeal**
- **1 tablespoon sugar**
- **1 teaspoon baking powder**
- **1 egg**
- **2 tablespoons milk**
- **2 teaspoons canola oil**

In a 5-qt. slow cooker, combine the first 10 ingredients. Cover and cook on high for 4-5 hours.

For dumplings, combine the flour, cheese, cornmeal, sugar and baking powder in a large bowl. In another bowl, combine the egg, milk and oil; add to dry ingredients just until moistened (batter will be stiff).

Drop by heaping tablespoons onto soup. Cover and cook on high 30 minutes longer (without lifting cover) or until a toothpick inserted in a dumpling comes out clean.

white bean fennel soup

PREP: 10 min. • **COOK:** 45 min.
YIELD: 5 servings.

For company dinners, I know I can count on this soup to dazzle my guests. Once they try it, they often request the recipe. A hint of fennel accents the flavor, and spinach and tomatoes add nice color.
donna quinn // round lake beach, illinois

- **1 large onion, chopped**
- **1 small fennel bulb, thinly sliced**
- **1 tablespoon olive oil**
- **5 cups reduced-sodium chicken broth *or* vegetable broth**
- **1 can (15 ounces) white kidney *or* cannellini beans, rinsed and drained**
- **1 can (14-1/2 ounces) diced tomatoes, undrained**
- **1 teaspoon dried thyme**
- **1/4 teaspoon pepper**
- **1 bay leaf**
- **3 cups shredded fresh spinach**

In a large saucepan, saute onion and fennel in oil until tender. Add the broth, beans, tomatoes, thyme, pepper and bay leaf; bring to a boil. Reduce heat; cover and simmer for 30 minutes or until fennel is tender.

Discard the bay leaf. Add spinach; cook 3-4 minutes longer or until the spinach is wilted.

vegetable bean soup

PREP: 30 min. • **COOK:** 6 hours • **YIELD:** 7 servings.

Kitchen staples and canned goods help me get this heartwarming soup on the table with very little preparation. Feel free to change the ingredients according to your tastes by adding a few of your favorite vegetables, or swap out some of the beans with the variety you like best. belinda moran // woodbury, tennessee

- **2 cans (14-1/2 ounces *each*) petite diced tomatoes**
- **1 can (16 ounces) kidney beans, rinsed and drained**
- **1 can (15-1/4 ounces) whole kernel corn, drained**
- **1 can (15 ounces) garbanzo beans *or* chickpeas, rinsed and drained**
- **1 can (15 ounces) black beans, rinsed and drained**
- **1 can (10 ounces) diced tomatoes and green chilies**
- **1 can (8 ounces) tomato sauce**
- **1 cup chopped green pepper**
- **1 cup chopped zucchini**
- **3/4 cup water**
- **1/2 cup chopped onion**
- **1/2 cup chopped celery**
- **2 tablespoons chili powder**
- **4 teaspoons dried oregano**
- **2 garlic cloves, minced**
- **1 teaspoon ground cumin**
- **1 teaspoon pepper**
- **1/2 teaspoon salt**
- **2 bay leaves**

In a 5-qt. slow cooker, combine all ingredients. Cover and cook on low for 6-8 hours or until vegetables are tender. Discard bay leaves.

DIFFERENT TWIST

After my bean soup has simmered in the slow cooker all day with ham and onions, I add a can of pureed pumpkin. This easy addition gives the soup an appealing color, more body and flavor plus extra vitamins.
loretta b. // le claire, iowa

refried bean soup

PREP/TOTAL TIME: 30 min. • **YIELD:** 8 servings (2 quarts).

My husband and I love this yummy soup. It's almost like a savory Southwestern dip that you eat with a spoon. It's very quick and easy to put together, and you can add any garnishes you like to vary the taste. barbara dean // littleton, colorado

- **1 can (28 ounces) crushed tomatoes**
- **1/2 cup chopped onion**
- **1/2 teaspoon minced garlic**
- **2 cans (16 ounces *each*) refried beans**
- **1 can (14-1/2 ounces) chicken broth**
- **1 tablespoon minced fresh cilantro**
- **5 corn tortillas (6 inches), cut into 1/2-inch strips, optional**
- **Sour cream and shredded Monterey Jack cheese, optional**

In a large saucepan, bring the tomatoes, onion and garlic to a boil. Reduce heat; simmer, uncovered, for 5 minutes. Stir in the refried beans, broth and cilantro; simmer for 15 minutes.

Meanwhile, if tortilla strips are desired, place strips on a baking sheet. Bake at 350° for 12-15 minutes or until crisp. Garnish soup with tortilla strips. Serve with sour cream and cheese if desired.

el paso bean soup

PREP: 10 min. • **COOK:** 30 min • **YIELD:** 6 servings (2-1/4 quarts).

We have so few bad-weather days in New Mexico that we like to celebrate cold rainy ones with bowls of hot soup. My family likes this ham and bean variety alongside green chili corn muffins. beverly peacock // santa teresa, new mexico

- **1 medium onion, chopped**
- **1 medium carrot, chopped**
- **2 garlic cloves, minced**
- **2 tablespoons olive oil**
- **4 cups reduced-sodium beef broth**
- **1 can (16 ounces) fat-free refried beans**
- **2 cans (15-1/2 ounces *each*) great northern beans, rinsed and drained**
- **1-1/3 cups cubed fully cooked lean ham**
- **1 teaspoon dried parsley flakes**
- **1 teaspoon ground cumin**
- **1 teaspoon chili powder**
- **1/4 teaspoon pepper**
- **2 medium tomatoes, chopped**

In a large saucepan, saute the onion, carrot and garlic in oil until tender. Stir in broth and refried beans; whisk until smooth. Stir in the beans, ham, parsley, cumin, chili powder and pepper. Bring to a boil. Reduce heat; cover and simmer for 15 minutes. Stir in the tomatoes and heat through.

bean cabbage soup

PREP: 15 min. • **COOK:** 35 min. • **YIELD:** 2 servings.

I used to love my Italian grandmother's homemade minestrone. She was very particular about ingredients and where she bought them. Since I cook for only my husband and myself, I have simplified her recipe and cut down on the amounts. If I do say so myself, it's almost as good as Nonna Teresa's.

joyce anderson // chico, california

- **2 tablespoons chopped celery**
- **1 tablespoon chopped onion**
- **1 teaspoon olive *or* 1 tablespoon canola oil**
- **1 garlic clove, minced**
- **1/3 cup cubed zucchini**
- **1/3 cup cubed peeled potato**
- **1/3 cup sliced carrot**
- **1 can (14-1/2 ounces) beef broth**
- **1/2 cup canned white kidney beans *or* cannellini beans, rinsed and drained**
- **2 teaspoons minced fresh basil *or* 1/2 teaspoon dried basil**
- **Dash pepper**
- **1/2 cup coarsely chopped cabbage**
- **1/4 cup cooked rice**
- **1 tablespoon grated Parmesan cheese**

In a saucepan, saute celery and onion in oil for 2-3 minutes. Add garlic and saute for 1 minute. Add the zucchini, potato and carrot; saute for 3 minutes. Stir in the beef broth, beans, basil and pepper. Bring to a boil. Stir in cabbage.

Reduce heat; cover and simmer for 20 minutes or until potatoes are tender. Just before serving, stir in rice and cheese.

campfire bean 'n' ham soup

PREP: 15 min. + standing • **GRILL:** 1-1/2 hours
YIELD: 12 servings (3 quarts).

These are the best beans and ham you'll ever taste—bar none! Friends rave about this hearty soup that I serve hot off the grill.

tom greaves // carrollton, illinois

- **1 pound dried navy beans**
- **2 small onions**
- **8 cups water**
- **4 cups cubed fully cooked lean ham (1-1/2 pounds)**
- **2 smoked ham hocks**
- **2 cups chopped celery**
- **1 cup chopped carrots**
- **1/2 teaspoon dried basil**
- **1/2 teaspoon pepper**

Place the beans in an ovenproof Dutch oven; add enough water to cover them by 2 in. Bring to a boil; boil for 2 minutes. Remove from the heat; cover and let stand for 1 to 4 hours or until beans are softened.

Chop one onion; slice second onion and separate into rings. Set onions aside. Drain and rinse beans, discarding liquid. Return beans to the pan. Add reserved onions; stir in the remaining ingredients. Cover pan and place on the grill rack over indirect medium heat.

Cover grill; cook for 1 hour or until beans are almost tender. Uncover Dutch oven; cover grill and cook 30 minutes longer or until beans are tender. Discard ham hocks.

EDITOR'S NOTE: For easy cleanup, consider covering the outside of your Dutch oven with heavy-duty foil first.

SAUSAGE CORN CHOWDER, PG. 257

SOUPS

cream soups, chowders & bisques

CHEESY VEGETABLE CHOWDER, PG. 229 CHEESEBURGER SOUP, PG. 259 SWEET POTATO AND PEAR SOUP, PG. 269

wild rice soup

PREP/TOTAL TIME: 20 min.
YIELD: 8 servings (about 2 quarts).

I tasted this thick and hearty soup at a food fair I helped judge. It didn't earn a ribbon, but I thought it was a real winner. The original recipe called for uncooked wild rice, but I use a quick-cooking rice blend instead.
kathy herink // gladbrook, iowa

- **1 pound ground beef**
- **2 cups chopped celery**
- **2 cups chopped onion**
- **3 cups hot water**
- **1 can (14-1/2 ounces) chicken broth**
- **1 can (10-3/4 ounces) condensed cream of mushroom soup, undiluted**
- **1 package (6.75 ounces) quick-cooking long grain and wild rice mix**
- **5 bacon strips, cooked and crumbled**

In a large saucepan, cook the beef, celery and onion over medium heat until the meat is no longer pink and vegetables are tender; drain.

Add the water, broth, soup, rice and contents of the seasoning packet. Bring to a boil. Reduce heat; cover and simmer for 5 minutes. Garnish with bacon.

simple shrimp chowder

PREP/TOTAL TIME: 30 min. • **YIELD:** 5 cups.

Shrimp fans will be bowled over by this tasty take on chowder. The creamy broth is full of vegetables. Chop up leftover cooked potatoes or use canned ones.
carolyn schmeling // brookfield, wisconsin

- **1/2 cup *each* chopped onion, celery, carrot and sweet red pepper**
- **1/4 cup butter, cubed**
- **1/4 cup all-purpose flour**
- **2 cups 2% milk**
- **1/2 pound cooked small shrimp, peeled and deveined**
- **1 can (14-1/2 ounces) diced potatoes, drained**
- **1 cup vegetable broth**
- **1 cup frozen corn, thawed**
- **2 teaspoons seafood seasoning**
- **1/2 teaspoon dried thyme**

In a large saucepan, saute the onion, celery, carrot and red pepper in butter for 5 minutes or until tender. Stir in flour until blended; gradually add milk. Bring to a boil; cook and stir for 2 minutes or until thickened.

Add the shrimp, potatoes, broth, corn, seafood seasoning and thyme. Reduce heat; cover and simmer for 10 minutes or until heated through.

butternut squash soup

PREP: 30 min. • **COOK:** 6-1/4 hours • **YIELD:** 14 servings (2-1/2 quarts).

The golden color, smooth and creamy texture and wonderful taste of this soup is a welcome addition on a chilly fall day. It has a slightly tangy flavor from the cream cheese, and the cinnamon really comes through. jackie campbell // stanhope, new jersey

- **1 medium onion, chopped**
- **2 tablespoons butter**
- **1 medium butternut squash (about 4 pounds), peeled and cubed**
- **3 cans (14-1/2 ounces *each*) vegetable broth**
- **1 tablespoon brown sugar**
- **1 tablespoon minced fresh gingerroot**
- **1 garlic clove, minced**
- **1 cinnamon stick (3 inches)**
- **1 package (8 ounces) cream cheese, softened and cubed**

In a small skillet, saute onion in butter until tender. Transfer to a 5-or 6-quart slow cooker; add squash. Combine the broth, brown sugar, ginger, garlic and cinnamon; pour over squash. Cover and cook on low for 6-8 hours or until squash is tender.

Cool slightly. Discard cinnamon stick. In a blender, process soup in batches until smooth. Return all to slow cooker. Whisk in cream cheese; cover and cook 15 minutes longer or until cheese is melted.

slow-cooked corn chowder

PREP: 10 min. • **COOK:** 6 hours • **YIELD:** 8 servings (2 quarts).

I combine and refrigerate the ingredients for this easy chowder the night before. In the morning, I pour the mixture into the slow cooker and turn it on before I leave for work. When I come home, a hot, tasty meal awaits.

mary hogue // rochester, pennsylvania

- **2-1/2 cups 2% milk**
- **1 can (14-3/4 ounces) cream-style corn**
- **1 can (10-3/4 ounces) condensed cream of mushroom soup, undiluted**
- **1-3/4 cups frozen corn**
- **1 cup frozen shredded hash brown potatoes**
- **1 cup cubed fully cooked ham**
- **1 large onion, chopped**
- **2 teaspoons dried parsley flakes**
- **2 tablespoons butter**
- **Salt and pepper to taste**

In a 3-qt. slow cooker, combine all ingredients. Cover and cook on low for 6 hours.

GOOD USE OF LEFTOVERS

When I have leftover scalloped potatoes, I either add them to corn chowder with other potatoes or replace the other spuds depending on how many leftovers I have. The resulting soup is always flavorful and filling.

jean j. // chula vista, california

creamy carrot-parsnip soup

PREP: 30 min. • **COOK:** 15 min. • **YIELD:** 4 cups.

My mom made this tasty soup for us many times to warm us up and fill us up. Whenever I make this soup, it brings me back to my mother's kitchen.

eleanor chilson // plantation, florida

- **1 can (14-1/2 ounces) chicken broth**
- **2 medium parsnips, peeled and sliced**
- **2 medium carrots, sliced**
- **1 small potato, peeled and sliced**
- **1 celery rib, sliced**
- **1/3 cup chopped onion**
- **1/4 teaspoon salt**
- **1 cup half-and-half cream**

In a small saucepan, combine the broth, parsnips, carrots, potato, celery, onion and salt. Bring to a boil. Reduce heat; cover and simmer for 10-12 minutes or until the vegetables are tender.

Using a slotted spoon, remove half of the vegetables to a bowl; cover the bowl and keep warm.

Cool remaining vegetables for 5 minutes. Transfer to a blender; cover and process for 30 seconds. Add cream; process until blended. Add reserved vegetables; pulse until vegetables are chopped. Return all to the saucepan; heat through.

basil tomato soup

PREP/TOTAL TIME: 20 min.
YIELD: 9 servings.

After bringing this six-ingredient soup to a teachers' function, I had so many requests for the recipe that it was published in the school newsletter. I serve the rich soup in mugs with a Caesar salad.

sarah perkins // southlake, texas

- **2 cans (28 ounces *each*) crushed tomatoes**
- **1 can (14-1/2 ounces) chicken broth**
- **18 to 20 fresh basil leaves, minced**
- **1 teaspoon sugar**
- **1 cup heavy whipping cream**
- **1/2 cup butter**

In a large saucepan, bring the tomatoes and broth to a boil. Reduce heat; cover and simmer for 10 minutes. Add basil and sugar. Reduce heat to low; stir in cream and butter. Cook until the butter is melted.

creamy turkey soup with wild rice

PREP: 10 min. • **COOK:** 1-1/4 hours • **YIELD:** 8 servings (2-3/4 quarts).

Our family loves this soup all year long but finds it especially comforting on cold days. If you want a less rich soup with fewer calories, substitute milk for the half-and-half. barbara schmid // cavalier, north dakota

- **1 cup uncooked wild rice**
- **7 cups chicken broth, *divided***
- **1/2 pound sliced fresh mushrooms**
- **1 medium onion, chopped**
- **1 celery rib, chopped**
- **1/4 cup butter, cubed**
- **1/2 cup all-purpose flour**
- **1/2 teaspoon salt**
- **1/2 teaspoon ground mustard**
- **1/2 teaspoon poultry seasoning**
- **1/4 teaspoon pepper**
- **4 cups cubed cooked turkey**
- **2 cups half-and-half cream**

In a large saucepan, bring rice and 3 cups broth to a boil. Reduce heat; cover and simmer for 50-60 minutes or until rice is tender.

In a Dutch oven, saute the mushrooms, onion and celery in butter until tender. Stir in flour and seasonings until blended. Gradually add remaining broth. Bring to a boil; cook and stir for 2 minutes or until thickened. Stir in the turkey, cream and cooked rice; heat through (do not boil).

WILD RICE HINTS

You can store wild rice in an airtight container indefinitely. Always rinse it before cooking. Wild rice may become tender without absorbing all the cooking liquid. If necessary, drain before serving or combining with other recipe ingredients. Leftover cooked wild rice freezes well. Defrost and reheat in the microwave for use in recipes calling for cooked rice or for a quick side dish.

cheesy vegetable chowder

PREP: 10 min. • **COOK:** 20 min. • **YIELD:** 8-10 servings.

Nutritious vegetables taste even better floating in a cheesy broth. This soothing soup is one you'll be inspired to make again and again. taste of home test kitchen

- **1/2 cup *each* finely chopped carrot, celery and onion**
- **1/4 cup chopped sweet red pepper**
- **8 tablespoons butter, *divided***
- **4 cups chicken broth**
- **3 cups fresh broccoli florets**
- **1 medium potato, peeled and diced**
- **3/4 teaspoon Worcestershire sauce**
- **1/2 teaspoon cayenne pepper**
- **1/4 cup all-purpose flour**
- **1 can (12 ounces) evaporated milk**
- **2 cups (8 ounces) shredded sharp cheddar cheese**
- **Additional shredded sharp cheddar cheese, optional**

In a Dutch oven, saute the carrot, celery, onion and red pepper in 4 tablespoons butter until vegetables are tender. Stir in the broth, broccoli, potato, Worcestershire and cayenne; bring to a boil. Reduce heat; cover and simmer 10-15 minutes or until broccoli and potato are tender.

Meanwhile in a large saucepan, melt remaining butter over medium heat. Whisk in flour until smooth. Gradually whisk in milk. Bring to a boil; cook and stir for 2 minutes or until thickened. Reduce heat. Add cheese; stir just until cheese is melted.

Slowly stir the cheese sauce into vegetable mixture. Garnish with additional cheese if desired.

BROCCOLI INFO

Broccoli comes from the Latin word brachium, which means branch or arm. When purchasing broccoli, look for bunches that have a deep green color, tightly closed buds and crisp leaves. Store in a resealable plastic bag in the refrigerator for up to 4 days. Wash just before using. One pound of broccoli yields about 2 cups florets.

cream of spinach soup

PREP/TOTAL TIME: 15 min.
YIELD: 4 servings.

This rich and creamy soup tastes like it's made by a professional chef. While I often use drained canned spinach in the recipe, frozen spinach works well, too.
patricia bradley
rohnert park, california

1 package (1.8 ounces) leek soup and dip mix
1 package (10 ounces) frozen chopped spinach, thawed and squeezed dry
1 cup (8 ounces) sour cream
1/4 teaspoon ground nutmeg
Lemon slices

Prepare soup mix according to package directions. Stir in spinach. Cover and simmer for 2 minutes. Remove from the heat; stir in sour cream and nutmeg. Garnish with lemon slices.

corn leek chowder

PREP: 10 min. • **COOK:** 35 min. • **YIELD:** 4 cups.

Leeks, onion, potatoes and cheese enrich my corn chowder. I developed it for our meatless Christmas Eve meal. stacey savoyski // southbury, connecticut

2 cups chopped leeks (white portion only)
3/4 cup chopped onion
2 garlic cloves, minced
1 tablespoon olive oil
3 cups reduced-sodium chicken broth
1-1/2 cups cubed peeled potatoes
1/4 to 1/2 teaspoon dill weed
3/4 cup frozen corn, thawed
1/4 teaspoon pepper
4 teaspoons cornstarch
1 tablespoon cold water
1/2 cup half-and-half cream
1/4 cup shredded cheddar cheese

In a large saucepan, saute the leeks, onion and garlic in oil until tender. Stir in the broth, potatoes and dill; cook for 10-15 minutes or until potatoes are tender.

Stir in the corn and pepper; cook 2 minutes longer. Combine the cornstarch and water until smooth; stir into the soup. Bring to a boil; cook and stir for 2 minutes or until thickened.

Stir in cream. Cook over medium heat for 1-2 minutes or until heated through. Garnish each serving with 1 tablespoon of cheese.

cream of walnut soup

PREP: 15 min. • **COOK:** 40 min. • **YIELD:** 3 cups.

Smooth and creamy, this mildly flavored soup makes a wonderful start to a meal. With its unique taste, it is not your run-of-the-mill soup. denise albers // freeburg, illinois

- **3 cups chicken broth**
- **1 cup chopped walnuts**
- **2 tablespoons chopped onion**
- **2 tablespoons chopped celery**
- **1/8 teaspoon ground nutmeg**
- **2 tablespoons butter**
- **2 tablespoons all-purpose flour**
- **1/2 cup 2% milk**
- **1 cup half-and-half cream**
- **Minced fresh parsley**

In a small saucepan, combine the first five ingredients. Bring to a boil. Reduce heat; cover and simmer for 30 minutes. Cool slightly. Transfer to a blender; cover and process until pureed. Strain.

In a large saucepan, melt butter over medium heat. Stir in flour until blended. Gradually whisk in milk. Bring to a boil; cook and stir for 1 minute or until thickened. Gradually stir in pureed mixture. Add cream; heat through (do not boil). Garnish with parsley.

hearty tomato bisque

PREP: 20 min. • **COOK:** 20 min. • **YIELD:** 6 servings.

Between the lycopene from the crushed tomatoes and soy protein from the tofu and soy milk, this soup offers a powerful, heart-healthy punch in a tasty bisque. You'll never want canned soup again. lisa renshaw // kansas city, missouri

- **1 medium onion, chopped**
- **1 tablespoon olive oil**
- **2 cans (15 ounces *each*) crushed tomatoes**
- **1 tablespoon honey**
- **1 teaspoon minced fresh rosemary *or* 1/4 teaspoon dried rosemary, crushed**
- **1/2 teaspoon salt**
- **1/4 teaspoon pepper**
- **8 ounces soft tofu, drained and crumbled (1 cup)**
- **1-1/2 cups soy milk**
- **3/4 cup salad croutons**

In a large saucepan, saute onion in oil for 4-6 minutes or until tender. Stir in the tomatoes, honey, rosemary, salt and pepper; bring to a boil. Reduce heat; simmer for 10 minutes, stirring occasionally.

Remove from the heat; stir in tofu and soy milk. Cool slightly. In a blender or food processor, process soup in batches until smooth. Return to the pan and heat through. Garnish with croutons.

SOY PRODUCT INSIGHT

Soybeans are made into many food products, and soybean products can be good sources of a variety of nutrients. When compared with many other legumes, soybeans have more protein and calcium, yet they're lower in complex carbohydrates. Common food products include soy milk and tofu. Soy milk is a nondairy beverage made from crushed, cooked soybeans. It is a good source of protein but has less calcium than cow's milk unless it has been calcium-fortified. Tofu is the processed bean curd. With a soft texture and bland taste, it's best mixed into stir-fries, casseroles, chili and other dishes in which it can take on other flavors.

garlic tomato soup

PREP: 30 min. • **COOK:** 30 min.
YIELD: about 4 cups.

Garlic is roasted in this recipe to add a mellow background flavor to this rich, creamy tomato soup. Canned tomatoes and puree make it an easy year-round favorite.
marilyn coomer // louisville, kentucky

- **12 garlic cloves, peeled and sliced**
- **1-1/2 teaspoons olive oil**
- **1 can (14-1/2 ounces) diced tomatoes, undrained**
- **1 cup tomato puree**
- **1 pint heavy whipping cream**
- **1/4 teaspoon dried oregano**
- **1/4 teaspoon minced fresh basil**
- **1/4 teaspoon salt**
- **1/8 teaspoon pepper**

In a 3-cup baking dish, combine garlic and oil. Cover; bake at 300° for 25-30 minutes or until lightly browned.

In a large saucepan, bring the garlic, tomatoes and tomato puree to a boil. Reduce the heat; cover and simmer for 30 minutes.

Add the cream, oregano, basil, salt and pepper. Cool slightly. Place half of the soup at a time in a blender; cover and process until pureed. Return to the pan; heat through.

red pepper carrot soup

PREP: 40 min. • **COOK:** 40 min. + cooling • **YIELD:** 4 servings.

This colorful soup is a tasty way to get a serving of vegetables without a lot of fat. Even my discerning teenagers happily eat it up. anna hartle // loveland, ohio

- **1 medium sweet red pepper**
- **1 pound carrots, sliced**
- **1 medium onion, chopped**
- **2 tablespoons uncooked long grain rice**
- **2 tablespoons butter**
- **2 cans (14-1/2 ounces *each*) chicken broth**
- **2 cups water**
- **1/3 cup orange juice**
- **4-1/2 teaspoons snipped fresh dill**
- **2 teaspoons grated orange peel**
- **1/2 teaspoon salt**
- **1/2 teaspoon *each* dried marjoram, thyme and rosemary, crushed**
- **1/2 teaspoon rubbed sage**
- **1/4 teaspoon pepper**

Broil red pepper 4 in. from the heat until skin is blistered, about 6 minutes. With tongs, rotate pepper a quarter turn. Broil and rotate until all sides are blistered and blackened. Immediately place pepper in a bowl; cover and let stand for 15-20 minutes. Peel and discard charred skin. Remove stem and seeds; set pepper aside.

In a large saucepan, cook the carrots, onion and rice in butter until onion is tender. Stir in the broth, water, orange juice, dill, orange peel, salt, marjoram, thyme, rosemary, sage and pepper. Bring to a boil. Reduce heat; cover and simmer for 20-25 minutes or until carrots and rice are tender. Cool for 10 minutes.

In a blender, puree carrot mixture and roasted pepper in small batches. Return to the pan; heat through.

white bean soup

PREP: 15 min. • **COOK:** 20 min. • **YIELD:** 2 servings.

Crunchy Parmesan crisps make a zippy topping for this rich, full-flavored soup. We love the Italian sausage garnish.

linda miranda // wakefield, rhode island

- **1/4 cup shredded Parmesan cheese**
- **Cayenne pepper**
- **1/4 pound bulk Italian sausage**
- **2 tablespoons chopped onion**
- **1 teaspoon olive oil**
- **1 garlic clove, minced**
- **1 can (15 ounces) white kidney *or* cannellini beans, rinsed and drained**
- **1 cup chicken broth**
- **1/4 cup heavy whipping cream**
- **2 teaspoons sherry, optional**
- **1 teaspoon minced fresh parsley**
- **1/8 teaspoon salt**
- **1/8 teaspoon dried thyme**

Spoon Parmesan cheese into six mounds 3 in. apart on a parchment paper-lined baking sheet. Spread into 1-1/2-in. circles. Sprinkle with a dash of cayenne. Bake at 400° for 5-6 minutes or until light golden brown. Cool.

In a saucepan, cook sausage and onion in oil over medium heat until meat is no longer pink; drain. Remove and keep warm.

In the same pan, saute garlic for 1-2 minutes or until tender. Stir in the beans, broth, cream, sherry if desired, parsley, salt, thyme and a dash of cayenne. Bring to a boil. Reduce heat; simmer, uncovered, for 12-15 minutes or until heated through. Cool slightly.

Transfer to a blender; cover and process on high until almost blended. Pour into soup bowls; sprinkle with sausage mixture and Parmesan crisps.

broccoli beer cheese soup

PREP: 15 min. • **COOK:** 40 min.
YIELD: 12 servings (3 quarts).

This soup tastes wonderful. I always make extra and pop individual servings in the fridge. lori lee // brooksville, florida

- **5 celery ribs, finely chopped**
- **3 medium carrots, finely chopped**
- **1 small onion, finely chopped**
- **3 tablespoons butter**
- **4 cans (14-1/2 ounces *each*) chicken broth**
- **4 cups fresh broccoli florets, chopped**
- **1/4 cup chopped sweet red pepper**
- **1 teaspoon salt**
- **1/2 teaspoon pepper**
- **1/2 cup all-purpose flour**
- **1/2 cup water**
- **3 cups (12 ounces) shredded cheddar cheese**
- **1 package (8 ounces) cream cheese, cubed**
- **1 bottle (12 ounces) beer *or* nonalcoholic beer**

Optional toppings: cooked and crumbled bacon, chopped green onions, shredded cheddar cheese, sour cream and salad croutons

In a Dutch oven, saute the celery, carrots and onion in butter until almost tender; add the broth, broccoli, red pepper, salt and pepper. Combine flour and water until smooth; stir into pan. Bring to a boil. Reduce heat; simmer, uncovered, for 30-40 minutes or until thickened and vegetables are tender.

Stir in the cheeses and beer; cook until heated through and cheese is melted, stirring occasionally (do not boil). Serve desired amount with toppings of your choice. Cool remaining soup; transfer to freezer containers. Freeze for up to 3 months.

TO USE FROZEN SOUP: Thaw in the refrigerator overnight. Transfer to a saucepan. Cover and cook over medium-low heat until heated through, stirring occasionally (do not boil).

creamy cauliflower soup

PREP/TOTAL TIME: 25 min. • **YIELD:** 5 servings.

Even people who don't care for cauliflower love this deliciously different soup! trisha kruse // eagle, idaho

- **1 package (16 ounces) frozen cauliflower**
- **1 cup frozen sliced carrots**
- **3 tablespoons dried minced onion**
- **1 tablespoon chicken bouillon granules**
- **2-1/4 cups water, *divided***
- **2 cups 2% milk**
- **1 can (10-3/4 ounces) condensed cream of potato soup, undiluted**
- **1/2 teaspoon garlic powder**
- **1/8 teaspoon ground nutmeg**
- **4 teaspoons cornstarch**
- **1 cup (4 ounces) shredded cheddar cheese**

In a large saucepan, combine the vegetables, onion, bouillon and 2 cups water. Bring to a boil. Reduce heat; cover and simmer for 4-6 minutes or until vegetables are tender.

Stir in the milk, soup, garlic powder and nutmeg. Combine the cornstarch and remaining water until smooth; gradually stir into soup. Bring to a boil; cook and stir for 2 minutes or until slightly thickened. Add cheese; stir until melted.

mushroom tomato bisque

PREP: 30 min. • **COOK:** 10 min. • **YIELD:** 4 servings.

I was out with friend and ordered this soup. After one spoonful, I knew I just had to re-create it at home. This was the result. The recipe might seem complicated, but it's really not. And I love the blend of flavors.

connie stevens // schaefferstown, pennsylvania

- **1-1/2 pounds plum tomatoes, halved lengthwise**
- **5 tablespoons olive oil, *divided***
- **2 garlic cloves, minced**
- **1/2 teaspoon salt**
- **1/2 teaspoon dried basil**
- **1/2 teaspoon dried oregano**
- **1/2 teaspoon pepper**
- **1/2 pound sliced fresh mushrooms**
- **1/2 cup finely chopped sweet onion**
- **1-1/4 cups chicken broth**
- **1/3 to 1/2 cup tomato paste**
- **Pinch sugar, optional**
- **3/4 cup heavy whipping cream**
- **2 tablespoons grated Parmesan cheese**

Place tomatoes cut side down in a greased 15-in. x 10-in. x 1-in. baking pan. Brush with 3 tablespoons oil. Mix garlic, salt, basil, oregano and pepper; sprinkle over tomatoes. Bake, uncovered, at 450° for 20-25 minutes or until edges are well browned.

Cool slightly. Place tomatoes and pan drippings in a blender. Cover and process until blended; process 1 minute longer.

In a large saucepan, saute mushrooms and onion in remaining oil for 5-8 minutes or until tender. Stir in broth, tomato paste, sugar if desired and tomato puree. Bring to a boil. Remove from the heat; stir in cream. Garnish with Parmesan cheese.

oh-so-easy tomato cream soup

PREP/TOTAL TIME: 20 min.
YIELD: 4 servings.

I like to make things that are quick, easy and tasty, and this creamy soup is all three.

eileen korecko
hot springs village, arkansas

- **2 cups 2% milk**
- **1 can (14-1/2 ounces) diced tomatoes, undrained**
- **1 package (8 ounces) cream cheese, softened**
- **1/4 cup coarsely chopped fresh basil**
- **1/2 teaspoon salt**
- **1/8 teaspoon pepper**

Place all ingredients in a blender; cover and process until smooth. Transfer to a large saucepan; heat through.

harvest corn chicken chowder

PREP: 20 min. • **COOK:** 35 min. • **YIELD:** 5 servings.

With lots of chicken and ham, this lightened-up corn chowder has become a favorite at my house. I like to use sweet corn I grow myself. janet boote // hull, iowa

- **1/2 cup chopped onion**
- **1/2 cup chopped sweet red pepper**
- **1 tablespoon olive oil**
- **1 cup cubed fully cooked ham**
- **2 garlic cloves, minced**
- **2 cups water**
- **2 cups cubed red potatoes**
- **1-1/2 cups fresh *or* frozen corn**
- **1 teaspoon reduced-sodium chicken bouillon granules**
- **3/4 teaspoon dried thyme**
- **1/2 teaspoon poultry seasoning**
- **1/2 teaspoon salt**
- **1/4 teaspoon pepper**
- **1 cup cubed cooked chicken breast**
- **1 can (12 ounces) fat-free evaporated milk**
- **3/4 cup 1% milk, *divided***
- **1/4 cup all-purpose flour**

In a large saucepan, saute onion and red pepper in oil until onion is tender. Add ham and garlic; cook 1 minute longer. Stir in the water, potatoes, corn, bouillon, thyme, poultry seasoning, salt and pepper. Bring to a boil. Reduce heat; cover and simmer for 15 minutes or until potatoes are tender.

Add chicken; heat through. Stir in evaporated milk and 1/2 cup milk; bring to a boil. Combine flour and remaining milk until smooth; slowly stir into soup. Cook and stir for 2 minutes or until thickened.

creamy fish chowder

PREP: 10 min. • **COOK:** 30 min. • **YIELD:** 3-1/2 cups.

We were tired of the same old vegetable soup, and I had some fish on hand that needed to be cooked, so this was the creation of our favorite fish chowder. Occasionally, I enhance it further by adding another vegetable, such as corn or peas, to add color and nutrition.

claudette mogle // federal way, washington

- **1/3 cup chopped onion**
- **1 tablespoon butter**
- **2 cups chicken broth**
- **1-1/2 cups diced potatoes**
- **1/2 teaspoon salt**
- **1/2 teaspoon pepper**
- **2 tablespoons all-purpose flour**
- **2 tablespoons mashed potato flakes**
- **2 cups milk**
- **1/2 pound cod *or* haddock fillets, cut into 1/2-inch pieces**
- **2 tablespoons minced fresh parsley**

In a large saucepan, saute onion in butter until tender. Add the broth, potatoes, salt and pepper. Bring to a boil. Reduce heat; cover and simmer for 20 minutes or until potatoes are tender.

In a bowl, combine the flour, potato flakes and milk until smooth. Stir into the potato mixture. Bring to a boil. Reduce heat; add fish and parsley. Cover and simmer for 5-10 minutes or until fish is opaque.

creamy zucchini soup

PREP: 10 min. • **COOK:** 25 min. • **YIELD:** 4 servings.

In our area, we use lots of zucchini. One day I decided to try a new recipe for it, and my family really liked the results.

mrs. thomas maust // berlin, pennsylvania

- **2 tablespoons chopped onion**
- **3 tablespoons butter**
- **3 tablespoons all-purpose flour**
- **2 cups 2% milk**
- **1 cup water**
- **1 teaspoon chicken bouillon granules**
- **1/2 teaspoon salt**
- **1/4 teaspoon pepper**
- **1 large zucchini, shredded**
- **1 cup (4 ounces) shredded cheddar cheese**

In a large saucepan, saute onion in butter until tender. Stir in flour until blended. Gradually stir in the milk, water, bouillon, salt and pepper. Bring to a boil; cook and stir for 2 minutes or until thickened. Add zucchini. Simmer, uncovered, for 10 minutes or until zucchini is tender. Stir in cheese until melted.

mushroom corn chowder

PREP/TOTAL TIME: 30 min. • **YIELD:** 8 servings.

Every spoonful of this thick, creamy chowder is brimming with veggies, ham and cheese. It 'll take the chill off even the nippiest of fall evenings. Try serving with fresh bread for scraping up every last bit. elaine krupsky // las vegas, nevada

- **1-1/4 cups sliced fresh carrots**
- **1 cup chopped celery with leaves**
- **3/4 cup sliced fresh mushrooms**
- **3 green onions, sliced**
- **1/4 cup butter, cubed**
- **1 can (10-3/4 ounces) condensed cream of mushroom soup, undiluted**
- **1-1/3 cups 2% milk**
- **1-1/2 cups frozen corn, thawed**
- **1/2 cup cubed fully cooked ham**
- **1/2 teaspoon seasoned salt**
- **1/2 cup cubed process cheese (Velveeta)**

In a large saucepan, saute the carrots, celery, mushrooms and onions in butter until tender. Stir in the soup, milk, corn, ham and seasoned salt. Bring to a boil. Reduce heat; stir in cheese. Cook and stir 3-5 minutes longer or until cheese is melted.

WHAT'S PROCESS CHEESE?

Process cheese is a blend of different cheeses that is similar in flavor to the natural cheese from which it's made. Generally, it is stable at room temperature and stays smooth and creamy when it is heated. The most common brand name of process American cheese is Velveeta.

vegetable tomato soup

PREP/TOTAL TIME: 20 min.
YIELD: 2 cups.

My husband and I love this quick, dressed-up tomato soup. The cloves give it a surprising little kick. Serve with grilled cheese sandwiches and you're sure to get a smile!
stacy myers // bristol, tennessee

1/4 cup chopped onion
1/4 cup chopped celery
1 tablespoon butter
1 can (10-3/4 ounces) condensed tomato soup, undiluted
1-1/4 cups water
1 tablespoon minced fresh parsley
2 teaspoons sugar
1/8 teaspoon salt
1/8 teaspoon pepper
Dash ground cloves

In a small saucepan, saute onion and celery in butter until tender. Stir in the remaining ingredients. Bring to a boil. Reduce heat; simmer, uncovered, for 5-7 minutes or until heated through.

spicy seafood bisque

PREP: 10 min. • **COOK:** 35 min. • **YIELD:** 10-12 servings (about 3 quarts).

This spicy soup, featuring shrimp, crabmeat and tomatoes, gets its zip from hot pepper sauce and cayenne pepper. It's easy to prepare and dresses up any meal. Of all the recipes I've borrowed from my mom, this soup is the one that I've made most often. kevin weeks // north palm beach, florida

1/2 cup chopped onion
1/2 cup chopped celery
2 tablespoons butter
4 cups chicken broth
3 cups tomato juice
1 can (14-1/2 ounces) diced tomatoes, undrained
1 tablespoon Worcestershire sauce
1 teaspoon seafood seasoning
1 teaspoon dried oregano
1/2 teaspoon garlic powder
1/2 teaspoon hot pepper sauce
1/4 teaspoon cayenne pepper
1 bay leaf
1/2 cup uncooked small shell pasta *or* elbow macaroni
1 pound uncooked medium shrimp, peeled and deveined
1 can (6 ounces) crabmeat, drained, flaked and cartilage removed

In a large saucepan, saute onion and celery in butter until tender. Add the broth, tomato juice, tomatoes, Worcestershire sauce and seasonings; bring to a boil. Reduce heat; cover and simmer for 20 minutes.

Discard bay leaf. Add pasta to the soup; cook, uncovered, until pasta is tender. Add shrimp and crab; simmer 5 minutes longer or until shrimp turn pink.

creamy bacon mushroom soup

PREP/TOTAL TIME: 30 min. • **YIELD:** 8 servings (2 quarts).

I've always enjoyed cooking and recently created this rich soup. It's always a hit. You can also garnish it with chopped green onion tops or shredded Swiss cheese. For a creamier, smoother consistency, try pouring the soup through a strainer.

toby mercer // inman, south carolina

- **10 bacon strips, diced**
- **1 pound sliced fresh mushrooms**
- **1 medium onion, chopped**
- **3 garlic cloves, minced**
- **1 quart heavy whipping cream**
- **1 can (14-1/2 ounces) chicken broth**
- **1-1/4 cups shredded Swiss cheese**
- **3 tablespoons cornstarch**
- **1/2 teaspoon salt**
- **1/2 teaspoon pepper**
- **3 tablespoons water**

In a large saucepan, cook bacon over medium heat until crisp. Using a slotted spoon, remove to paper towels; drain, reserving 2 tablespoons drippings. In the drippings, saute the mushrooms, onion and garlic. Stir in cream and broth. Gradually add the cheese, stirring until melted.

In a small bowl, combine the cornstarch, salt, pepper and water until smooth. Stir into soup. Bring to a boil; cook and stir for 2 minutes or until thickened. Garnish with the bacon.

haddock chowder

PREP: 30 min. • **COOK:** 35 min. • **YIELD:** 5 servings.

Warming bowls of this chilly-weather chowder can include most any type of seafood or whitefish. We especially like it with haddock, cod or grouper. Crispy rolls and a green salad complete the meal. eleanor atteridg // rolesville, north carolina

- **1/2 pound bacon strips, diced**
- **1 large onion, chopped**
- **2 medium carrots, sliced**
- **1 bay leaf**
- **2 whole cloves**
- **1 medium potato, peeled and cubed**
- **2 cups water**
- **1/4 cup white wine *or* chicken broth**
- **1 pound haddock fillets, cut into chunks**
- **1 teaspoon dill weed**
- **1/2 teaspoon salt**
- **1/8 teaspoon white pepper**
- **1 tablespoon all-purpose flour**
- **2 tablespoons cold water**
- **1 cup half-and-half cream**
- **1 tablespoon minced fresh parsley**

In a large saucepan, cook bacon over medium heat until crisp. Using a slotted spoon, remove to paper towels; drain, reserving 1 tablespoon drippings. In the drippings, saute onion and carrots until tender.

Place bay leaf and cloves on a double thickness of cheesecloth; bring up corners of cloth and tie with string to form a bag. Add to saucepan. Stir in the potato, water and wine. Bring to a boil. Reduce heat; cover and simmer for 15-20 minutes or until the potatoes are tender.

Add the haddock, dill, salt and pepper. Bring to a boil. Reduce heat; cook for 5-10 minutes or until fish flakes easily with a fork.

Combine flour and cold water until smooth; gradually stir into chowder. Bring to a boil; cook and stir for 2 minutes or until thickened. Add cream; heat through (do not boil). Discard spice bag. Stir in bacon. Garnish with parsley.

mexican shrimp bisque

PREP/TOTAL TIME: 30 min. • **YIELD:** 3 cups.

I enjoy both Cajun and Mexican cuisine, and this rich, elegant soup combines the best of both.
karen harris // castle rock, colorado

- **1/2 cup chopped onion**
- **1 tablespoon olive oil**

- 2 garlic cloves, minced
- 1 tablespoon all-purpose flour
- 1 cup water
- 1/2 cup heavy whipping cream
- 1 tablespoon chili powder
- 2 teaspoons chicken bouillon granules
- 1/2 teaspoon ground cumin
- 1/2 teaspoon ground coriander
- 1/2 pound uncooked medium shrimp, peeled and deveined
- 1/2 cup sour cream
- Fresh cilantro and cubed avocado, optional

In a large saucepan, saute onion in oil until tender. Add garlic; cook 1 minute longer. Stir in flour until blended. Stir in the water, cream, chili powder, bouillon, cumin and coriander; bring to a boil. Reduce heat; cover and simmer for 5 minutes.

Cut the shrimp into bite-size pieces; add to soup. Simmer for 5 minutes or until shrimp turn pink. Gradually stir 1/2 cup hot soup into sour cream; return all to the pan, stirring constantly. Heat through (do not boil). Garnish with cilantro and avocado if desired.

northwest seafood corn chowder

PREP: 45 min. • **COOK:** 45 min.
YIELD: 8 servings (2 quarts).

This chowder showcases wonderful Northwest seafood; it's all in here, from bay scallops to snapper.

barbara sidway // baker city, oregon

- 2 large ears sweet corn in husks
- 14 fresh cherrystone clams
- 6 bacon strips, chopped
- 1/3 cup butter, cubed
- 2 large onions, chopped
- 1 celery rib, chopped
- 1 tablespoon chopped shallot
- 2 garlic cloves, minced
- 1/2 cup all-purpose flour
- 2 cups water
- 1 bottle (8 ounces) clam juice
- 3/4 pound potatoes, cubed

- 1/4 cup clam stock
- 2 tablespoons minced fresh parsley
- 1 bay leaf
- 1/2 teaspoon salt
- 1/2 teaspoon white pepper
- 1/4 teaspoon dried thyme
- 1/2 pound bay scallops
- 1/2 pound uncooked small shrimp, peeled and deveined
- 1-1/2 cups heavy whipping cream

Carefully peel back husks from corn to within 1 in. of bottom; remove silk. Rewrap corn in husks. Place on a baking sheet. Bake at 375° for 30-35 minutes or until tender.

Meanwhile, tap clams; discard any that do not close. Place in a large saucepan; cover with water. Bring to a boil. Reduce heat; cover and simmer for 5-6 minutes or until clams open. Drain. Remove meat from clams; chop and set aside.

In a Dutch oven, cook bacon over medium heat until crisp. Add the butter, onion, celery, shallot and garlic; cook until tender. Stir in flour until blended; cook and stir for 10 minutes or until browned (do not burn). Gradually add water and clam juice. Bring to a boil; cook and stir for 2 minutes or until thickened.

Remove corn from cobs. Stir the corn, potatoes, clam stock, parsley, bay leaf, salt, pepper and thyme into soup. Bring to a boil. Reduce heat; simmer, uncovered, for 30 minutes. Add the scallops, shrimp and clams; cook 3-4 minutes longer or until shrimp turn pink and scallops are opaque. Stir in cream; heat through. Discard bay leaf.

chicken asparagus soup

PREP: 1 hour • **COOK:** 45 min. • **YIELD:** 10 servings (about 2 quarts).

Asparagus stars in this flavorful soup, a favorite recipe from my Italian grandmother. I have fond memories of chopping veggies and cooking with her as a child. sandy clayton // visalia, california

- **2 pounds thin fresh asparagus**
- **2 large potatoes, peeled and diced**
- **1 large onion, chopped**
- **2 celery ribs, chopped**
- **1 medium carrot, chopped**
- **2 teaspoons dried parsley flakes**
- **1 garlic clove, minced**
- **2 tablespoons canola oil**
- **2 cans (14-1/2 ounces *each*) chicken broth**
- **1 teaspoon salt**
- **1/2 teaspoon pepper, *divided***
- **1 bay leaf**
- **2 cups cubed cooked chicken**
- **2 cups half-and-half cream**
- **Shaved Parmesan cheese, optional**

Cut tips from asparagus spears; set aside. Place stalks in a large skillet; cover with water. Bring to a boil. Reduce heat; cover and simmer for 40 minutes. Strain, reserving 4 cups cooking liquid. Discard stalks.

In a Dutch oven, saute the potatoes, onion, celery, carrot, parsley and garlic in oil until vegetables are tender. Stir in the broth, salt, 1/4 teaspoon pepper, bay leaf and reserved cooking liquid. Bring to a boil. Reduce heat; simmer, uncovered, for 30 minutes. Discard bay leaf. Cool slightly.

In a blender, cover and puree soup in batches until smooth. Return to the pan. Add the chicken, cream, remaining pepper and reserved asparagus tips. Bring to a boil. Reduce heat; simmer, uncovered, for 5 minutes or until asparagus is tender. Garnish with Parmesan cheese if desired.

HANDLING ASPARAGUS

The peak months for buying asparagus are April and May. When buying, look for firm, straight, uniform-size spears. The tips should be closed with crisp stalks. It's best to use asparagus within a few days of purchase. For a little longer storage, place bundled stalks upright in a bowl filled with 1 inch of water; refrigerate. Or wrap the cut ends in moist paper towels. Cover the towel with plastic wrap; refrigerate. To clean, soak asparagus in cold water. Cut or snap off the tough white portion.

fiesta chicken chowder

PREP: 30 min. • **COOK:** 15 min. • **YIELD:** 10 servings (2-1/2 quarts).

I entered the recipe for this hearty soup in a contest sponsored by my hometown newspaper. I won first place and donated the prize money to the area shelter for women and children. beth jenkins-horsley // belmont, north carolina

- **3 tablespoons all-purpose flour**
- **1 envelope fajita seasoning, *divided***
- **1 pound boneless skinless chicken breasts, cut into 1-inch cubes**
- **3 tablespoons canola oil**
- **1 medium onion, chopped**
- **2 garlic cloves, minced**
- **3 cups water**
- **1 can (15 ounces) black beans, rinsed and drained**
- **1 can (14-1/2 ounces) Mexican stewed tomatoes, undrained**
- **1 can (11 ounces) Mexicorn, drained**
- **1 cup uncooked instant brown rice**
- **1 can (4 ounces) chopped green chilies**
- **1 can (11 ounces) condensed nacho cheese soup, undiluted**
- **3 tablespoons minced fresh cilantro**
- **1 tablespoon lime juice**

In a large resealable plastic bag, combine flour and 2 tablespoons fajita seasoning; add chicken. Seal bag and shake to coat. In a large saucepan, saute chicken in oil until no longer pink. Remove and keep warm.

In the same pan, saute onion until tender; add garlic, cook 1 minute longer. Stir in the water, beans, tomatoes, corn, rice, chilies and remaining fajita seasoning. Bring to a boil. Reduce heat; cover and simmer for 5 minutes or until rice is tender.

Stir in the soup, cilantro, lime juice and chicken; heat through.

salmon chowder

PREP/TOTAL TIME: 20 min.
YIELD: 8 servings.

This comforting chowder really hits the spot. Enjoy it with a side salad or a freshly baked loaf of bread for a complete meal.

pat waymire // yellow springs, ohio

- 1 cup thinly sliced green onions
- 2 celery ribs, thinly sliced
- 2 tablespoons butter
- 2 tablespoons all-purpose flour
- 1/2 teaspoon salt
- 1/2 teaspoon dill weed
- 4 cups milk
- 2 cups cauliflowerets, cooked
- 1 can (14-3/4 ounces) salmon, drained, skin and bones removed
- 1 package (10 ounces) frozen peas, thawed
- 1/2 cup shredded Swiss cheese
- 1/2 cup shredded cheddar cheese

In a large saucepan, saute onions and celery in butter until tender. Stir in the flour, salt and dill until blended. Gradually add milk. Bring to a boil; cook and stir for 2 minutes or until thickened. Add the cauliflower, salmon and peas; heat through. Stir in the cheeses until melted. Serve immediately.

creamy asparagus soup

PREP/TOTAL TIME: 30 min. • **YIELD:** 4 servings.

I think this asparagus soup tastes like spring—so fresh and colorful. Pureed to a smooth, creamy texture and nicely seasoned with thyme, it's sure to please asparagus lovers.

adele long // sterling heights, michigan

- 2 green onions, chopped
- 1 garlic clove, minced
- 1 tablespoon butter
- 2 cans (14-1/2 ounces *each*) reduced-sodium chicken broth *or* vegetable broth
- 1 pound fresh asparagus, trimmed and cut into 1-inch pieces
- 1/2 teaspoon salt
- 1/2 to 3/4 teaspoon dried thyme
- 1/8 teaspoon pepper
- 1 bay leaf
- 2 tablespoons all-purpose flour
- 3 tablespoons water
- 1/4 cup reduced-fat sour cream
- 1 teaspoon grated lemon peel

In a large saucepan, saute onions and garlic in butter. Add the broth, asparagus, salt, thyme, pepper and bay leaf. Bring to a boil. Reduce heat; cover and simmer for 8-10 minutes or until asparagus is tender. Drain asparagus, reserving cooking liquid. Discard bay leaf. Cool slightly.

In a food processor, combine asparagus and 1/2 cup cooking liquid; cover and process until smooth. Return pureed asparagus and remaining cooking liquid to pan.

Combine the flour and water until smooth; stir into soup. Bring to a boil; cook and stir for 1-2 minutes or until thickened. Garnish each serving with sour cream and lemon peel.

cream of potato soup

PREP/TOTAL TIME: 30 min. • **YIELD:** 2 servings.

Here's a recipe that proves you don't have to make a big batch of soup to enjoy home-style flavor. It's the perfect way to warm up on chilly nights...just add some hot biscuits. nancy mosher // sun city, california

- **1 medium potato, peeled and cubed**
- **1/2 cup water**
- **1 celery rib, diced**
- **2 tablespoons finely chopped onion**
- **2 tablespoons butter**
- **3/4 cup evaporated milk**
- **1 teaspoon dried parsley flakes**
- **1/4 teaspoon salt**
- **Dash pepper**

In a small saucepan, bring the potato and water to a boil. Reduce heat; cover and cook for 10-15 minutes or until tender.

In a small skillet, saute celery and onion in butter until tender. Add to potato mixture. Stir in the milk, parsley, salt and pepper; heat through.

chicken chowder

PREP/TOTAL TIME: 30 min. • **YIELD:** 8 servings (3 quarts).

Served over tortilla chips or with corn bread as a side, this hearty chowder is wonderful. Packed with chicken (or turkey) and veggies, it makes a nutritious and satisfying meal. heather hamilton // bunker hill, west virginia

- **1 can (14-1/2 ounces) reduced-sodium chicken broth**
- **1 can (10-3/4 ounces) condensed cream of chicken soup, undiluted**
- **1 can (10-3/4 ounces) condensed cream of potato soup, undiluted**
- **1-1/2 cups milk**
- **2 cans (14-1/2 ounces *each*) diced tomatoes, undrained**
- **2 cups cubed cooked chicken**
- **1 can (11 ounces) Mexicorn, drained**
- **1/3 cup chopped onion**
- **1 can (4 ounces) chopped green chilies**
- **1-1/2 cups (6 ounces) shredded Monterey Jack cheese**

In a large saucepan, combine the broth, soups and milk. Stir in the tomatoes, chicken, Mexicorn, onion and chilies. Bring to a boil. Reduce heat; simmer, uncovered, for 10-15 minutes or until onion is tender. Garnish with cheese.

SHRED YOUR OWN CHEESE

It's usually cheaper to buy cheese in blocks than in shredded form. So I buy large quantities of cheddar, Monterey Jack and mozzarella, then shred them myself in my food processor. I store the shredded cheese in the freezer in heavy-duty resealable plastic bags, so I have it at my fingertips whenever it's needed. evelyn o. // parma, ohio

baked potato soup

PREP: 30 min. • **COOK:** 10 min. • **YIELD:** 2 servings.

You'll get a little zippy flavor with each spoonful of this tasty soup. A few drops of hot pepper sauce and a sprinkle of basil make my version stand out from other potato soup recipes. kristi teague // southside, tennessee

- **1 large potato**
- **1 bacon strip, diced**
- **2 tablespoons chopped onion**
- **1 small garlic clove, minced**
- **5 teaspoons all-purpose flour**
- **1/2 teaspoon dried basil**
- **1/4 teaspoon pepper**
- **1-1/2 cups chicken broth**
- **1/2 cup half-and-half cream**
- **6 to 8 drops hot pepper sauce, optional**
- **2 tablespoons shredded cheddar cheese**
- **2 teaspoons minced fresh parsley**

Scrub and pierce potato. Microwave on high for 4-6 minutes or bake at 400° for 50-75 minutes or until tender, turning once. When cool enough to handle, peel and cube potato; set aside.

In a small saucepan, cook bacon over medium heat until crisp. Using a slotted spoon, remove to paper towels to drain.

In the drippings, saute onion and garlic until tender. Stir in the flour, basil and pepper until blended. Gradually add broth. Bring to a boil; cook and stir for 2 minutes.

Add the cream, cubed potato and hot pepper sauce if desired; heat through (do not boil). Top each serving with bacon, cheese and parsley.

EDITOR'S NOTE: This recipe was tested in a 1,100-watt microwave.

PERK UP SOUP'S COLOR

I like to add some grated carrots to my creamy potato soup. It complements the flavor of cream soup nicely and adds appealing flecks of color. marie w. // prince george, british columbia

creamy chicken potato soup

PREP/TOTAL TIME: 30 min. • **YIELD:** 6 servings.

Any time I serve this thick, comforting soup, someone asks for the recipe. Because it is loaded with chunks of potatoes and chicken, no one suspects that it's lower in fat.

carla reid // charlottetown, prince edward island

- **1 medium onion, chopped**
- **2 tablespoons butter**
- **3 cups reduced-sodium chicken broth**
- **1 pound potatoes, (about 2 medium), cut into 1/2-inch cubes**
- **1-1/2 cups diced cooked chicken breast**
- **1/2 teaspoon salt**
- **1/4 teaspoon pepper**
- **1/4 cup all-purpose flour**
- **1 cup fat-free milk**
- **1 cup reduced-fat evaporated milk**
- **1 teaspoon minced fresh parsley**
- **1 teaspoon minced chives**

In a large saucepan, saute onion in butter until tender. Stir in broth and potatoes. Bring to a boil. Reduce heat; cover and simmer for 10-15 minutes or until potatoes are tender. Stir in the chicken, salt and pepper.

Combine flour and fat-free milk until smooth; stir into saucepan. Add evaporated milk. Bring to a boil; cook and stir for 2 minutes or until thickened. Sprinkle with parsley and chives.

pepperoni cheese soup

PREP: 45 min. • **COOK:** 25 min.
YIELD: 10 servings (2-1/2 quarts).

Children and adults will be equally thrilled by my creative soup, which tastes like pizza in a bowl. It's just as fresh and flavorful as pizza, and you don't have to fuss with making a crust.

debbie reid // clearwater, florida

- **1 pint grape tomatoes**
- **2 tablespoons olive oil, *divided***
- **1/2 teaspoon dried oregano**
- **1/2 teaspoon pepper, *divided***
- **3/4 cup chopped sweet onion**
- **3/4 cup chopped carrots**
- **3/4 cup chopped green pepper**
- **1 carton (32 ounces) reduced-sodium chicken broth**
- **1-1/4 cups cubed peeled potatoes**
- **3 cups (12 ounces) shredded part-skim mozzarella cheese, *divided***
- **2 cups (8 ounces) shredded white cheddar cheese**
- **1 package (8 ounces) cream cheese, cubed**
- **1 cup milk**
- **2 teaspoons pizza *or* Italian seasoning**
- **1/4 teaspoon crushed red pepper flakes**
- **2 packages (one 8 ounces, one 3-1/2 ounces) sliced pepperoni, chopped, *divided***

Place tomatoes in a greased 15-in. x 10-in. x 1-in. baking pan; drizzle with 1 tablespoon oil, oregano and 1/4 teaspoon pepper; toss gently. Bake at 400° for 10-15 minutes or until tender; set aside.

In a Dutch oven, saute onion in remaining oil until tender. Add the carrots, green pepper and remaining pepper; saute 4 minutes longer. Add broth and potatoes. Bring to a boil. Reduce heat; cover and cook for 10-15 minutes or until potatoes are tender. Cool slightly.

In a blender, process soup in batches until smooth. Return all to the pan; heat through. Stir in 2 cups mozzarella cheese, cheddar cheese, cream cheese, milk, pizza seasoning and pepper flakes until cheeses are melted. Add 1-1/3 cups pepperoni and reserved tomatoes; heat through. Serve with remaining mozzarella cheese and pepperoni.

sausage corn chowder

PREP: 10 min. • **COOK:** 45 min. • **YIELD:** 4 servings.

Warm up with this comforting chowder. I love sausage and sweet corn, so I put them together, and voila! This is a perfect meal to serve on a blustery day.
kay nichols // wellsburg, west virginia

- **1/2 pound bulk sage-flavored sausage *or* sausage of your choice**
- **1/4 cup chopped onion**
- **1/4 cup chopped celery**
- **3 cups water**
- **2 medium red potatoes, cut into 1/2-inch cubes**
- **2 teaspoons chicken bouillon granules**
- **1 cup frozen corn**
- **3 tablespoons butter**
- **1/4 cup all-purpose flour**
- **1/8 teaspoon pepper**
- **1-1/2 cups 2% milk**

In a large saucepan, cook the sausage, onion and celery over medium heat until meat is no longer pink; drain.

Stir in water, potatoes and bouillon. Bring to a boil. Reduce heat; simmer, uncovered, for 20 minutes. Add corn; simmer 10 minutes longer or until potatoes are tender.

Meanwhile, in a small saucepan, melt butter; stir in flour and pepper until smooth. Gradually stir in milk. Bring to a boil; cook and stir for 1-2 minutes or until thickened. Stir into the sausage mixture.

tomato crab soup

PREP: 20 min. • **COOK:** 30 min.
YIELD: 10 servings (2-1/2 quarts).

You'll enjoy crabmeat and veggies in every bite of my so-easy soup. The rich dish is sure to please anyone who enjoys seafood. The fresh basil gives it a nice herb flavor.
clinton liu // edmonds, washington

- **1 small onion, chopped**
- **1/4 cup chopped sweet red pepper**
- **4 garlic cloves, minced**
- **3 tablespoons butter**
- **4 plum tomatoes, finely chopped**
- **1/4 cup all-purpose flour**
- **1/2 teaspoon pepper**
- **1/8 teaspoon salt**
- **3 cans (14-1/2 ounces *each*) reduced-sodium chicken broth**
- **1 can (6 ounces) tomato paste**
- **2 cans (6 ounces *each*) crabmeat, drained, flaked and cartilage removed**
- **3 tablespoons minced fresh basil**
- **1 cup milk**

In a large saucepan, saute onion, red pepper and garlic in butter for 3 minutes. Stir in the tomatoes; cook 2-3 minutes longer or until the onion is tender.

Whisk in the flour, pepper and salt until blended. Gradually stir in the broth and tomato paste. Bring to a boil; cook and stir for 2 minutes or until thickened. Stir in crab and basil. Gradually stir in the milk; heat through.

cheeseburger soup

PREP: 45 min. • **COOK:** 10 min. • **YIELD:** 8 servings (2-1/4 quarts).

A local restaurant serves a similar soup but wouldn't share its recipe with me. So I developed my own by modifying a recipe for potato soup. I was really pleased at how good this "all-American" dish turned out. joanie shawhan // madison, wisconsin

- **1/2 pound ground beef**
- **3/4 cup chopped onion**
- **3/4 cup shredded carrots**
- **3/4 cup diced celery**
- **1 teaspoon dried basil**
- **1 teaspoon dried parsley flakes**
- **4 tablespoons butter, *divided***
- **3 cups chicken broth**
- **4 cups diced peeled potatoes (1-3/4 pounds)**
- **1/4 cup all-purpose flour**
- **2 cups (8 ounces) process cheese (Velveeta)**
- **1-1/2 cups milk**
- **3/4 teaspoon salt**
- **1/4 to 1/2 teaspoon pepper**
- **1/4 cup sour cream**

In a large saucepan, brown beef; drain and set aside. In the same saucepan, saute the onion, carrots, celery, basil and parsley in 1 tablespoon butter until vegetables are tender, about 10 minutes. Add the broth, potatoes and beef; bring to a boil. Reduce heat; cover and simmer for 10-12 minutes or until potatoes are tender.

Meanwhile, in a small skillet, melt remaining butter. Add flour; cook and stir for 3-5 minutes or until bubbly. Add to soup; bring to a boil. Cook and stir for 2 minutes. Reduce heat to low. Stir in the cheese, milk, salt and pepper; cook and stir until cheese is melted. Remove from the heat; blend in sour cream.

HANDY SHREDDED CARROTS

I shred carrots and freeze them in plastic bags in 1-cup portions. When I have a recipe that calls for shredded carrots, I just pull a bag out of the freezer. It's a big time-saver. candace z. // eagar, arizona

broccoli potato soup

PREP: 25 min. • **COOK:** 4-1/2 hours • **YIELD:** 8 cups (2 quarts).

For a very comforting soup with a creamy texture, try this one with nutritious broccoli and chunks of potato. The red pepper flakes add a hint of spice, and the fresh herbs make this a truly delicious blend. crystal kelso // sandy, oregon

- **1 pound small red potatoes, cubed**
- **1 large onion, chopped**
- **1 large carrot, coarsely chopped**
- **7 garlic cloves, minced**
- **3 cups water**
- **1 can (14-1/2 ounces) condensed cream of broccoli soup, undiluted**
- **1 teaspoon *each* minced fresh thyme, basil and parsley**
- **1 teaspoon garlic powder**
- **1/2 teaspoon salt**
- **1/2 teaspoon crushed red pepper flakes**
- **1/4 teaspoon pepper**
- **2 cups frozen chopped broccoli, thawed and drained**
- **1 cup (4 ounces) shredded Havarti cheese**

Place the potatoes, onion, carrot and garlic in a 4- or 5-qt. slow cooker. Add the water, soup and seasonings. Cover and cook on low for 4-5 hours or until heated through.

Stir in broccoli and cheese. Cover and cook for 30 minutes or until broccoli is tender.

HOW TO FREEZE BROCCOLI

When fresh broccoli is on sale, buy extra and freeze for use in recipes later. To freeze broccoli, choose young tender stalks. Trim off the large leaves and tough parts of the stems. Wash stalks thoroughly and cut lengthwise into uniform pieces, leaving florets about 1-1/2 inches across. Heat in rapidly boiling water for 3 minutes, or in a steamer basket over boiling water for 5 minutes. Immediately plunge broccoli into ice-cold water to stop cooking. Without proper cooling, frozen broccoli will develop bigger ice crystals and a limp texture. Package broccoli in sturdy resealable plastic bags, removing any air pockets before sealing. Use within 10 months.

potato clam chowder

PREP/TOTAL TIME: 30 min.
YIELD: 8 servings (2 quarts).

I got this recipe from an old college friend. Serve it piping hot with a loaf of sourdough bread and coleslaw.
kristy doty // riverside, california

- **1/2 pound sliced bacon, diced**
- **2 large onions, chopped**
- **3 cans (6-1/2 ounces *each*) minced clams**
- **3 cups diced unpeeled potatoes**
- **1/2 cup chicken broth**
- **1 can (10-3/4 ounces) condensed cream of celery soup, undiluted**
- **1-1/4 cups milk**
- **1 cup heavy whipping cream**
- **1 teaspoon salt**
- **1/2 teaspoon pepper**

In a Dutch oven or soup kettle, cook bacon over medium heat until crisp. Using a slotted spoon, remove to paper towels; drain, reserving 2 tablespoons drippings. In the drippings, saute onions until tender.

Drain clams, reserving juice. Set clams aside. Add the potatoes, clam juice and broth to the onions. Cook over medium heat for 15 minutes or until potatoes are tender. Stir in clams, soup, milk, cream, salt, pepper and bacon; heat through.

reuben soup

PREP: 20 min. • **COOK:** 15 min. • **YIELD:** about 6 servings.

When we're lucky (or have been good, I'm not certain which), the cafeteria staff at our school serves this soup. The cooks have served it for years, and it remains a special favorite with the students. mary lindell // sanford, michigan

- **1/2 cup chopped onion**
- **1/2 cup sliced celery**
- **2 tablespoons butter**
- **1 cup chicken broth**
- **1/2 teaspoon baking soda**
- **2 tablespoons cornstarch**
- **2 tablespoons water**
- **3/4 cup sauerkraut, rinsed and drained**
- **2 cups half-and-half cream**
- **2 cups chopped cooked corned beef**
- **1 cup (4 ounces) shredded Swiss cheese**

Salt and pepper to taste
Rye croutons, optional

In a large saucepan, saute onion and celery in butter until tender. Add broth and baking soda. Combine cornstarch and water until smooth; gradually add to pan. Bring to a boil; cook and stir for 2 minutes or until thickened.

Reduce heat. Add sauerkraut, cream and corned beef; simmer and stir for 15 minutes. Add cheese; stir until melted. Add salt and pepper. Garnish with croutons if desired.

roasted onion & garlic soup

PREP: 1 hour • **COOK:** 10 min.
YIELD: 8 servings (2 quarts).

My low-fat soup, made with Vidalias or other sweet onions, is a cold-weather tonic for my husband and me.

nancy mueller // menomonee falls, wisconsin

- **6 medium sweet onions**
- **1 whole garlic bulb**
- **3 cups reduced-sodium chicken broth, *divided***
- **1/2 cup buttermilk**
- **1 tablespoon minced fresh thyme *or* 1 teaspoon dried thyme**
- **1/2 teaspoon coarsely ground pepper**
- **1/2 cup shredded Swiss cheese**

Place the unpeeled onions and garlic bulb in a 15-in. x 10-in. x 1-in. baking pan coated with cooking spray. Spritz with cooking spray. Bake, uncovered, at 450° for 50-60 minutes or until tender.

When cool enough to handle, peel the onions and garlic. Place in a blender; add 1 cup of broth. Cover and process until smooth; transfer to a large saucepan. Add the buttermilk, thyme, pepper and remaining broth; heat through. Garnish with cheese.

seafood chowder

PREP: 45 min. • **COOK:** 25 min.
YIELD: 12 servings (4-1/2 quarts).

Chock-full of fish, shrimp and scallops, this comforting chowder has been pleasing my family for a long time. The seasoned oyster crackers add a fun bit of spice.

virginia anthony // jacksonville, florida

- **1 tablespoon unsalted butter, melted**
- **1 tablespoon marinade for chicken**
- **1 teaspoon hot pepper sauce**
- **1/4 teaspoon curry powder**
- **1/4 teaspoon paprika**
- **1-1/4 cups oyster crackers**

CHOWDER:

- **8 bacon strips, chopped**
- **1-1/2 pounds red potatoes, cut into 1/2-inch cubes**
- **2 cups thinly sliced leeks (white portion only)**
- **1/4 cup all-purpose flour**
- **3/4 teaspoon dried thyme**
- **1 carton (32 ounces) reduced-sodium chicken broth**
- **4 cups clam juice**
- **1 package (12 ounces) frozen corn**
- **1-1/2 cups diced zucchini**
- **1 pound grouper *or* tilapia fillets, cut into 1-inch cubes**
- **3/4 pound uncooked medium shrimp, peeled and deveined**
- **1/2 pound bay scallops**
- **1 cup half-and-half cream**
- **1 teaspoon salt**
- **1/4 teaspoon white pepper**

In a small bowl, combine the butter, marinade for chicken, pepper sauce, curry and paprika. Add the crackers; toss to coat.

Transfer to a greased 15-in. x 10-in. x 1-in. baking pan. Bake at 350° for 8-10 minutes or until golden brown; stirring twice. Set aside.

Meanwhile, in a stockpot, cook bacon over medium heat until crisp. Using a slotted spoon, remove to paper towels to drain.

Saute potatoes and leeks in drippings; stir in flour and thyme until blended. Gradually whisk in broth and clam juice. Bring to a boil, stirring constantly. Cook and stir 1-2 minutes longer. Reduce heat; cover and simmer for 10 minutes or until potatoes are tender.

Add the corn, zucchini, grouper, shrimp and scallops; cook for 2-4 minutes or until fish flakes easily with a fork. Stir in the cream, salt and pepper; heat through. Serve with crackers and bacon.

EDITOR'S NOTE: This recipe was tested with Lea & Perrins Marinade for Chicken.

zesty potato cheese soup

PREP/TOTAL TIME: 10 min. • **YIELD:** 6 servings.

I really like to make potato cheese soup from scratch. But one night, we were in a hurry, so I added a few ingredients to a can of potato soup instead. It was so good and so quick and easy that I now constantly keep a few cans on hand. Serve it in bread bowls, which is always a big hit with kids.
karen pigmon // corning, california

- **3 cans (10-3/4 ounces *each*) condensed cream of potato soup, undiluted**
- **2 cans (12 ounces *each*) evaporated milk**
- **3/4 cup shredded cheddar cheese**
- **3/4 cup shredded pepper Jack cheese**
- **6 slices ready-to-serve fully cooked bacon, crumbled**

In a large saucepan, combine the potato soup and milk. Cook over medium heat for 5-7 minutes or until heated through. Ladle into serving bowls. Sprinkle with cheeses and bacon.

mushroom meatball soup

PREP/TOTAL TIME: 10 min. • **YIELD:** 6 servings.

After a busy day of running errands and cleaning, I wanted something fast but hearty for dinner. I combined prepared meatballs with canned soup, mushrooms and seasonings. My husband loved my creation and thought I spent hours cooking it. sue fuller // quincy, michigan

- **2 cans (10-3/4 ounces *each*) condensed cream of mushroom soup, undiluted**
- **2-2/3 cups milk**
- **1/2 teaspoon dried oregano**
- **1/8 to 1/4 teaspoon pepper**
- **1 package frozen fully cooked Italian meatballs (12 ounces) , thawed**
- **1 jar (4-1/2 ounces) sliced mushrooms, drained**

In a large saucepan, whisk the soup, milk, oregano and pepper until blended. Add the meatballs and mushrooms. Cover and cook until heated through.

cream of asparagus soup

PREP/TOTAL TIME: 25 min. • **YIELD:** 6 servings.

Kids may not want to try a vegetable soup, but once they spoon up a mouthful of this cheesy variety, the flavor will keep them coming back for more. muriel lerdal // humboldt, iowa

- **2 packages (12 ounces *each*) frozen cut asparagus**
- **1/4 cup butter**
- **2 tablespoons all-purpose flour**
- **4 cups milk**
- **1 cup (4 ounces) shredded Monterey Jack cheese**
- **4 to 5 drops hot pepper sauce**
- **1-1/2 teaspoons salt**
- **3/4 to 1 teaspoon pepper**

Prepare asparagus according to package directions; drain and set aside. In a large saucepan, melt butter. Stir in flour until smooth; gradually add milk. Bring to a boil; cook and stir for 2 minutes or until thickened. Cool slightly.

Pour half of the milk mixture into a blender; add half of the asparagus. Cover and process until blended. Strain and discard pulp; return soup to the saucepan. Repeat with remaining milk mixture and asparagus. Stir in the cheese, hot pepper sauce, salt and pepper; heat through (do not boil).

creamy garlic & mushroom soup

PREP: 15 min. • **COOK:** 30 min. • **YIELD:** 13 servings (1 cup each).

Cool, crisp winter evenings call for comforting bowls of rich, distinctive soup. It's a terrific first course at holiday meals. mandy howison // glenshaw, pennsylvania

- **1 pound medium fresh mushrooms, halved**
- **1 pound sliced baby portobello mushrooms**
- **1/2 pound sliced fresh shiitake mushrooms**
- **7 tablespoons butter**
- **12 garlic cloves, minced**
- **2 green onions, chopped**
- **1/2 cup all-purpose flour**
- **2 cans (14-1/2 ounces *each*) chicken broth**
- **3-1/3 cups 2% milk**
- **1-2/3 cups heavy whipping cream**
- **4 teaspoons minced fresh thyme *or* 1-1/2 teaspoons dried thyme**
- **2 teaspoons minced fresh basil *or* 3/4 teaspoon dried basil**
- **1 teaspoon salt**
- **1 teaspoon pepper**
- **Minced fresh parsley**

In a Dutch oven, saute mushrooms in butter in batches until tender. Return all to the pan; add garlic and onions. Cook and stir for 2 minutes. Sprinkle with flour; stir until blended.

Gradually stir in broth and milk. Bring to a boil; cook and stir for 2 minutes or until thickened. Stir in the cream, thyme, basil, salt and pepper; heat through. Sprinkle each serving with parsley.

broccoli-cheese noodle soup

PREP/TOTAL TIME: 25 min.
YIELD: 4-5 servings.

My husband's aunt shared this creamy soup with me. It tastes like I spent all day cooking. It's very filling with a salad and bread. We spoon leftovers over baked potatoes.

trinity nicholas
mt. carbon, west virginia

- **3 cups frozen chopped broccoli**
- **2 ounces angel hair pasta, broken into small pieces**
- **1/4 cup butter, cubed**
- **1 tablespoon all-purpose flour**
- **1 cup water**
- **3/4 cup milk**
- **1/8 teaspoon pepper**
- **6 ounces process cheese (Velveeta), cubed**
- **1/2 cup sour cream**

Cook both broccoli and pasta according to package directions; drain. In a large saucepan, melt butter; stir in flour until smooth. Gradually stir in the water, milk and pepper. Bring to a boil; cook and stir for 2 minutes or until thickened.

Reduce heat; add cheese, stirring until melted. Stir in broccoli, pasta and sour cream; heat through (do not boil).

mushroom-spinach cream soup

PREP/TOTAL TIME: 25 min.
YIELD: 10 servings (2-1/2 quarts).

Fresh mushrooms are a surprise for the palate in this creamy spinach soup. You can make it in advance and reheat it just before serving.

patricia kile
elizabethtown, pennsylvania

- **1 pound sliced fresh mushrooms**
- **2 small onions, chopped**
- **6 tablespoons butter, cubed**
- **1/2 cup all-purpose flour**
- **2 teaspoons Italian seasoning**
- **1/2 teaspoon onion powder**
- **1/2 teaspoon pepper**
- **1/8 teaspoon paprika**
- **4 cups milk**
- **1 carton (32 ounces) chicken broth**
- **2 packages (10 ounces *each*) frozen chopped spinach, thawed and squeezed dry**

In a large saucepan, saute mushrooms and onions in butter until tender. Stir in flour and seasonings until blended; gradually add milk and broth. Bring to a boil; cook and stir for 2 minutes or until thickened.

Stir in the spinach. Reduce heat; cover and simmer for 5 minutes or until heated through.

rich clam chowder

PREP: 45 min. • **COOK:** 25 min. • **YIELD:** 22 servings (1 cup each).

Several years ago, I came across a chowder recipe I liked. I have made just enough changes to give it a unique flavor and feed a pretty large crowd. People always go back for seconds—then they ask for the recipe.

teresa dastrup // meridian, idaho

- **6 cups diced peeled red potatoes**
- **3 large onions, finely chopped**
- **6 celery ribs, finely chopped**
- **3 cups water**
- **6 cans (6-1/2 ounces *each*) minced clams**
- **1-1/2 cups butter, cubed**
- **1-1/2 cups all-purpose flour**
- **8 cups half-and-half cream**
- **1/4 cup red wine vinegar**
- **2 tablespoons minced fresh parsley**
- **3 teaspoons salt**
- **1/4 teaspoon pepper**

In a stockpot, combine the potatoes, onions, celery and water. Drain clams, reserving juice; set clams aside. Add juice to potato mixture. Bring to a boil. Reduce heat; cover and simmer for 10 minutes or until potatoes are tender.

Meanwhile, in a large saucepan, melt butter over medium heat. Whisk in flour. Cook and stir for 5 minutes or until lightly browned. Gradually stir in cream. Bring to a boil; cook and stir for 2 minutes or until thickened. Gradually stir into potato mixture.

Add the vinegar, parsley, salt, pepper and clams. Cook 5-10 minutes longer or until heated through.

crab chowder

PREP/TOTAL TIME: 25 min. • **YIELD:** 6 servings.

You're sure to enjoy this satisfying chowder. To make it thicker, use heavy cream or half-and-half. taste of home test kitchen

- **1/2 pound sliced fresh mushrooms**
- **1/2 cup chopped celery**
- **1/2 cup chopped onion**
- **1/4 cup butter, cubed**
- **1/4 cup all-purpose flour**
- **2 cups milk**
- **2 cans (6 ounces *each*) crabmeat, drained, flaked and cartilage removed**
- **1 can (14-1/2 ounces) vegetable broth**
- **1 can (14-1/2 ounces) whole potatoes, drained and cut into 1/2-inch cubes**
- **1 cup frozen corn, thawed**
- **1 teaspoon salt**
- **1/2 teaspoon dill weed**
- **1/2 teaspoon pepper**
- **2 tablespoons sherry**

In a Dutch oven, saute the mushrooms, celery and onion in butter until tender. Stir in flour until blended; gradually add milk. Bring to a boil; cook and stir for 2 minutes or until thickened.

Add the crab, broth, potatoes, corn, salt, dill and pepper. Reduce heat; cover and simmer for 10 minutes or until heated through. Stir in sherry.

EASY VARIATIONS

A classic potato and corn chowder recipe can be very versatile. I like to use my basic chowder as a hearty base and then add ham, clams, fish or crab to make several delicious versions.

mary jo e. // cedar rapids, iowa

sweet potato and pear soup

PREP: 15 min. • **COOK:** 30 min. • **YIELD:** 5 servings.

I'm an adventurous cook who loves to try new recipes. This tasty cold-weather soup has garnered many warm compliments from family and friends. They rave over it. dr. cristy shank // summersville, west virginia

- **1-3/4 pounds sweet potatoes (about 4 medium), peeled and cubed**
- **1-3/4 cups water**
- **1 teaspoon salt, *divided***
- **1/4 teaspoon ground cinnamon**
- **2 large pears, peeled and sliced**
- **1 large onion, chopped**
- **2 tablespoons butter**
- **1/2 cup white grape juice**
- **1 cup half-and-half cream**
- **1/4 teaspoon white pepper**

In a large saucepan, combine the sweet potatoes, water, 3/4 teaspoon salt and cinnamon. Bring to a boil. Reduce heat; simmer, uncovered, for 15-20 minutes or until tender.

Meanwhile, in another large saucepan, cook and stir the pears and onion in butter over medium heat for 5 minutes. Stir in grape juice; bring to a boil. Reduce heat; simmer, uncovered, for 5 minutes. Stir into the sweet potato mixture. Cool slightly.

In a blender, cover and puree soup in batches; return all to one of the pans. Stir in the cream, pepper and remaining salt; heat through (do not boil).

SWEET POTATOES OR YAMS?

Sweet potatoes and yams are similar in many ways, so they're often confused with one another. To add to the confusion, canned sweet potatoes are often labeled yams. The sweet potato is a member of the morning glory family and native to Central America. Two varieties are readily available. One has pale skin with a light yellow flesh and a dry, mealy texture. The other has dark skin with dark orange flesh that cooks to a moist texture. This variety is often commonly known as a yam. True yams, though, are not readily available in this country and are seldom grown here. However, they are available throughout Latin America, Asia, India, West Africa, the South Pacific and the Caribbean. Though you're not likely to find true yams at your grocery store, yams and sweet potatoes are interchangeable in most recipes.

special clam chowder

PREP: 15 min. • **COOK:** 30 min.
YIELD: 9 servings (about 2 quarts).

I serve this cheesy chowder every Christmas or New Year's. Throughout the year, I substitute the potatoes and clams with broccoli and find that even the grandchildren enjoy it.

joy schuster // glentana, montana

- **4 cups cubed red potatoes**
- **3 cups water**
- **1 medium carrot, grated**
- **1 small onion, chopped**
- **2 teaspoons chicken bouillon granules**
- **1 teaspoon dried parsley flakes**
- **1/2 teaspoon pepper**
- **2 tablespoons all-purpose flour**
- **1/2 cup cold water**
- **3 cans (6-1/2 ounces *each*) chopped clams, drained**
- **2/3 cup cubed process cheese (Velveeta)**
- **1 can (12 ounces) evaporated milk**

In a large saucepan, combine the first seven ingredients. Bring to a boil. Reduce heat; cover and simmer for 20 minutes or until potatoes are tender.

In a small bowl, combine flour and cold water until smooth. Stir into potato mixture. Bring to a boil; cook and stir for 2 minutes or until thickened. Reduce heat. Add clams and cheese; cook and stir until cheese is melted. Stir in milk; heat through (do not boil).

cheddar potato soup

PREP: 25 min. • **COOK:** 25 min.
YIELD: 10-12 servings (about 2-1/2 quarts).

Here's a dish I created as an alternative to plain potato soup. Hearty and comforting, it disappears quickly when I serve it to my family or guests. Team it with bread and a fruit salad, and you have a complete meal.

susan peck // republic, missouri

- **1 large onion, chopped**
- **3/4 cup chopped celery**
- **1/4 cup butter**
- **5 cups cubed peeled potatoes**
- **3 cups water**
- **3 cups 2% milk, *divided***
- **4 teaspoons chicken bouillon granules**
- **1/2 teaspoon salt**
- **1/2 teaspoon pepper**
- **1/4 cup all-purpose flour**
- **4 cups (16 ounces) shredded cheddar cheese**
- **1/2 pound sliced bacon, cooked and crumbled**

In a large Dutch oven, saute onion and celery in butter for 5 minutes. Add potatoes and water. Bring to a boil. Reduce heat; cover and simmer for 15 minutes or until potatoes are tender.

Stir in 2 cups milk, bouillon, salt and pepper. Combine flour and remaining milk until smooth; gradually stir into soup. Bring to a boil; cook and stir for 2 minutes or until thickened. Reduce heat. Add cheese and bacon; stir until cheese is melted.

cheeseburger chowder

PREP/TOTAL TIME: 25 min. • **YIELD:** 4 servings.

After tasting a wonderful chowder at a restaurant, I dressed up can of cheese soup to see if I could capture the same flavors. I then took things a step further by adding chilies and Southwestern spices. I hope you enjoy it as much as I do.

lori risdal // sioux city, iowa

- **1/2 pound ground beef**
- **1 can (10-3/4 ounces) condensed cheddar cheese soup, undiluted**
- **1-3/4 cups milk**
- **1 cup frozen shredded hash brown potatoes**
- **1 can (4 ounces) chopped green chilies**
- **1 tablespoon taco seasoning**
- **1 tablespoon dried minced onion**
- **1/2 teaspoon chili powder**
- **Coarsely crushed corn chips, shredded Monterey Jack cheese and chopped green onions, optional**

In a large saucepan, cook beef over medium heat until no longer pink; drain. Stir in the soup, milk, potatoes, chilies, taco seasoning, onion and chili powder until blended. Bring to a boil. Reduce heat; simmer, uncovered, for 5 minutes or until heated through. Garnish with corn chips, cheese and green onions if desired.

broccoli barley soup

PREP: 15 min. • **COOK:** 50 min.
YIELD: 8 servings (about 2 quarts).

The addition of barley makes this both a flavorful and hearty broccoli soup. It's a delicious way to warm up right to your toes.

cindy sutton // holbein, saskatchewan

- **2 medium onions, chopped**
- **2 garlic cloves, minced**
- **4 ounces sliced fresh mushrooms**
- **3 tablespoons butter**
- **3 cups chicken broth**
- **3 cups vegetable broth**
- **3/4 cup uncooked medium pearl barley**
- **1/4 to 1/2 teaspoon dried rosemary, crushed**
- **1 pound fresh broccoli, cut into florets**
- **2 tablespoons cornstarch**
- **1/4 cup cold water**
- **2 cups half-and-half cream**
- **Salt and pepper**
- **Grated Parmesan cheese**

In a large saucepan or Dutch oven, saute the first three ingredients in butter until tender. Add the chicken and vegetable broths, barley and rosemary. Bring to a boil. Reduce heat; cover and simmer for 30 minutes or until barley is tender. Add broccoli; cover and cook for 10 minutes or until broccoli is tender.

In a small bowl, combine cornstarch and cold water until smooth; stir into the soup. Bring to a boil; cook and stir for 2 minutes or until thickened. Reduce heat; stir in the cream, salt and pepper (do not boil). Sprinkle with the Parmesan cheese.

marvelous mushroom soup

PREP/TOTAL TIME: 30 min.
YIELD: 9 servings (about 2 quarts).

Some mushroom soups seem to have more broth than mushrooms. That's why I love this version brimming with superb "shrooms!"
laura mahaffey // annapolis, maryland

- **3 medium onions, chopped**
- **2 garlic cloves, minced**
- **1/4 cup butter**
- **2 pounds fresh mushrooms, chopped**
- **2 cups heavy whipping cream**
- **2 cups beef broth**
- **1/2 teaspoon salt**
- **1/2 teaspoon pepper**
- **Grated Parmesan cheese and minced fresh parsley, optional**

In a large saucepan, cook onions and garlic in butter over medium-low heat until tender. Reduce heat to low; add the mushrooms. Cook for 8-10 minutes or until tender, stirring occasionally.

Add the cream, broth, salt and pepper; cook and stir over low heat until heated through. Garnish with Parmesan cheese and parsley if desired.

veggie potato soup

PREP: 20 min. • **COOK:** 5-1/2 hours • **YIELD:** 11 servings (2-3/4 quarts).

Chock-full of potatoes, this vegetarian soup is as filling as it is flavorful. Serve with fresh bread or take a thermos of it to work; with this in store, you'll really look forward to lunch! hannah thompson // scotts valley, california

- **6 medium potatoes, cubed**
- **3 cans (14-1/2 ounces *each*) vegetable broth**
- **1 medium carrot, thinly sliced**
- **1 large leek (white portion only), chopped**
- **1/4 cup butter, cubed**
- **1 garlic clove, minced**
- **1 teaspoon dried thyme**
- **3/4 teaspoon salt**
- **1/4 teaspoon dried marjoram**
- **1/4 teaspoon pepper**
- **1/4 cup all-purpose flour**
- **1-1/2 cups half-and-half cream**
- **1 cup frozen peas, thawed**

In a 5-qt. slow cooker, combine the first 10 ingredients. Cover and cook on low for 5-6 hours or until vegetables are tender.

In a small bowl, combine flour and cream until smooth; add to slow cooker. Stir in peas. Cover and cook on high for 30 minutes or until slightly thickened.

creamy tomato soup

PREP/TOTAL TIME: 15 min. • **YIELD:** 4 servings.

I had this when I was dining out and was able to persuade the waiter to share the ingredients. I modified it, and now people say it's the best tomato soup they've had! I almost hate to share the recipe since it reveals how easy it is!

beth ann slough // mountville, pennsylvania

1 can (29 ounces) tomato sauce
1 cup heavy whipping cream
1-1/2 teaspoons brown sugar
1 teaspoon Italian seasoning
1/4 teaspoon salt
1/8 teaspoon white pepper
Dash hot pepper sauce
Salad croutons, shredded cheddar cheese, quartered grape tomatoes *and/or* thinly sliced green onions

In a large saucepan, combine the first seven ingredients. Cook and stir over medium heat until heated through (do not boil). Garnish with croutons, cheese, tomatoes and/or onions.

chunky salmon chowder

PREP: 10 min. • **COOK:** 30 min. • **YIELD:** 14 servings.

The salmon in this recipe is a change from traditional chowder, but it sure is delicious! cindy st. martin // portland, oregon

- **2 pounds red potatoes, peeled and cubed**
- **1 large onion, chopped**
- **6 cups reduced-sodium chicken broth**
- **1 pound salmon fillets, cut into 1-inch pieces**
- **1/2 pound sliced bacon, cooked and crumbled**
- **2 cups whole milk**
- **1 cup half-and-half cream**
- **1 tablespoon butter**
- **1/2 teaspoon salt**
- **Pepper to taste**

In a Dutch oven, combine the potatoes, onion and broth. Bring to a boil. Reduce heat; cover and cook for 10-15 minutes or until potatoes are tender. Add salmon and bacon; cook over medium heat until fish flakes easily with a fork.

Reduce heat; stir in the milk, cream, butter, salt and pepper; heat through (do not boil). Thicken if desired.

creamy vegetable soup

PREP/TOTAL TIME: 30 min. • **YIELD:** 4 servings.

With colorful bits of veggies and a mild cheese flavor, Creamy Vegetable Soup brightens up a dreary day. marcia orlando // boyertown, pennsylvania

- **2 cups chicken broth**
- **1/4 cup diced carrot**
- **1/4 cup diced celery**
- **1/4 cup finely chopped onion**
- **2 tablespoons butter**
- **1/4 cup all-purpose flour**
- **Dash salt**
- **2 cups 2% milk**
- **1/2 cup cubed process cheese (Velveeta)**

In a small saucepan, bring broth to a boil. Add carrot and celery; simmer, uncovered, for 5 minutes or until tender.

In a large saucepan, saute onion in butter until tender. Stir in the flour and salt until blended. Gradually add milk. Bring to a boil over medium heat; cook and stir for 2 minutes or until thickened and bubbly. Stir in carrot mixture. Remove from the heat; add cheese and stir until melted.

potato ham chowder

PREP/TOTAL TIME: 30 min.
YIELD: 2 servings.

I find that homemade is always best, especially when it comes to soup. This rich and hearty broth features chunks of potatoes, ham and lots of dill flavor.
esther j. danielson
san marcos, california

- **3/4 cup cubed fully cooked ham**
- **1/4 cup chopped onion**
- **2 tablespoons chopped celery**
- **1 tablespoon butter**
- **1 cup chicken broth**
- **1 cup cubed peeled potatoes**
- **4 teaspoons all-purpose flour**
- **1-1/3 cups 2% milk**
- **1/4 teaspoon dill weed**
- **1/8 teaspoon pepper**

In a small saucepan, saute the ham, onion and celery in butter for 5 minutes or until the ham is lightly browned and vegetables are tender. Add the broth and potatoes; bring to a boil. Reduce heat; cover and simmer for 15-20 minutes or until potatoes are tender.

In a small bowl, combine flour and milk until smooth; stir into chowder. Add dill and pepper. Bring to a boil; cook and stir for 1 minute or until thickened.

chunky veggie chowder

PREP: 15 min. • **COOK:** 30 min.
YIELD: 8 servings (2 quarts).

We enjoy this colorful chowder year-round. The light but flavorful soup is loaded with vegetables and pleasantly seasoned with thyme.

diane molberg // calgary, alberta

- **2 medium onions, finely chopped**
- **2 garlic cloves, minced**
- **2 tablespoons butter**
- **3 medium carrots, chopped**
- **2 celery ribs, sliced**
- **2 medium potatoes, cubed**
- **1 small zucchini, cubed**
- **2 cans (10-1/2 ounces *each*) condensed chicken broth, undiluted**
- **1/4 cup minced fresh parsley**
- **3/4 teaspoon dried thyme**
- **1 cup frozen peas**
- **1 cup frozen corn**
- **1/4 cup all-purpose flour**
- **3 cups milk**
- **Salt and pepper to taste**

In a large saucepan or Dutch oven, saute onions and garlic in butter until tender. Add carrots, celery, potatoes, zucchini, broth, parsley and thyme. Bring to a boil. Reduce heat; cover and simmer until vegetables are tender, about 20 minutes. Stir in peas and corn.

In a large bowl, combine the flour, milk, salt if desired and pepper until smooth; gradually add to soup. Bring to a boil; cook and stir for 2 minutes or until soup is thickened.

vegetable cheese soup

PREP: 15 min. • **COOK:** 25 min. • **YIELD:** 5 cups.

This is one of my family's favorite soups. It's creamy, smooth and easy to make. I serve it with sandwiches or crackers and dip.

katie peat // palmer, illinois

- **1 medium potato, peeled and diced**
- **1/4 cup *each* chopped onion, celery and carrot**
- **1 teaspoon chicken bouillon granules**
- **2-1/2 cups water**
- **1-1/3 cups frozen mixed vegetables**
- **1 can (10-3/4 ounces) condensed cream of chicken soup, undiluted**
- **1/2 pound process cheese (Velveeta), cubed**

In a large saucepan, combine the potato, onion, celery, carrot, bouillon and water. Bring to a boil. Reduce heat; cover and simmer for 10-15 minutes or until potatoes are almost tender.

Stir in mixed vegetables and chicken soup. Bring to a boil. Reduce heat; cover and simmer for 5-10 minutes or until vegetables are tender. Stir in cheese just until melted (do not boil).

rich broccoli cream soup

PREP: 10 min. • **COOK:** 65 min. • **YIELD:** 6-8 servings.

Go ahead and indulge in a bowl of this rich and creamy soup! It's deliciously thick, flavorful and full of broccoli. Homemade soup never tasted so good!

carol macagno // fresno, california

- **4 celery ribs, chopped**
- **1 large onion, chopped**
- **3 tablespoons butter**
- **2 bunches broccoli, trimmed and coarsely chopped (about 8 cups)**
- **1-1/2 cups chicken broth**
- **2 teaspoons garlic salt**
- **1/2 teaspoon pepper**
- **2 tablespoons cornstarch**
- **1/4 cup cold water**
- **1 pint heavy whipping cream**

In a large saucepan, saute celery and onion in butter until tender. Add the broccoli, broth, garlic salt and pepper; bring to a boil. Reduce heat; cover and simmer for 45 minutes or until broccoli is tender.

In a small bowl, combine cornstarch and water until smooth. Stir into soup. Bring to a boil; cook and stir for 2 minutes or until thickened. Reduce heat to low. Stir in cream; cook 10 minutes longer or until heated through.

spring pea soup

PREP: 10 min. • **COOK:** 35 min.
YIELD: 16 servings (4 quarts).

I've had this tried-and-true recipe for years. The pleasing pea soup is easy to prepare and has wonderful texture and flavor.

denise patterson // bainbridge, ohio

- **4 cups cubed peeled potatoes**
- **1/4 cup butter, cubed**
- **12 cups chicken broth**
- **4 cups fresh *or* frozen peas**
- **1/4 cup minced chives**

In a Dutch oven, saute potatoes in butter until lightly browned. Stir in broth. Bring to a boil. Reduce heat; cover and simmer for 12 minutes. Stir in peas; cook 5-8 minutes longer or until potatoes and peas are tender. Cool slightly. In a blender, process soup in batches until smooth. Return all to pan and heat through. Sprinkle with chives.

CHILLED SUMMER BERRY BISQUE, PG. 283

SOUPS

chilled fruit & veggie soups

CHILLED RASPBERRY SOUP, PG. 286

GAZPACHO, PG. 289

COOL AS A CUCUMBER SOUP, PG. 291

chilled blueberry soup

PREP: 20 min. + chilling
YIELD: 6 servings.

When I serve this fruit soup on a warm summer evening, my guests are always delighted. Compliments abound for this sweet and creamy meal starter.
sue tucker // brush prairie, washington

- **4 cups fresh *or* frozen blueberries**
- **3 cups water**
- **2/3 cup sugar**
- **1/4 teaspoon ground allspice**
- **2 cups (16 ounces) plain yogurt**
- **Sour cream *or* additional yogurt, optional**

In a large saucepan, combine the blueberries, water, sugar and allspice. Bring to a boil, stirring occasionally. Remove from the heat. Cool slightly.

In batches, process blueberry mixture and yogurt until smooth. Cover and refrigerate until chilled. Serve with sour cream or yogurt if desired.

starry fruit soup

PREP: 20 min. + chilling • **YIELD:** 6 servings.

If you want to make a soup that your children will love, try this cool and refreshing summer blend. The impressive star design is simple to create with sweetened sour cream. edie despain // logan, utah

- **1 can (15 ounces) sliced pears, undrained**
- **1 package (10 ounces) frozen sweetened raspberries, thawed**
- **1 can (6 ounces) frozen orange juice concentrate, thawed**
- **2 medium ripe bananas, cut into chunks**
- **1/4 cup lemon juice**
- **1 to 2 teaspoons grated orange peel**
- **1/8 to 1/4 teaspoon ground coriander, optional**
- **1/2 cup sour cream**
- **2 tablespoons confectioners' sugar**

In a blender, combine the first seven ingredients; cover and process until smooth. Strain to remove seeds if desired. Chill until serving.

Combine sour cream and sugar until smooth; place in a heavy-duty resealable plastic bag. Cut a small hole in a corner of bag. Pipe two thin concentric circles 1/2 in. apart on top of each bowl of soup. Beginning with the center circle, gently pull a toothpick through both circles toward outer edge. Wipe toothpick clean. Draw toothpick from outer edge of bowl back to center. Repeat to complete star pattern.

chilled strawberry soup

PREP: 10 min. + chilling • **YIELD:** 2 servings.

After a day outdoors, my husband and I find that there's nothing more refreshing than a bowl of this chilled soup.

alice butcher // penticon, british columbia

- **1 pint fresh strawberries, hulled**
- **2 tablespoons sugar**
- **1/3 cup white wine *or* white grape juice**

In a food processor, combine all the ingredients; cover and process for 30 seconds or until smooth. Pour into a bowl. Refrigerate until chilled.

chilled summer berry bisque

PREP: 20 min. + chilling • **YIELD:** 8 servings.

A blend of yogurt and spices thickens this cold blueberry soup and tempers the sweetness. It makes an attractive and healthy first course for a special menu. arlene knick // newport news, virginia

- **4-1/2 cups fresh *or* frozen blueberries, thawed, *divided***
- **1 cup unsweetened apple juice**
- **1 cup orange juice**
- **1/4 cup honey**
- **2 teaspoons minced fresh gingerroot**
- **1 teaspoon grated orange peel**
- **1/4 teaspoon ground cinnamon**
- **1/8 teaspoon ground nutmeg**
- **2 cups (16 ounces) plain yogurt**
- **Fresh mint leaves**

In a large saucepan, combine 4 cups blueberries, apple juice, orange juice, honey, ginger, orange peel, cinnamon and nutmeg. Bring to a boil, stirring occasionally. Cool slightly.

In a blender, process blueberry mixture and yogurt in batches until smooth. Refrigerate until chilled. Just before serving, garnish with mint and remaining blueberries.

BEST BLUEBERRIES

Look for fresh blueberries that are firm, dry, plump, smooth-skinned and relatively free from leaves and stems. Berries should be deep purple-blue to blue-black. Reddish berries aren't completely ripe but may be used in cooking if desired.

succulent strawberry soup

PREP: 30 min. + chilling • **YIELD:** 4 servings.

Treat family and friends to a perfect summertime treat by making a batch of this cool, creamy fruit soup. The strawberry base with a hint of orange appeals to all palates! paula pelis // lenhartsville, pennsylvania

- **2 quarts fresh strawberries, *divided***
- **1/2 cup water**
- **5 tablespoons sugar**
- **1 tablespoon all-purpose flour**
- **1 teaspoon grated orange peel**
- **1 cup heavy whipping cream**
- **Fresh mint and additional strawberries, optional**

Mash half of the strawberries with a potato masher or fork; set aside.

In a blender, combine remaining strawberries, water, sugar, flour and orange peel; process until smooth. Pour into a large saucepan. Bring to a boil over medium heat; boil for 2 minutes, stirring constantly. Add mashed strawberries. Reduce heat; simmer, uncovered, for 10 minutes, stirring constantly. Chill for at least 1 hour.

Stir in cream. Cover and chill overnight. Serve with mint and strawberries if desired.

GRATING CITRUS PEEL

The outer peel or rind of citrus fruits like oranges and lemons can also be called the zest. The zest does not include the bitter white membrane attached to the fruit. Zest is used often in recipes. To remove the zest, peel thin strips with a small sharp knife, being careful not to include the white membrane, and mince finely. You can also take the whole fruit and rub it over a hand grater to remove the zest.

chilled raspberry soup

PREP: 20 min. + chilling • **YIELD:** 12 servings.

Family and friends enjoy sipping this lovely, chilled soup. I often use sugar substitute and reduced-fat sour cream to make it a little lighter. amy wenger // severance, colorado

1/3 cup cranberry juice
1/3 cup sugar
5-1/3 cups plus 12 fresh raspberries, *divided*
1-1/3 cups plus 2 tablespoons sour cream, *divided*

In a blender, combine the cranberry juice, sugar and 5-1/3 cups raspberries; cover and process until blended. Strain and discard seeds. Stir in 1-1/3 cups sour cream. Cover and refrigerate for at least 2 hours.

To serve, pour 1/4 cup of soup into 12 cordial glasses. Top each with a raspberry and 1/2 teaspoon sour cream.

chilled peach soup

PREP: 10 min. + chilling • **YIELD:** 4 servings.

Here's a peachy way to begin a ladies' luncheon or brunch. The toasted almonds on top are a nice complement to the sweet-tart flavor. A serving of this fruit soup is surprisingly filling.

lane mcloud // siloam springs, arkansas

3 cups chopped peeled fresh peaches
1 cup (8 ounces) fat-free plain yogurt
1 teaspoon lemon juice
1/8 to 1/4 teaspoon almond extract
6 tablespoons sliced almonds, toasted
Fresh mint, optional

In a blender or food processor, combine the peaches, yogurt, lemon juice and extract; cover and process until smooth. Refrigerate until chilled. Serve with almonds and mint if desired.

chilled asparagus soup

PREP: 10 min. • **COOK:** 1 hour + chilling
YIELD: 8-10 servings.

When the hot weather rolls around, try this cool asparagus soup. The curry seasoning comes through just right.

kim gilliland // simi valley, california

1 pound fresh asparagus, trimmed
5 cups chicken broth
1/2 cup water
1/4 cup butter, cubed
1/4 cup all-purpose flour
3 egg yolks, beaten
3/4 cup heavy whipping cream
1 teaspoon curry powder
1/8 teaspoon pepper
Dash lemon juice

Cut asparagus into 1-in. pieces; set tips aside. Place the remaining asparagus in a saucepan; add broth. Bring to a boil; reduce heat. Cover and simmer for 40-45 minutes. Cool slightly.

Process in batches in a blender or food processor until smooth; set aside. In a small saucepan, bring water to a boil. Add the asparagus tips; cook for 2-3 minutes or until tender. Drain and chill until serving.

In a large saucepan, melt butter. Stir in flour until smooth. Gradually add pureed asparagus. Bring to a boil; cook and stir for 2 minutes or until thickened. Remove from the heat. Stir a small amount of hot soup into egg yolks; return all to the pan, stirring constantly. Cook over low heat for 5 minutes or until mixture is heated through and reaches 160°. Stir in the cream, curry powder, pepper and lemon juice.

Remove from the heat; cool slightly. Cover and chill until serving. Garnish with asparagus tips, gently adding to each bowl.

danish fruit soup

PREP/TOTAL TIME: 30 min. • **YIELD:** 4-6 servings.

I've been making this colorful dessert since 1961, and my whole family just loves it. It's a great way to enjoy fruit in winter.

ellie marsh // lewistown, pennsylvania

1 package (3 ounces) raspberry gelatin
1/8 teaspoon salt
1 cup boiling water
1 package (12 ounces) frozen unsweetened raspberries
1-1/2 cups cold water
2 tablespoons lemon juice
Sour cream and ground nutmeg, optional

In a large bowl, combine gelatin and salt. Gradually stir in boiling water until gelatin is dissolved. Stir in the raspberries, cold water and lemon juice. Refrigerate for 15-20 minutes.

Just before serving, stir soup. Garnish with sour cream and nutmeg if desired.

summertime melon soup

PREP: 15 min. + chilling • **YIELD:** 6-8 servings.

I get a sweet response when I bring out servings of this special summertime soup. Guests never fail to request the recipe. To make it look even more impressive for parties, I sometimes serve it in cantaloupe bowls.

valerie black // fairfield bay, arkansas

- **5 cups seeded cubed watermelon**
- **1 pint fresh strawberries, hulled and cut in half**
- **1/4 cup sour cream**
- **2 tablespoons milk**
- **2 tablespoons sugar**
- **3 to 4 cantaloupes, optional**
- **Additional fresh strawberries, optional**

In a small bowl, combine watermelon and strawberries. Puree in batches in a blender, adding the sour cream, milk and sugar to the last batch. Pour into a 2-qt. container and mix well. Cover and chill for at least 3 hours.

To serve soup in cantaloupe bowls, cut cantaloupes in half; hollow out melon and seeds, leaving about a 1-1/2-in. shell if desired. Cut a decorative edge if desired. Add soup; garnish with a strawberry if desired.

raspberry-cranberry soup

PREP: 25 min. • **COOK:** 10 min. • **YIELD:** 4 servings.

Served hot, this tangy, beautiful soup helps beat the winter blahs. On a sunny summer day, it's refreshing cold. I have fun serving it, because people are so intrigued with the idea of a fruit soup. Even doubters scrape their bowls clean.
susan stull // chillicothe, missouri

- **2 cups fresh *or* frozen cranberries**
- **2 cups unsweetened apple juice**
- **1 cup fresh *or* frozen unsweetened raspberries, thawed**
- **1/2 to 1 cup sugar**
- **1 tablespoon lemon juice**
- **1/4 teaspoon ground cinnamon**
- **1 tablespoon cornstarch**
- **2 cups half-and-half cream**
- **Whipped cream, additional raspberries and mint, optional**

In a large saucepan, bring cranberries and apple juice to a boil. Reduce heat and simmer, uncovered, for 10 minutes. Press through a sieve; return to the pan. Also press the raspberries through the sieve; discard skins and seeds. Add to cranberry mixture; bring to a boil. Add the sugar, lemon juice and cinnamon; remove from the heat.

Cool 4 minutes. Combine cornstarch and cream until smooth; gradually stir into the pan. Bring to a gentle boil; cook and stir for 2 minutes or until thickened. Serve hot or chilled. Serve with whipped cream, raspberries and mint if desired.

gazpacho

PREP: 20 min. + chilling • **YIELD:** 8 servings (2 quarts).

For summer meals, you're going to want to make this handy dish. It's so colorful and refreshing. I prepare it a day ahead using garden vegetables. The flavor gets even better as it sits in the refrigerator overnight. pat waymire // yellow springs, ohio

- **4 cups tomato juice**
- **2 cups chopped seeded peeled tomatoes**
- **1 cup diced green pepper**
- **1 cup diced celery**
- **1 cup diced seeded cucumber**
- **2 garlic cloves, minced**
- **1/2 cup diced onion**
- **1/3 cup tarragon vinegar**
- **2 tablespoons minced fresh parsley**
- **1 tablespoon minced chives**
- **1 teaspoon Worcestershire sauce**
- **1 teaspoon salt, optional**
- **1/2 teaspoon pepper**
- **2 tablespoons olive oil**

In a large bowl, combine the first 13 ingredients. Cover and chill for 4 hours or until chilled. Stir in oil just before serving.

pretty peach soup

PREP: 10 min. + chilling
YIELD: 4 servings.

A delightful change of pace, this cool, fruity soup is always the hit of a dinner party.
laura stoltzfus // leola, pennsylvania

- **1 cup fresh *or* frozen raspberries, thawed**
- **3 cups fresh *or* frozen peaches, thawed**
- **3 tablespoons lemon juice**
- **1 cup peach nectar**
- **1 cup (8 ounces) plain yogurt**
- **1/4 cup sugar, optional**
- **1 teaspoon almond extract**

Place raspberries in a blender; cover and process until blended. Strain and discard seeds. Cover and refrigerate puree. Place peaches and lemon juice in the blender; cover and process until smooth. Transfer to a bowl; stir in the nectar, yogurt, sugar if desired and extract. Cover and refrigerate for 2 hours or until chilled.

To garnish as shown in photo, drizzle 1 tablespoon raspberry puree in a 3 in. circle on top of each serving. Use a toothpick to draw six lines toward the center of circle, forming a flower.

summer fruit soup

PREP: 15 min. + chilling • **YIELD:** 6 servings.

I've served this delightful medley for 37 years, and it has never failed to elicit raves from those eating it. gladys de boer // castleford, idaho

- **1/2 cup sugar**
- **3 tablespoons quick-cooking tapioca**
- **2-1/2 cups water, *divided***
- **1 can (6 ounces) frozen orange juice concentrate**
- **1 package (10 ounces) frozen sweetened sliced strawberries, thawed**
- **2 cups fresh *or* frozen sliced peaches, thawed and cut into bite-size pieces**
- **1 can (11 ounces) mandarin oranges, drained**
- **2 medium ripe bananas, sliced**
- **1 pint lime sherbet, optional**

In a large saucepan, combine the sugar, tapioca and 1-1/2 cups water. Cook over medium heat for 5-6 minutes or until thickened and clear.

Remove from the heat; stir in orange juice concentrate and remaining water until the concentrate is thawed. Stir in the strawberries, peaches and oranges. Cover and refrigerate for 2 hours.

Just before serving, stir in the bananas. Top each serving with a scoop of sherbet if desired.

cool as a cucumber soup

PREP: 15 min. + standing • **YIELD:** 7 servings.

This chilled soup makes a wonderful appetizer or side on a hot summer day. Bright bursts of dill provide a pleasant contrast to the milder flavor of cucumber. deirdre dee cox // milwaukee, wisconsin

- **1 pound cucumbers, peeled, seeded and sliced**
- **1/2 teaspoon salt**
- **1-1/2 cups fat-free plain yogurt**
- **1 green onion, coarsely chopped**
- **1 garlic clove, minced**
- **4-1/2 teaspoons snipped fresh dill**
- **Additional chopped green onion and snipped fresh dill**

In a colander set over a bowl, toss cucumbers with salt. Let stand for 30 minutes. Squeeze and pat dry.

Place the cucumbers, yogurt, onion and garlic in a food processor; cover and process until smooth. Stir in dill. Serve immediately in chilled bowls. Garnish with additional onion and dill.

cold plum soup

PREP: 30 min. + chilling • **YIELD:** 13 servings (2-1/2 quarts).

When my husband and I were first married, we ate at an inn that served a flavorful plum soup. This is my own tasty version!
carol klein // franklin square, new york

2 cans (15 ounces *each*) plums
1 cup water
1/2 cup sugar, *divided*
1 cinnamon stick (3 inches)
1/4 teaspoon white pepper
Dash salt
1 tablespoon cornstarch
1/2 cup heavy whipping cream
1/2 cup dry red wine *or* grape juice
1 cup (8 ounces) sour cream
1/3 cup creme de cassis *or* cranberry-raspberry juice
2 tablespoons lemon juice
1 teaspoon grated lemon peel
Sour cream, optional

Drain plums, reserving juice. Pit plums; puree in a blender with juice. Transfer to a Dutch oven. Stir in the water, 1/4 cup sugar, cinnamon stick, pepper and salt. Bring to a boil. Reduce heat; cover and simmer for 10 minutes.

In a small bowl, combine cornstarch and remaining sugar; stir in cream and wine or grape juice until smooth. Gradually add to plum mixture until blended. Bring to a boil; cook and stir for 2 minutes or until thickened, stirring constantly. Remove from the heat; discard cinnamon stick. Stir in the sour cream, creme de cassis or cranberry-raspberry juice and lemon juice.

Strain half of the soup through a fine mesh strainer over a 1-1/2-qt. bowl. Repeat with remaining soup. Stir in lemon peel. Cover and refrigerate overnight. Garnish with sour cream if desired.

chilled cantaloupe soup

PREP: 10 min. + chilling • **YIELD:** 6 servings.

A friend shared the recipe for this chilled melon soup that's spiced with cinnamon. Most people are skeptical when I describe it, but after one spoonful, they're hooked.
m. mcneil // germantown, tennessee

1 medium cantaloupe, peeled, seeded and cubed
2 cups orange juice, *divided*
1 tablespoon lime juice
1/4 to 1/2 teaspoon ground cinnamon
Fresh mint, optional

Place cantaloupe and 1/2 cup orange juice in a blender or food processor; cover and process until smooth. Transfer to a large bowl; stir in lime juice, cinnamon and remaining orange juice. Cover and refrigerate for at least 1 hour. Serve with mint if desired.

honeydew soup

PREP: 15 min. + chilling • **YIELD:** 2 servings.

Crisp and refreshing, this honeydew soup is sure to cool off those warm summer days. I like to add fresh blueberries for an extra burst of flavor. earle davis // pittsburgh, pennsylvania

1-1/2 cups diced cantaloupe, *divided*
1-1/4 cups diced honeydew
4-1/2 teaspoons sugar
1 teaspoon minced fresh mint
1/4 cup white wine *or* white grape juice
3 tablespoons plain yogurt
1 tablespoon half-and-half cream
Mint sprigs, optional

In a blender, combine 1-1/4 cups cantaloupe, honeydew, sugar and mint; cover and process for 1 minute. Add the wine or grape juice, yogurt and cream; cover and process for 1-2 minutes or until smooth. Refrigerate for at least 2 hours.

Pour into soup bowls. Garnish with remaining cantaloupe and mint if desired.

chilled bean soup

PREP: 15 min. + chilling • **YIELD:** 7 servings.

I combined crunchy fresh veggies with black beans and a splash of hot pepper sauce to create this spicy chilled soup. I often serve this during the warm summer months, when tomatoes are in season. It tastes best when you let it mellow overnight in the refrigerator. betty nickels // tampa, florida

- **4 cups chopped seeded tomatoes**
- **2 cups spicy hot V8 juice**
- **1 can (15 ounces) black beans, rinsed and drained**
- **1 cup chopped cucumber**
- **1 cup chopped sweet red *or* yellow pepper**
- **1/2 cup chopped red onion**
- **2 tablespoons balsamic vinegar**
- **1 teaspoon sugar**
- **1/4 to 1/2 teaspoon hot pepper sauce**
- **1/4 teaspoon ground cumin**
- **1/4 teaspoon salt**
- **1/4 teaspoon pepper**
- **7 tablespoons reduced-fat sour cream**
- **Sliced cucumber, optional**

In a blender, combine tomatoes and V8 juice; cover and process just until blended.

Transfer to a large bowl. Stir in the beans, chopped cucumber, sweet pepper, onion, vinegar, sugar and seasonings.

Cover and refrigerate for at least 4 hours or overnight. Serve with sour cream. Garnish with sliced cucumber if desired.

swedish fruit soup

PREP: 5 min. + standing
COOK: 20 min. + chilling
YIELD: 6-8 servings.

Our children expect me to make this sweet soup for the holidays. It's a delicious dessert served with pound cake and whipped cream—or offer it as a fruit compote for brunch.

dolores bean
baldwinsville, new york

- **4 cups cranberry-apple juice**
- **1/4 cup quick-cooking tapioca**
- **1 medium lemon, thinly sliced**
- **6 whole cloves**
- **1/4 teaspoon ground nutmeg**
- **1 can (20 ounces) pineapple chunks, drained**
- **1 can (11 ounces) mandarin oranges, drained**
- **1 package (10 ounces) frozen sweetened sliced strawberries, thawed**
- **1/3 cup maraschino cherry juice *or* grenadine syrup, optional**
- **1/8 teaspoon salt**

In a large saucepan, combine the first five ingredients; let stand for 10 minutes. Bring to a boil over medium heat. Reduce heat; cook and stir for 15 minutes or until thickened and clear. Remove from the heat; discard lemon slices and cloves. Stir in remaining ingredients. Cover and refrigerate for at least 4 hours.

LENTIL BARLEY STEW, PG. 297

stews

HOME-STYLE STEW, PG. 296 SUNDAY BEEF STEW, PG. 308 PUEBLO GREEN CHILI STEW, PG. 313

home-style stew

PREP: 20 min. • **COOK:** 6 hours
YIELD: 5 servings.

My husband and I both work full time and we have three daughters, so quick meals are important. This speedy stew always tastes great, so it's a regular menu item for us.

marie shanks // terre haute, indiana

- **2 packages (16 ounces *each*) frozen vegetables for stew**
- **1-1/2 pounds beef stew meat, cut into 1-inch cubes**
- **1 can (10-3/4 ounces) condensed cream of mushroom soup, undiluted**
- **1 can (10-3/4 ounces) condensed tomato soup, undiluted**
- **1 envelope reduced-sodium onion soup mix**

Place vegetables in a 5-qt. slow cooker. In a large nonstick skillet coated with cooking spray, brown beef on all sides.

Transfer to slow cooker. Combine the remaining ingredients; pour over top.

Cover and cook on low for 6-8 hours or until beef is tender.

sweet potato pork stew

PREP: 10 min. • **COOK:** 40 min. • **YIELD:** 2 servings.

Unusual ingredients add up to a delicious, stick-to-your-ribs stew with a touch of brown sugar sweetness in this easy recipe. It's sure to become a fall favorite!

susan schlenvogt // waukesha, wisconsin

- **3/4 pound pork chop suey meat**
- **1 tablespoon Dijon mustard**
- **3 tablespoons all-purpose flour**
- **1 tablespoon brown sugar**
- **1 small garlic clove, minced**
- **1 tablespoon canola oil**
- **1 cup chicken broth**
- **1 small onion, quartered**
- **1 medium sweet potato, peeled and cubed**
- **1/4 teaspoon salt**
- **1/8 teaspoon pepper**
- **1 tablespoon minced fresh parsley**

In a small bowl, toss pork with mustard. In a large resealable plastic bag, combine flour and brown sugar; add pork and shake to coat.

In a large saucepan coated with cooking spray, cook pork and garlic in oil until pork is browned on all sides. Stir in broth. Bring to a boil. Reduce heat; cover and simmer for 15 minutes.

Stir in the onion, sweet potato, salt and pepper. Return to a boil. Reduce heat; cover and simmer 15-20 minutes longer or until meat is no longer pink and vegetables are tender. Stir in parsley.

EDITOR'S NOTE: If you can't find pork chop suey meat, use 1-inch cubes of boneless pork chops or pork loin roast.

lentil barley stew

PREP: 10 min. • **COOK:** 50 min. • **YIELD:** 2 servings.

Green chilies and fresh ginger add zip to this thick meatless stew. It can be served as is or with a tablespoon of sour cream on top. erin monroe // oviedo, florida

- **1 medium carrot, chopped**
- **1 small onion, chopped**
- **1 celery rib, chopped**
- **1 teaspoon minced fresh gingerroot**
- **2 teaspoons olive oil**
- **1 garlic clove, minced**
- **1/4 cup dried lentils, rinsed**
- **1/4 cup medium pearl barley**
- **1 can (10 ounces) diced tomatoes with mild green chilies**
- **1 cup water**
- **1 cup vegetable broth**
- **1/4 teaspoon ground cumin**
- **1 tablespoon reduced-sodium soy sauce**

In a large saucepan, saute the carrot, onion, celery and ginger in oil until crisp-tender. Add garlic; cook 1 minute longer. Add lentils and barley; cook for 3 minutes, stirring occasionally.

Stir in the tomatoes, water, broth and cumin. Bring to a boil. Reduce heat; cover and simmer for 20 minutes, stirring occasionally. Add soy sauce; simmer 20-30 minutes longer or until lentils and barley are tender.

tuscan pork stew

PREP: 15 min. • **COOK:** 8-1/2 hours • **YIELD:** 8 servings.

Tender chunks of pork slowly cook in a nicely seasoned, wine-infused sauce in this recipe. Add some crushed red pepper flakes for a little added kick. penny hawkins // mebane, north carolina

- **1 boneless whole pork loin roast (1-1/2 pounds), cut into 1-inch cubes**
- **2 tablespoons olive oil**
- **2 cans (14-1/2 ounces *each*) Italian diced tomatoes, undrained**
- **2 cups reduced-sodium chicken broth**
- **2 cups frozen pepper stir-fry vegetable blend, thawed**
- **1/2 cup dry red wine *or* additional reduced-sodium chicken broth**
- **1/4 cup orange marmalade**
- **2 garlic cloves, minced**
- **1 teaspoon dried oregano**
- **1/2 teaspoon fennel seed**
- **1/2 teaspoon pepper**
- **1/8 teaspoon crushed red pepper flakes, optional**
- **2 tablespoons cornstarch**
- **2 tablespoons cold water**
- **Hot cooked fettuccine, optional**

In a large skillet, brown the pork in oil until no longer pink; drain. Transfer to a 5-qt. slow cooker.

In a large bowl, combine the tomatoes, broth, vegetable blend, wine, marmalade, garlic, oregano, fennel seed, pepper and pepper flakes if desired; pour over pork. Cover and cook on low for 8-10 hours or until meat is tender.

Combine cornstarch and water until smooth; gradually stir into stew. Cover and cook on high for 30 minutes or until gravy is thickened. Serve with fettuccine if desired.

USING ORANGE MARMALADE

To make an excellent glaze for chicken, turkey or pork, I combine half a cup of orange marmalade with a tablespoon of Dijon mustard. I also stir in a little brown sugar to balance the tartness. Then I just brush this glaze on the meat before it goes in the oven. Delicious! isabel k. // longville, minnesota

apple cider beef stew

PREP: 20 min. • **COOK:** 6-1/4 hours • **YIELD:** 12 servings.

I created this slow-cooker recipe with convenience products to save time chopping vegetables and browning beef. Apple cider and cinnamon are the unique additions that give down-home flavor to this economical and oh-so-easy dish.

margaret wilson // sun city, california

- **4 cups frozen vegetables for stew (about 24 ounces), thawed**
- **1 can (8 ounces) sliced water chestnuts, drained**
- **1 jar (4-1/2 ounces) sliced mushrooms, drained**
- **1 tablespoon dried minced onion**
- **2 envelopes brown gravy mix**
- **2 tablespoons onion soup mix**
- **2 teaspoons steak seasoning**
- **1/8 teaspoon ground cinnamon**
- **2 pounds beef stew meat, cut into 1-inch cubes**
- **1 can (14-1/2 ounces) beef broth**
- **1-1/4 cups apple cider *or* unsweetened apple juice**
- **1 can (8 ounces) tomato sauce**
- **1 bay leaf**
- **3 tablespoons cornstarch**
- **1/3 cup cold water**

Place the vegetables, water chestnuts, mushrooms and onion in a 5-qt. slow cooker. In a large resealable plastic bag, combine the gravy mix, soup mix, steak seasoning and cinnamon; add beef, a few pieces at a time, and shake to coat. Add to slow cooker.

Combine the broth, cider and tomato sauce; pour over beef. Add bay leaf. Cover and cook on low for 6-7 hours or until meat is tender.

Combine cornstarch and water until smooth; stir into stew. Cover and cook on high for 15 minutes or until thickened. Discard bay leaf.

EDITOR'S NOTE: This recipe was tested with McCormick's Montreal Steak Seasoning. Look for it in the spice aisle.

turkey noodle stew

PREP/TOTAL TIME: 30 min.
YIELD: 6 servings.

Just half an hour and eight ingredients make a terrific turkey noodle dinner.

traci maloney // toms river, new jersey

- **2 turkey breast tenderloins (about 1/2 pound *each*), cut into 1/4-inch slices**
- **1 medium onion, chopped**
- **1 tablespoon canola oil**
- **1 can (14-1/2 ounces) chicken broth**
- **1 can (10-3/4 ounces) condensed cream of chicken soup, undiluted**
- **2 cups frozen mixed vegetables**
- **1/2 to 1 teaspoon lemon-pepper seasoning**
- **3 cups uncooked extra-wide egg noodles**

In a large skillet, cook turkey and onion in oil for 5-6 minutes or until turkey is no longer pink; drain.

In a large bowl, combine the broth, soup, vegetables and lemon pepper. Add to the skillet; bring to a boil. Stir in noodles. Reduce heat; cover and simmer for 10 minutes or until noodles and vegetables are tender.

wintertime braised beef stew

PREP: 40 min. • **BAKE:** 2 hours • **YIELD:** 8 servings (2 quarts).

This easy beef stew has a deep, rich taste. Since it's even better a day or two later, you may want to make a double batch.
michaela rosenthal // woodland hills, california

- 2 tablespoons all-purpose flour
- 2 teaspoons steak seasoning
- 2 pounds boneless beef sirloin steak, cut into 1-inch cubes
- 2 tablespoons olive oil, *divided*
- 1 large onion, chopped
- 2 celery ribs, chopped
- 2 medium parsnips, peeled and cut into 1-1/2-inch pieces
- 2 medium carrots, peeled and cut into 1-1/2-inch pieces
- 2 garlic cloves, minced
- 1 can (14-1/2 ounces) diced tomatoes, undrained
- 1 cup dry red wine *or* reduced-sodium beef broth
- 2 tablespoons red currant jelly
- 2 bay leaves
- 2 fresh oregano sprigs
- 1 can (15 ounces) white kidney *or* cannellini beans, rinsed and drained

In a large resealable plastic bag, combine flour and steak seasoning. Add beef, a few pieces at a time, and shake to coat. Heat 1 tablespoon oil in an ovenproof Dutch oven; brown beef in batches on all sides. Remove and keep warm.

In the same pan, saute the onion, celery, parsnips and carrots in remaining oil until crisp-tender. Add garlic; cook 1 minute longer. Add the tomatoes, wine, jelly, bay leaves, oregano and beef; bring to a boil.

Cover and bake at 350° for 1-1/2 hours. Stir in beans; cover and bake 30-40 minutes longer or until the beef and vegetables are tender. Discard bay leaves and oregano.

EDITOR'S NOTE: This recipe was tested with McCormick's Montreal Steak Seasoning. Look for it in the spice aisle.

SPEEDY BEEF STEW

When steak is on sale I stock up and use some to make a great stew. I cut the beef into small cubes and brown it in olive oil in a skillet. Then I stir in some flour until blended. Next, I add cubed potatoes, sliced carrots, diced onion, water and beef bouillon. I simmer it until the vegetables are tender, stirring frequently. This makes a quick, delicious meal served with hot biscuits. jeanetta s. // st. george, kansas

northwoods beef stew

PREP: 30 min. • **COOK:** 8 hours • **YIELD:** 11 servings (2-3/4 quarts).

I live in northern Wisconsin, where we appreciate hot and hearty meals during our cold winters. Conveniently prepared in a slow cooker, this stew is superb for company. janice christofferson // eagle river, wisconsin

- 3 large carrots, cut into 1-inch pieces
- 3 celery ribs, cut into 1-inch pieces
- 1 large onion, cut into wedges
- 1/4 cup all-purpose flour
- 1/2 teaspoon salt
- 1/4 teaspoon pepper
- 3-1/2 pounds beef stew meat
- 1 can (10-3/4 ounces) condensed tomato soup, undiluted
- 1/2 cup dry red wine *or* beef broth
- 2 tablespoons quick-cooking tapioca
- 1 tablespoon Italian seasoning
- 1 tablespoon paprika
- 1 tablespoon brown sugar
- 1 tablespoon beef bouillon granules
- 1 tablespoon Worcestershire sauce
- 1/2 pound sliced baby portobello mushrooms
- Hot cooked egg noodles

Place the carrots, celery and onion in a 5-qt. slow cooker. In a large resealable plastic bag, combine the flour, salt and pepper. Add beef, a few pieces at a time, and shake to coat. Place beef over vegetables.

In a small bowl, combine the soup, wine, tapioca, Italian seasoning, paprika, brown sugar, bouillon and Worcestershire sauce. Pour over the top.

Cover and cook on low for 8-10 hours or until the meat and vegetables are tender, adding the mushrooms during the last hour. Serve with noodles.

BLANCH AND FREEZE MUSHROOMS

Fresh mushrooms should be used within a few days of purchase. If that's not possible, you can blanch them in a jiffy, then freeze for up to a month for use in soups, stews, sauces and casseroles. To blanch mushrooms, slice larger mushrooms or use small whole mushroom caps. Bring 1 quart of water to a boil; add mushrooms and 1 tablespoon lemon juice to prevent darkening. Cook in boiling water (3 minutes for slices, or 4 minutes for mushroom caps). Immediately remove mushrooms with a slotted spoon and cool in ice water for 3 to 4 minutes. Drain well and pack into freezer containers. Freeze mushrooms in recipe-size portions for added convenience.

squash 'n' chicken stew

PREP: 15 min. • **COOK:** 6 hours
YIELD: 5 servings.

We know you'll love this satisfying stew—it's colorful, full-flavored and family-friendly. Chicken thighs are slowly simmered with stewed tomatoes, butternut squash, green peppers and onion for meal-in-one convenience.
taste of home test kitchen

- **2 pounds boneless skinless chicken thighs, cut into 1/2-inch pieces**
- **1 can (28 ounces) stewed tomatoes, cut up**
- **3 cups cubed butternut squash**
- **2 medium green peppers, cut into 1/2-inch pieces**
- **1 small onion, sliced and separated into rings**
- **1 cup water**
- **1 teaspoon salt**
- **1 teaspoon ground cumin**
- **1/2 teaspoon ground coriander**
- **1/2 teaspoon pepper**
- **2 tablespoons minced fresh parsley**
- **Hot cooked couscous, optional**

In a 5-qt. slow cooker, combine the first 10 ingredients. Cover and cook on low for 6-7 hours or until chicken is no longer pink. Sprinkle with the parsley. Serve with couscous if desired.

baked stew with root vegetables

PREP: 35 min. • **BAKE:** 2-1/2 hours • **YIELD:** 8 servings (3 quarts).

This hearty, savory stew will fill you up without emptying your wallet! It's a classic with economical ingredients. barb templin // norwood, minnesota

- **1 cup all-purpose flour, *divided***
- **3/4 teaspoon salt**
- **1/2 teaspoon pepper**
- **2 pounds boneless beef chuck roast, cut into 1-inch cubes**
- **1/4 cup canola oil**
- **1 large onion, chopped**
- **3 tablespoons butter**
- **2 garlic cloves, minced**
- **5 cups beef broth**
- **1 bay leaf**
- **3 celery ribs**
- **3 medium parsnips, peeled**
- **3 medium carrots**
- **1 small rutabaga, peeled**

In a large resealable plastic bag, combine 3/4 cup flour, salt and pepper. Add beef, a few pieces at a time, and shake to coat. In an ovenproof Dutch oven, brown beef in oil in batches. Remove and keep warm.

In the same pan, saute onion in butter until crisp-tender. Add garlic; cook 1 minute longer. Stir in remaining flour until blended. Gradually add broth; stir in bay leaf and beef. Bring to a boil.

Cover and bake at 350° for 1 hour. Cut vegetables into 1-in. pieces; stir into stew. Cover and bake 1-1/2 to 2 hours longer or until beef and vegetables are tender. Skim fat and discard bay leaf.

loaded vegetable beef stew

PREP: 40 min. • **COOK:** 8-1/2 hours • **YIELD:** 12 servings (1-1/3 cups each).

I first had this dish during a trip to Argentina a few years ago. It inspired me to re-create it at home. It turned out so well, I wrote "Yum!" on the recipe card! kari caven // post falls, idaho

- **8 bacon strips, diced**
- **3 pounds beef stew meat, cut into 1-inch cubes**
- **6 medium carrots, cut into 1-inch pieces**
- **6 medium tomatoes, peeled and cut into wedges**
- **4 medium potatoes, peeled and cubed**
- **3 cups cubed peeled butternut squash**
- **2 medium green peppers, chopped**
- **2 teaspoons dried thyme**
- **2 garlic cloves, minced**
- **2 cans (14-1/2 ounces *each*) beef broth**
- **6 cups chopped cabbage**
- **1/2 teaspoon pepper**

In a large skillet, cook bacon over medium heat until crisp. Using a slotted spoon, remove to paper towels to drain. In the drippings, brown beef in batches. Refrigerate the bacon until serving.

In a 5-qt. slow cooker, combine carrots, tomatoes, potatoes, squash, green peppers, thyme and garlic. Top with beef. Pour broth over the top. Cover and cook on low for 8-10 hours.

Stir in cabbage and pepper. Cover and cook on high for 30 minutes or until cabbage is tender. Sprinkle each serving with bacon.

jamaican-style beef stew

PREP: 25 min. • **COOK:** 1-1/2 hours • **YIELD:** 5 servings.

My delicious stew makes a hearty supper with a lighter touch. The leaner cut of meat, herbs and seasonings and fresh vegetables make it so flavorful that you'll want to go back for seconds! james hayes // ridgecrest, california

- 1 tablespoon canola oil
- 1 tablespoon sugar
- 1-1/2 pounds beef top sirloin steak, cut into 3/4-inch cubes
- 5 plum tomatoes, finely chopped
- 3 large carrots, cut into 1/2-inch slices
- 3 celery ribs, cut into 1/2-inch slices
- 4 green onions, chopped
- 3/4 cup reduced-sodium beef broth
- 1/4 cup barbecue sauce
- 1/4 cup reduced-sodium soy sauce
- 2 tablespoons steak sauce
- 1 tablespoon garlic powder
- 1 teaspoon dried thyme
- 1/4 teaspoon ground allspice
- 1/4 teaspoon pepper
- 1/8 teaspoon hot pepper sauce
- 1 tablespoon cornstarch
- 2 tablespoons cold water
- Hot cooked rice *or* mashed potatoes, optional

In a Dutch oven, heat oil over medium-high heat. Add sugar; cook and stir for 1 minute or until lightly browned. Add beef and brown on all sides.

Stir in the vegetables, broth, barbecue sauce, soy sauce, steak sauce and seasonings. Bring to a boil. Reduce heat; cover and simmer for 1 to 1-1/4 hours or until meat and vegetables are tender.

Combine cornstarch and water until smooth; stir into stew. Bring to a boil; cook and stir for 2 minutes or until thickened. Serve with rice or potatoes if desired.

FLUFFY RICE

For fluffy long grain white rice, combine 1 cup rice, 1 tablespoon butter or margarine, 1 teaspoon salt (if desired) and 2 cups water in a 2- to 3-quart saucepan. Heat to boiling, stirring once or twice. Reduce heat; cover and simmer for 15 minutes. It's best not to peek while the rice is cooking. If the water is not absorbed after 15 minutes, cover and continue to cook for another 2-4 minutes. Fluff with a fork before serving. For variety, substitute chicken, beef or vegetable broth for the water.

italian pork stew

PREP: 30 min. • **COOK:** 2-1/2 hours
YIELD: 8 servings (2 quarts).

Don't skip the anchovy paste! It gives a good, salty flavor but doesn't taste fishy at all. Add a salad and garlic bread for an incredible meal. lynne german // norcross, georgia

- **2/3 cup all-purpose flour**
- **2 pounds boneless pork loin, cut into 1-inch pieces**
- **4 tablespoons olive oil, *divided***
- **1 large onion, chopped**
- **5 garlic cloves, crushed**
- **1 can (28 ounces) diced tomatoes, undrained**
- **1 cup dry red wine *or* beef broth**
- **3 bay leaves**
- **1 cinnamon stick (3 inches)**
- **1 tablespoon *each* tomato paste and red wine vinegar**
- **1 teaspoon anchovy paste**
- **1 teaspoon *each* dried oregano, basil and sage leaves**
- **1/2 teaspoon salt**
- **1/2 teaspoon crushed red pepper flakes**
- **1/4 teaspoon pepper**
- **1/4 cup minced fresh parsley**
- **Hot cooked bow tie pasta**
- **Grated Parmesan cheese**

Place flour in a large resealable plastic bag. Add pork, a few pieces at a time, and shake to coat. In a Dutch oven, brown pork in 3 tablespoons oil in batches. Remove and keep warm.

In the same pan, saute onion in remaining oil until crisp-tender. Add garlic; cook 1 minute longer. Stir in the tomatoes, wine, bay leaves, cinnamon, tomato paste, vinegar, anchovy paste, herbs, salt, pepper flakes, pepper and pork; bring to a boil.

Reduce the heat; cover and simmer for 1-1/2 hours, stirring occasionally. Stir in parsley. Cover and cook for 30-60 minutes or until meat is tender. Skim fat; discard bay leaves and cinnamon. Serve with pasta; sprinkle with cheese.

sunday beef stew

PREP: 25 min. • **COOK:** 6 hours • **YIELD:** 6 servings.

We had an aunt who served this savory stew whenever we all got together for a special occasion. It brings back wonderful memories. The cinnamon adds a unique flavor.
jeanette lazary // rochester, new york

- **1/3 cup all-purpose flour**
- **3/4 teaspoon salt**
- **3/4 teaspoon ground cinnamon**
- **1/2 teaspoon pepper**
- **2 pounds beef stew meat, cut into 1-inch cubes**
- **2 tablespoons canola oil**
- **1 package (14 ounces) frozen pearl onions**
- **1 cup dry red wine *or* beef broth**
- **3/4 cup water**
- **2 tablespoons red wine vinegar**
- **2 tablespoons tomato paste**
- **1 tablespoon honey**
- **2 bay leaves**
- **1 garlic clove, minced**

In a large resealable plastic bag, combine the flour, salt, cinnamon and pepper. Add beef, a few pieces at a time, and shake to coat. In a large skillet, brown beef in oil. Transfer to a 3-qt. slow cooker. Stir in the remaining ingredients.

Cover and cook on low for 6-8 hours or until beef and onions are tender. Discard bay leaves.

mexican beef stew

PREP: 30 min. • **COOK:** 6 hours • **YIELD:** 8 servings (4-1/2 quarts).

Instead of chuck roast, you can use eye of round for this recipe. To change it up a little, I sometimes serve it with noodles, rice or flour tortillas.

pat dazis // charlotte, north carolina

- **4 medium potatoes, peeled and cubed**
- **1 can (16 ounces) fat-free refried beans**
- **1 can (14-1/2 ounces) reduced-sodium beef broth**
- **1 can (10 ounces) enchilada sauce**
- **2 cups frozen corn**
- **1 large red onion, chopped**
- **1 can (4 ounces) chopped green chilies**
- **2 tablespoons chopped pickled jalapeno slices**
- **1 tablespoon lime juice**
- **1 teaspoon ground cumin**
- **Dash crushed red pepper flakes**
- **1 boneless beef chuck roast (3 to 4 pounds)**
- **Sour cream**

In a 5-qt. slow cooker, combine the first 11 ingredients. Cut roast in half; transfer to slow cooker.

Cover and cook on low for 6-8 hours or until meat and vegetables are tender.

Remove meat; cool slightly. Cut meat into bite-sized pieces and return to slow cooker; heat through. Serve with sour cream.

louisiana red beans and rice

PREP: 20 min. • **COOK:** 8 hours
YIELD: 9 servings.

Smoked turkey sausage and red pepper flakes add zip to this saucy, slow-cooked version of the New Orleans classic. For extra heat, add red pepper sauce at the table.

julia bushree // georgetown, texas

- **4 cans (16 ounces *each*) kidney beans, rinsed and drained**
- **1 can (14-1/2 ounces) diced tomatoes, undrained**
- **1 package (14 ounces) smoked turkey sausage, sliced**
- **1 cup chicken broth**
- **3 celery ribs, chopped**
- **1 large onion, chopped**
- **1 medium green pepper, chopped**
- **1 small sweet red pepper, chopped**
- **6 garlic cloves, minced**
- **1 bay leaf**
- **1/2 teaspoon crushed red pepper flakes**
- **2 green onions, chopped**
- **Hot cooked rice**

In a 4-qt. slow cooker, combine the first 11 ingredients. Cover and cook on low for 8-10 hours or until heated through. Stir before serving. Discard bay leaf.

Sprinkle each serving with onions. Serve with rice.

beef and lamb stew

PREP: 50 min. + marinating • **COOK:** 8-1/2 hours • **YIELD:** 12 servings (3 quarts).

I tracked down this recipe after a recent trip to South Africa with my church. Traditionally served with brown rcie or pumpkin fritters, the stew includes lots of fresh garden vegetables and two kinds of meat. I've made it for my friends several times. They thought it was great and enjoyed the interesting combination of flavors. dennis kuyper // creston, iowa

- **1/2 cup dry red wine *or* beef broth**
- **1/2 cup olive oil**
- **4 garlic cloves, minced, *divided***
- **1-1/2 teaspoons salt, *divided***
- **1-1/2 teaspoons dried thyme, *divided***
- **1-1/4 teaspoons dried marjoram, *divided***
- **3/4 teaspoon dried rosemary, crushed, *divided***
- **3/4 teaspoon pepper, *divided***
- **1 pound beef stew meat, cut into 1- inch cubes**
- **1 pound lamb stew meat, cut into 1-inch cubes**
- **10 small red potatoes, halved**
- **1/2 pound medium fresh mushrooms, halved**
- **2 medium onions, thinly sliced**
- **2 cups fresh cauliflowerets**
- **1 can (16 ounces) kidney beans, rinsed and drained**
- **1-1/2 cups fresh green beans, trimmed and cut in half**
- **3 medium carrots, cut into 1/2-inch slices**
- **1 celery rib, thinly sliced**
- **1 cup beef broth**
- **2 tablespoons minced fresh parsley**
- **2 teaspoons sugar**
- **3 tablespoons cornstarch**
- **1/4 cup cold water**
- **6 cups cooked brown rice**

In a large resealable plastic bag, combine wine, oil, 2 minced garlic cloves, 1/2 teaspoon salt, 1 teaspoon thyme, 3/4 teaspoon marjoram, 1/2 teaspoon rosemary and 1/4 teaspoon pepper; add beef and lamb. Seal bag and turn to coat; refrigerate for 8 hours.

In a 5- or 6-qt. slow cooker, layer the potatoes, mushrooms, onions, cauliflower, kidney beans, green beans, carrots and celery.

Drain and discard marinade. Place meats over vegetables. Combine the broth, parsley, sugar and remaining garlic, salt, thyme, marjoram, rosemary and pepper; pour over the meats.

Cover and cook on low for 8-10 hours or until meat and vegetables are tender. Combine cornstarch and water until smooth; stir into stew. Cover and cook for 30 minutes longer or until thickened. Serve with rice.

irish beef stew

PREP: 40 min. • **COOK:** 3-1/4 hours
YIELD: 15 servings (3-3/4 quarts).

Rich and hearty, this dish is my husband's favorite. The beef is incredibly tender. It's an ideal cool-weather meal served with fresh bread and perfect for any Irish holiday.
carrie karleen // st. nicolas, quebec

- **8 bacon strips, diced**
- **1/3 cup all-purpose flour**
- **1 teaspoon salt**
- **1/2 teaspoon pepper**
- **3 pounds beef stew meat, cut into 1-inch cubes**
- **1 pound whole fresh mushrooms, quartered**
- **3 medium leeks (white portion only), chopped**
- **2 medium carrots, chopped**
- **1/4 cup chopped celery**
- **1 tablespoon canola oil**
- **4 garlic cloves, minced**
- **1 tablespoon tomato paste**
- **4 cups reduced-sodium beef broth**
- **1 cup dark stout beer *or* additional reduced-sodium beef broth**
- **2 bay leaves**
- **1 teaspoon dried thyme**
- **1 teaspoon dried parsley flakes**
- **1 teaspoon dried rosemary, crushed**
- **2 pounds Yukon Gold potatoes, cut into 1-inch cubes**
- **2 tablespoons cornstarch**
- **2 tablespoons cold water**
- **1 cup frozen peas**

In a stock pot, cook bacon over medium heat until crisp. Using a slotted spoon, remove to paper towels. In a large resealable plastic bag, combine the flour, salt and pepper. Add beef, a few pieces at a time, and shake to coat. Brown beef in the bacon drippings. Remove and set aside.

In the same pan, saute the mushrooms, leeks, carrots and celery in oil until tender. Add garlic; cook 1 minute longer. Stir in tomato paste until blended. Add the broth, beer, bay leaves, thyme, parsley and rosemary. Return beef and bacon to pan. Bring to a boil. Reduce heat; cover and simmer for 2 hours or until beef is tender.

Add potatoes. Return to a boil. Reduce heat; cover and simmer 1 hour longer or until potatoes are tender. Combine cornstarch and water until smooth; stir into stew. Bring to a boil; cook and stir for 2 minutes or until thickened. Add peas; heat through. Discard bay leaves.

hearty sausage stew

PREP/TOTAL TIME: 30 min. • **YIELD:** 4 servings.

My daughters shared this recipe with me, and I've since shared it with many others. It saves both time and money. Plus, it tastes fantastic! nellie lamb // muskogee, oklahoma

- **1/2 pound fresh kielbasa *or* Polish sausage links, cut into 1/2-inch slices**
- **1/2 pound Italian sausage links, cut into 1/2-inch slices**
- **1 medium onion, chopped**
- **1 medium green pepper, chopped**
- **3-1/2 cups beef broth**
- **1 can (14-1/2 ounces) diced tomatoes, undrained**
- **1 cup apple juice**
- **1 tablespoon minced fresh parsley**
- **1 garlic clove, minced**
- **1/4 teaspoon dried basil**
- **1/4 teaspoon dried oregano**
- **4 ounces uncooked spiral pasta**

In a large saucepan, cook the sausage over medium heat until no longer pink. Remove with a slotted spoon; drain, reserving 2 tablespoons drippings.

In the drippings, saute onion and pepper until crisp-tender. Stir in the broth, tomatoes, apple juice, parsley, garlic, basil, oregano and sausages. Bring to a boil; add pasta. Reduce heat; cover and simmer for 10-15 minutes or until pasta is tender.

pueblo green chili stew

PREP: 15 min. • **COOK:** 1-1/4 hour • **YIELD:** 8 servings (about 2-1/2 quarts).

Green chilies add a little spice to a flavorful pork stew that also features corn, potatoes and tomatoes.

helen labrake // rindge, new hampshire

- **2 pounds lean boneless pork, cut into 1-1/2 inch cubes**
- **1 tablespoon canola oil**
- **3 cans (11 ounces *each*) whole kernel corn, drained**
- **2 celery ribs, chopped**
- **2 medium potatoes, peeled and chopped**
- **2 medium tomatoes, coarsely chopped**
- **3 cans (4 ounces *each*) chopped green chilies**
- **4 cups chicken broth**
- **2 teaspoons ground cumin**
- **1 teaspoon dried oregano**
- **1 teaspoon salt, optional**

In a large Dutch oven, brown pork in batches in oil over medium-high heat. Add all the remaining ingredients. Bring to a boil. Reduce heat; cover and simmer for 1 hour or until pork is tender.

low country boil

PREP: 20 min. • **COOK:** 40 min. • **YIELD:** 4 servings.

Ideal for camping and relaxing trips to the beach, this crowd-pleasing recipe includes a combination of shrimp, crab, sausage, corn and potatoes. mageswari elagupillai // victorville, california

- 2 quarts water
- 1 bottle (12 ounces) beer
- 2 tablespoons seafood seasoning
- 1-1/2 teaspoons salt
- 4 medium red potatoes, cut into wedges
- 1 medium sweet onion, cut into wedges
- 4 medium ears sweet corn, cut in half
- 1/3 pound smoked chorizo *or* kielbasa, cut into 1-inch slices
- 3 tablespoons olive oil
- 6 large garlic cloves, minced
- 1 tablespoon ground cumin
- 1 tablespoon minced fresh cilantro
- 1/2 teaspoon paprika
- 1/2 teaspoon pepper
- 1 pound uncooked large shrimp, deveined
- 1 pound uncooked snow crab legs

Optional condiments: seafood cocktail sauce, lemon wedges and melted butter

In a stockpot, combine the water, beer, seafood seasoning and salt; add potatoes and onion. Bring to a boil. Reduce heat; simmer, uncovered, for 10 minutes. Add corn and chorizo; simmer 10-12 minutes longer or until potatoes and corn are tender.

Meanwhile, in a small skillet, heat oil. Add the garlic, cumin, cilantro, paprika and pepper. Cook and stir over medium heat for 1 minute.

Stir the shrimp, crab legs and garlic mixture into the stockpot; cook for 4-6 minutes or until shrimp and crab turn pink. Drain; transfer seafood mixture to a large serving bowl. Serve with condiments of your choice.

EASY COCKTAIL SAUCE

For a tasty seafood cocktail sauce, combine 1 cup of ketchup, 1/2 cup of chili sauce, 1 tablespoon of lemon juice, 1 tablespoon of prepared horseradish and 1/8 teaspoon of hot pepper sauce. Makes about 1-1/2 cups of sauce to serve with shrimp and crab.

pork tenderloin stew

PREP: 20 min. • **COOK:** 40 min. • **YIELD:** 8 servings.

My family frequently requests this thick, creamy stew. It does a good job of warming us up on cold winter days.

janet allen // belleville, illinois

- **2 pork tenderloins (1 pound *each*), cut into 1-inch cubes**
- **1 tablespoon olive oil**
- **1 medium onion, chopped**
- **1 garlic clove, minced**
- **1 can (14-1/2 ounces) reduced-sodium chicken broth**
- **2 pounds red potatoes, peeled and cubed**
- **1 cup sliced fresh carrots**
- **1 cup sliced celery**
- **1/2 pound sliced fresh mushrooms**
- **2 tablespoons cider vinegar**
- **2 teaspoons sugar**
- **1-1/2 teaspoons dried tarragon**
- **1 teaspoon salt**
- **2 tablespoons all-purpose flour**
- **1/2 cup fat-free milk**
- **1/2 cup reduced-fat sour cream**

In a large nonstick skillet over medium heat, cook pork in batches in oil until no longer pink; remove and keep warm.

In the same pan, saute onion until crisp-tender. Add garlic; cook 1 minute longer. Add the broth, vegetables, vinegar, sugar, tarragon and salt; bring to a boil. Reduce heat; cover and simmer for 25-30 minutes or until vegetables are tender.

Combine the flour and milk until smooth; gradually stir into the vegetable mixture. Bring to a boil; cook and stir for 2 minutes or until thickened. Add pork and heat through. Reduce heat; stir in sour cream just before serving (do not boil).

red flannel stew

PREP: 25 min. • **COOK:** 1-1/2 hours • **YIELD:** 5 servings.

When I was child, every Saturday night was Red Flannel Night. Grandpa and I wore our red flannel underwear to supper and Grandma, the cook, dressed in a long calico dress and sunbonnet. We'd eat Red Flannel Stew spooned over fluffy Southern-style biscuits. Grandma had learned to make the stew from earlier generations.

kathy padgett // diamond city, arkansas

- **2 whole fresh beets, washed, trimmed and halved**
- **6 cups water, *divided***
- **1 pound corned beef brisket, trimmed and cut into 1-inch pieces**
- **4 small carrots, sliced**
- **1 large potato, cubed**
- **1 small turnip, peeled and cubed**
- **1 small onion, chopped**
- **1 teaspoon *each* dried parsley flakes, basil and thyme**
- **1/4 teaspoon salt**
- **1/8 teaspoon pepper**

In a large saucepan, bring beets and 4 cups water to a boil. Reduce heat; simmer, uncovered, for 20-25 minutes or until tender. Drain, reserving 2 cups cooking liquid. Peel and dice beets; set aside.

In same pan, combine the corned beef, vegetables, seasonings, remaining water and reserved cooking liquid. Bring to a boil. Reduce heat; cover and simmer for 1-1/4 to 1-1/2 hours or until meat is tender. Stir in diced beets; heat through.

burgundy beef stew

PREP: 25 min. • **COOK:** 8 hours • **YIELD:** 6 servings.

This stew is brimming with home-cooked comfort. I dress up the dish by using sirloin steak, turkey bacon and a variety of herbs, making it special enough for company. mindy ilar // st. albans, west virginia

- **1/2 cup all-purpose flour**
- **1 pound beef top sirloin steak, cut into 1/2-inch pieces**
- **3 turkey bacon strips, diced**
- **8 small red potatoes, halved**
- **2 medium carrots, cut into 1-inch pieces**
- **1 cup sliced fresh mushrooms**
- **3/4 cup frozen pearl onions, thawed**
- **3 garlic cloves, minced**
- **1 bay leaf**
- **1 teaspoon dried marjoram**
- **1/2 teaspoon salt**
- **1/2 teaspoon dried thyme**
- **1/4 teaspoon pepper**
- **1/2 cup reduced-sodium beef broth**
- **1 cup Burgundy wine *or* additional reduced-sodium beef broth**
- **6 cups hot cooked egg noodles**

Place flour in a large resealable plastic bag. Add beef, a few pieces at a time, and shake to coat. In a large skillet coated with cooking spray, brown beef and bacon in batches on all sides.

Place beef and bacon in a 5-qt. slow cooker. Stir in the vegetables, garlic, seasonings, broth and wine or additional broth. Cover and cook on low for 8-9 hours or until meat is tender.

Discard bay leaf. Thicken cooking juices if desired. Serve with noodles.

STOVETOP BURGUNDY BEEF STEW: Using a Dutch oven, prepare beef as directed in first step of the recipe. Add the bacon, vegetables, garlic, bay leaf, marjoram, salt, thyme, pepper, broth and wine. Bring to a boil. Reduce heat; cover and simmer for 1 hour or until beef is tender. Discard bay leaf. Thicken cooking juices if desired. Serve with noodles.

beer-braised beef

PREP: 20 min. • **COOK:** 6 hours • **YIELD:** 8 servings.

I modified the ingredients in this main dish to suit my family's tastes. It's quick to put together in the morning, and at the end of the day, all that's left to do is cook the noodles and eat! The recipe can easily be doubled or tripled to serve large crowds.

geri faustich // appleton, wisconsin

- 3 bacon strips, diced
- 2 pounds beef stew meat, cut into 1-inch cubes
- 1/2 teaspoon pepper
- 1/4 teaspoon salt
- 2 tablespoons canola oil
- 1 medium onion, cut into wedges
- 1 teaspoon minced garlic
- 1 bay leaf
- 1 can (12 ounces) beer *or* nonalcoholic beer
- 1 tablespoon soy sauce
- 1 tablespoon Worcestershire sauce
- 1 teaspoon dried thyme
- 2 tablespoons all-purpose flour
- 1/4 cup water
- Hot cooked noodles

In a large skillet, cook bacon over medium heat until crisp. Using a slotted spoon, remove bacon to paper towels; drain, discarding drippings. Sprinkle beef with pepper and salt. In the same skillet, brown beef on all sides in oil in batches; drain.

Transfer to a 5-qt. slow cooker. Add the bacon, onion, garlic and bay leaf. In a small bowl, combine the beer, soy sauce, Worcestershire sauce and thyme. Pour over beef mixture.

Cover and cook on low for 5-1/2 to 6 hours or until the meat is tender.

In a small bowl, combine flour and water until smooth. Gradually stir into slow cooker. Cover and cook on high for 30 minutes longer or until thickened. Discard bay leaf. Serve beef with noodles.

chicken stew with gnocchi

PREP: 25 min. • **COOK:** 6-1/2 hours
YIELD: 8 servings (3 quarts).

My chicken stew makes the house smell wonderful as it gently bubbles in the slow cooker. One whiff and my family heads to the kitchen to see when it'll be ready.

marge drake // juniata, nebraska

- 3 medium parsnips, peeled and cut into 1/2-inch pieces
- 2 large carrots, cut into 1/2-inch slices
- 2 celery ribs, chopped
- 1 large sweet potato, peeled and cut into 1-inch cubes
- 4 green onions, chopped
- 3 pounds bone-in chicken thighs, skin removed
- 1/2 teaspoon dried sage leaves
- 1/4 teaspoon salt
- 1/4 teaspoon pepper
- 4 cups chicken broth
- 1 cup water
- 3 tablespoons cornstarch
- 1/4 cup cold water
- 1 package (16 ounces) potato gnocchi
- Hot pepper sauce, optional

Place the parsnips, carrots, celery, sweet potato and onions in a 5-qt. slow cooker. Top with chicken; sprinkle with the sage, salt and pepper. Add broth and water. Cover and cook on low for 6 hours or until chicken is tender.

Remove chicken; when cool enough to handle, remove meat from bones and discard bones. Cut meat into bite-size pieces and return to the slow cooker.

Mix cornstarch and cold water until smooth; stir into stew. Add gnocchi. Cover and cook on high for 30 minutes or until thickened. Season with hot pepper sauce if desired.

STOVETOP CHICKEN STEW WITH GNOCCHI: Cover and simmer the chicken, broth, water and seasonings in a Dutch oven for 1 hour. Add the vegetables; cover and simmer 30 minutes longer. Cut chicken and add cornstarch mixture as directed. Add gnocchi. Bring to a boil; cook and stir for 2-3 minutes or until thickened and gnocchi float to the top. Season as directed.

beef stew with dilly dumplings

PREP: 40 min. • **COOK:** 2 hours • **YIELD:** 8 servings.

For a comforting meal on a chilly weeknight, try this savory stew. The combination of fluffy seasoned dumplings and tender meat and vegetables is so good, you'll want to serve it not only to family, but to guests, too. bernadine dirmeyer // harpster, ohio

- 1/3 cup all-purpose flour
- 1-1/8 teaspoons salt, *divided*
- 1/4 teaspoon pepper
- 2 pounds beef stew meat, cut into 1-inch cubes
- 2 tablespoons canola oil
- 4 cups water
- 2 cups sliced fresh carrots
- 2 cups cubed peeled potatoes
- 2 medium onions, chopped
- 1-1/2 cups sliced celery
- 2 tablespoons minced fresh parsley
- 1/2 teaspoon dried thyme
- 1 bay leaf

DUMPLINGS:

- 1-1/2 cups all-purpose flour
- 1 tablespoon minced fresh parsley
- 3 teaspoons baking powder
- 1/2 teaspoon salt
- 1/4 teaspoon dried thyme
- 1/4 teaspoon dill weed
- 1 egg, lightly beaten
- 2/3 cup fat-free milk
- 1 tablespoon canola oil

In a large resealable plastic bag, combine the flour, 1/8 teaspoon salt and pepper. Add meat; seal bag and shake to coat.

In a Dutch oven, brown beef in oil in batches. Add water, stirring to loosen browned bits from pan. Return meat to the pan. Bring to a boil. Reduce heat; cover and simmer for 1 hour.

Add the carrots, potatoes, onions, celery, parsley, thyme, bay leaf and remaining salt. Bring to a boil. Reduce heat; cover and simmer for 45 minutes or until meat and vegetables are tender. Discard bay leaf.

For dumplings, in a large bowl, combine the flour, parsley, baking powder, salt, thyme and dill. Combine the egg, milk and oil; stir into dry ingredients just until moistened.

Drop by tablespoonfuls onto simmering stew. Cover and simmer for 15-20 minutes or until a toothpick inserted in a dumpling comes out clean (do not lift the cover while simmering).

VEGETABLE BEEF STEW WITH DILLY DUMPLINGS: Omit the carrots. Just before adding dumplings, stir in 3 cups frozen mixed vegetables. Return stew to a simmer. Proceed as directed.

simple chicken stew

PREP: 20 min. • **COOK:** 6 hours
YIELD: 2 servings.

This wonderful stew was one of my husband's experiments. It turned out to be one of our favorite dishes for Sunday dinners.
amy dulling // rockwood, tennessee

- **1 can (10-3/4 ounces) condensed cream of chicken soup, undiluted**
- **1 cup water**
- **1/2 pound boneless skinless chicken breasts, cut into cubes**
- **1 large potato, peeled and cut into 3/4-inch cubes**
- **2 medium carrots, cut into 1/4-inch slices**
- **1/2 cup sliced fresh mushrooms**
- **1/4 cup chopped onion**
- **1 teaspoon chicken bouillon granules**
- **1/4 teaspoon poultry seasoning**

In a 3-qt. slow cooker, combine all ingredients. Cover and cook on low for 6-7 hours or until chicken is no longer pink and vegetables are tender.

tortellini meatball stew

PREP: 40 min. • **COOK:** 45 min. • **YIELD:** 6 servings (2-1/2 quarts).

Loaded with meatballs, tortellini, tomatoes and kidney beans, this hearty meal is sure to warm you up on cold winter days. Sprinkle servings with shredded Parmesan for even more flavor. lori martin // marysville, michigan

- **1 egg, lightly beaten**
- **1 package (10 ounces) frozen chopped spinach, thawed and squeezed dry**
- **1/4 cup seasoned bread crumbs**
- **1/2 teaspoon salt**
- **1/4 teaspoon pepper**
- **1 pound lean ground beef**
- **2 tablespoons canola oil, *divided***
- **1 large onion, chopped**
- **1 cup chopped celery**
- **1 cup chopped carrots**
- **4 cups beef broth**
- **1 can (16 ounces) kidney beans, rinsed and drained**
- **1 can (14-1/2 ounces) Italian diced tomatoes, undrained**
- **1/2 teaspoon dried basil**
- **1/2 teaspoon dried oregano**
- **1 package (9 ounces) refrigerated cheese tortellini**
- **1/4 cup shredded Parmesan cheese**

In a large bowl, combine the egg, spinach, bread crumbs, salt and pepper. Crumble beef over mixture and mix well. Shape into 3/4-in. balls.

In a large saucepan, brown meatballs in batches in 1 tablespoon oil; drain. Remove meatballs and keep warm.

In the same pan, saute onion in remaining oil for 2 minutes. Add celery and carrots; saute 2 minutes longer. Stir in the broth, beans, tomatoes, basil and oregano. Add meatballs; bring to a boil. Reduce heat; cover and simmer for 10 minutes.

Return to a boil. Add tortellini; cook for 7-9 minutes or until tender, stirring several times. Garnish with Parmesan cheese.

all-american beef stew

PREP: 40 min. • **COOK:** 1-3/4 hours
YIELD: 8 servings (2-1/2 quarts).

My mother was born and raised in Japan and wasn't familiar with many American dishes when she married and moved to the States. My paternal grandmother gave her the recipe for this mouthwatering dish. frances aldal // antelope, california

- **3/4 cup all-purpose flour, *divided***
- **1/2 teaspoon seasoned salt**
- **1/2 teaspoon pepper, *divided***
- **2 pounds beef stew meat, cut into 1-inch cubes**
- **1 tablespoon olive oil**
- **4-1/2 cups water, *divided***
- **1 large onion, halved and sliced**
- **2 tablespoons Worcestershire sauce**
- **1 tablespoon lemon juice**
- **2 garlic cloves, minced**
- **1 teaspoon sugar**
- **1/2 teaspoon salt**
- **1/2 teaspoon paprika**
- **1/8 teaspoon ground allspice**
- **1 bay leaf**
- **4 medium potatoes, cubed**
- **6 medium carrots, sliced**

Place 1/2 cup flour, seasoned salt and 1/4 teaspoon pepper in a large resealable plastic bag. Add beef, a few pieces at a time, and shake to coat.

In a Dutch oven, brown meat in oil in batches. Remove and set aside. Add 4 cups water to the pan, stirring to loosen browned bits. Add the onion, Worcestershire sauce, lemon juice, garlic, sugar, salt, paprika, allspice, bay leaf and remaining pepper. Return beef to the pan. Bring to a boil. Reduce heat; cover and simmer for 1 hour.

Stir in potatoes and carrots. Bring to a boil. Reduce heat; cover and simmer for 30-35 minutes or until the meat and vegetables are tender.

Combine remaining flour and water until smooth; stir into the pan. Bring to a boil; cook and stir for 2 minutes or until thickened. Discard bay leaf.

quick chicken and dumplings

PREP/TOTAL TIME: 30 min. • **YIELD:** 6 servings.

With precooked chicken and ready-made biscuits, this hearty dish is comfort food made simple. It's a great way to stay cozy in the cold months. akeya astwood // schenectady, new york

- **6 individually frozen biscuits**
- **1/4 cup chopped onion**
- **1/4 cup chopped green pepper**
- **1 tablespoon olive oil**
- **4 cups shredded rotisserie chicken**
- **2 cans (14-1/2 ounces *each*) reduced-sodium chicken broth**
- **1 can (4 ounces) mushroom stems and pieces, drained**
- **1 teaspoon chicken bouillon granules**
- **1 teaspoon minced fresh parsley**
- **1/2 teaspoon dried sage leaves**
- **1/4 teaspoon dried rosemary, crushed**
- **1/4 teaspoon pepper**

Cut each biscuit into fourths; set aside. In a large saucepan, saute onion and green pepper in oil until tender. Stir in the chicken, broth, mushrooms, bouillon granules, parsley, sage, rosemary and pepper.

Bring to a boil. Reduce heat; add biscuits for dumplings. Cover and simmer for 10 minutes or until a toothpick inserted near the center of a dumpling comes out clean (do not lift the cover while simmering).

chicken 'n' sweet potato stew

PREP/TOTAL TIME: 30 min. • **YIELD:** 2 servings.

Are you tired of the same old dinnertime fare? Then spice it up with this Malaysian-inspired dish. Served on a bed of couscous, this stew is as good as it gets. agnes ward // stratford, ontario

- **2/3 pound boneless skinless chicken breasts, cut into 1-inch cubes**
- **1/2 teaspoon minced fresh gingerroot**
- **1 garlic clove, minced**
- **1/2 teaspoon olive oil**
- **1/2 cup chopped onion**
- **1/2 cup chopped sweet red pepper**
- **1/2 teaspoon ground coriander**
- **1/2 teaspoon ground cumin**
- **1/2 teaspoon curry powder**
- **Dash ground cinnamon**
- **1-1/2 cups cubed peeled sweet potatoes**
- **3/4 cup chicken broth**
- **1 cup water**
- **1 tablespoon thawed orange juice concentrate**
- **1/2 cup uncooked couscous**
- **1 tablespoon cornstarch**
- **6 tablespoons light coconut milk**
- **1 tablespoon minced fresh cilantro**

In a large skillet, saute the chicken, ginger and garlic in oil until chicken juices run clear. Add the onion, pepper and seasonings; saute 4-5 minutes longer. Add sweet potatoes and broth. Bring to a boil. Reduce heat; cover and simmer for 10-12 minutes or until sweet potatoes are tender tender.

Meanwhile, in a small saucepan, bring water and orange juice concentrate to a boil. Stir in couscous. Cover and remove from the heat; let stand for 5-10 minutes or until water is absorbed. Fluff with a fork.

Combine the cornstarch and coconut milk until smooth. Stir into the chicken mixture. Bring to a boil; cook and stir for 2 minutes or until thickened. Stir in the cilantro. Serve with couscous.

SWEET POTATO SECRETS

Select sweet potatoes that are firm, with no cracks or bruises. If stored in a cool, dark, well-ventilated place, they'll remain fresh for about two weeks. If the temperature is above 60 degrees, they'll sprout sooner or become woody. Once cooked, sweet potatoes can be stored for up to one week in the refrigerator.

oven beef stew

PREP: 20 min. • **BAKE:** 2-1/4 hours • **YIELD:** 6 servings.

I love this cold-weather meal because everything's in one pot. Add a good loaf of bread and you're all set.

bettina turner // kernersville, north carolina

- **6 tablespoons all-purpose flour, *divided***
- **1/4 teaspoon salt, optional**
- **1/2 teaspoon pepper, *divided***
- **1-1/2 pounds boneless beef chuck roast, cut into 1-inch cubes**
- **1 tablespoon canola oil**
- **1 medium onion, chopped**
- **3 garlic cloves, minced**
- **3 cups beef broth**
- **1 can (14-1/2 ounces) stewed tomatoes, cut up**
- **3/4 teaspoon dried thyme**
- **3 large potatoes, peeled and cut into 1-inch cubes**
- **3 medium carrots, cut into 1/4-inch slices**
- **1/2 cup frozen peas, thawed**

In a large resealable plastic bag, combine 4 tablespoons flour, salt if desired and 1/4 teaspoon pepper. Add beef, a few pieces at a time, and shake to coat.

In a Dutch oven over medium-high heat, brown beef in oil in batches. Remove and set aside. Add onion to the pan and cook until tender. Add garlic; cook 1 minute longer. Stir in remaining flour and pepper until blended. Gradually stir in the broth, tomatoes and thyme. Cover and bake at 350° for 1-1/4 hours.

Add the potatoes and carrots. Cover and bake 1 hour longer or until meat and vegetables are tender. Stir in peas; cover and let stand for 5 minutes before serving.

creole black beans 'n' sausage

PREP: 25 min. • **COOK:** 6 hours • **YIELD:** 10 servings.

Whenever I want to serve up a touch of Louisiana for dinner, I turn to this entree. I brown the meat, cut up veggies and measure spices the night before, and then assemble and start it cooking the next morning. When I get home, I make the rice—and dinner is served!

cheryl landers // latour, missouri

- **2 pounds smoked sausage, cut into 1-inch slices**
- **3 cans (15 ounces *each*) black beans, rinsed and drained**
- **1-1/2 cups *each* chopped onion, celery and green pepper**
- **1 cup water**
- **1 can (8 ounces) tomato sauce**
- **4 garlic cloves, minced**
- **2 teaspoons dried thyme**
- **1 teaspoon chicken bouillon granules**
- **1 teaspoon white pepper**
- **1/4 teaspoon cayenne pepper**
- **2 bay leaves**

Hot cooked rice

In a large skillet, brown sausage over medium heat; drain. Transfer to a 5-qt. slow cooker.

In a large bowl, combine the beans, onion, celery, green pepper, water, tomato sauce, garlic, thyme, bouillon, white pepper, cayenne and bay leaves; pour over sausage. Cover and cook on low for 6 hours or until vegetables are tender. Discard bay leaves. Serve with rice.

speedy jambalaya

PREP/TOTAL TIME: 30 min. • **YIELD:** 8 servings.

Spicy sausage and colorful sweet peppers make this classic Cajun dish look as appetizing as it tastes. It's impossible to say no to seconds!

nicole filizetti // grand marais, michigan

- **1-1/3 cups uncooked long grain rice**
- **1 large onion, halved and sliced**
- **1 medium green pepper, sliced**
- **1 medium sweet red pepper, sliced**
- **2 teaspoons olive oil**
- **3 garlic cloves, minced**
- **1 can (28 ounces) diced tomatoes, undrained**
- **3 bay leaves**
- **1 teaspoon salt**
- **1 teaspoon paprika**
- **1/2 teaspoon dried thyme**
- **1/2 teaspoon pepper**
- **1/4 teaspoon hot pepper sauce**
- **2 cans (15-1/2 ounces *each*) black-eyed peas, rinsed and drained**
- **3/4 pound fully cooked andouille *or* Italian sausage links, sliced**
- **1/4 cup minced fresh parsley**

Cook rice according to package directions. Meanwhile, in a large skillet, saute onion and peppers in oil for 4 minutes. Add garlic; cook 1 minute longer. Stir in the tomatoes, bay leaves, salt, paprika, thyme, pepper and pepper sauce. Bring to a boil.

Reduce heat; simmer, uncovered, for 5 minutes. Stir in peas and sausage; heat through. Discard bay leaves. Serve with rice. Sprinkle each serving with parsley.

bavarian meatball stew

PREP: 35 min. • **COOK:** 35 min.
YIELD: 8 servings.

Meatballs are a delicious addition to a this stew and go so well with the kraut. We like it any time of year, but the flavors really speak to fall and winter.

janice mitchell // aurora, colorado

- **1 egg, lightly beaten**
- **1/2 cup soft bread crumbs**
- **3 tablespoons dried parsley flakes**
- **1/4 teaspoon ground allspice**
- **1/4 teaspoon ground nutmeg**
- **1/4 teaspoon pepper**
- **1-1/2 pounds ground beef**
- **2 cans (14-1/2 ounces *each*) beef broth**
- **1 can (14-1/2 ounces) diced tomatoes, undrained**
- **1 can (14 ounces) Bavarian sauerkraut, rinsed and well drained**
- **2 medium potatoes, peeled and cubed**
- **2 medium carrots, sliced**
- **2 celery ribs, sliced**
- **1 envelope onion soup mix**
- **1 tablespoon sugar**
- **1/2 teaspoon pepper**
- **1 bay leaf**

In a large bowl, combine the first six ingredients. Crumble beef over mixture and mix well. Shape into 1-in. balls. Place on a greased rack in a shallow baking pan. Bake at 400° for 15 minutes; drain.

In a large saucepan, combine remaining ingredients. Add meatballs. Bring to a boil. Reduce heat; cover and simmer for 30-35 minutes or until the vegetables are tender. Discard bay leaf.

irish stew

PREP: 15 min. • **COOK:** 1-1/2 hours • **YIELD:** 8 servings (2-1/2 quarts).

Lamb is an excellent source of protein and adds delicious flavor to this classic stew. If you can't find it at your grocery store, try using beef stew meat instead. taste of home test kitchen

- **1/3 cup plus 1 tablespoon all-purpose flour, *divided***
- **1-1/2 pounds lamb stew meat, cut into 1-inch cubes**
- **3 tablespoons olive oil, *divided***
- **3 medium onions, chopped**
- **3 garlic cloves, minced**
- **4 cups reduced-sodium beef broth**
- **2 medium potatoes, peeled and cubed**
- **4 medium carrots, cut into 1-inch pieces**
- **1 cup frozen peas**
- **1 teaspoon salt**
- **1 teaspoon dried thyme**
- **1/2 teaspoon pepper**
- **1/2 teaspoon Worcestershire sauce**
- **2 tablespoons water**

Place 1/3 cup flour in a large resealable plastic bag. Add lamb, a few pieces at a time, and shake to coat.

In a Dutch oven, brown lamb in batches in 2 tablespoons oil. Remove and set aside. In the same pan, saute onions in remaining oil until tender. Add garlic; cook 1 minute longer.

Add broth, stirring to loosen browned bits from pan. Return lamb to the pan. Bring to a boil. Reduce heat; cover and simmer for 1 hour or until meat is tender.

Add potatoes and carrots; cover and cook for 20 minutes. Stir in peas; cook 5-10 minutes longer or until vegetables are tender.

Add seasonings and Worcestershire sauce. Combine remaining flour with water until smooth; stir into stew. Bring to a boil; cook and stir for 2 minutes or until thickened.

HEARTY IRISH STEW: Add 1 cup cubed turnip to pan along with potatoes. Add 1/2 teaspoon each crushed dried rosemary and marjoram to the seasonings.

TENDER LAMB

Try pouring a cup of black coffee over a lamb roast, or lamb for stew, before cooking. The aroma is always delightful, and I think it helps tenderize the meat. helen a. // walden, vermont

harvest stew

PREP: 20 min. • **COOK:** 40 min.
YIELD: 6 servings.

You'll find all the fabulous flavors of the autumn harvest in this special pork stew. Everyone around your table will surely ask for seconds!
taste of home test kitchen

- **1-1/2 pounds boneless pork loin roast, cut into 1-inch cubes**
- **1 medium onion, chopped**
- **2 tablespoons butter**
- **2 garlic cloves, minced**
- **3 cups chicken broth**
- **3/4 teaspoon salt**
- **1/4 teaspoon dried rosemary, crushed**
- **1/4 teaspoon rubbed sage**
- **1 bay leaf**
- **1 medium butternut squash, peeled and cubed (3 cups)**
- **2 medium apples, peeled and cubed**

In a large saucepan, cook pork and onion in butter until meat is no longer pink. Add garlic; cook 1 minute longer. Drain. Add the broth, salt, rosemary, sage and bay leaf. Cover and simmer for 20 minutes.

Stir in squash and apples; simmer, uncovered, for 20 minutes or until squash and apples are tender. Discard bay leaf.

sausage & rice stew

PREP: 20 min. • **COOK:** 30 min. • **YIELD:** 6 servings.

Sausage is one of my husband's favorite foods, so I find ways to serve it with healthy ingredients, like beans and spinach. I'm sure you'll enjoy this hearty recipe just as much as he does. kelly young // cocoa, florida

- **1 package (14 ounces) smoked turkey kielbasa, halved lengthwise and sliced**
- **1 large sweet onion, chopped**
- **2 shallots, chopped**
- **1 tablespoon chopped pickled jalapeno slices**
- **3 garlic cloves, minced**
- **1 tablespoon canola oil**
- **2 cups water**
- **1 can (14-1/2 ounces) reduced-sodium chicken broth**
- **2 cans (15 ounces *each*) white kidney *or* cannellini beans, rinsed and drained**
- **1 cup uncooked long grain rice**
- **1 teaspoon dried oregano**
- **1 teaspoon dried thyme**
- **1/2 teaspoon pepper**
- **2 cups fresh baby spinach**

In a Dutch oven, saute the kielbasa, onion, shallots, jalapeno and garlic in oil until onion is tender. Add the water, broth, beans, rice and seasonings. Bring to a boil. Reduce heat; cover and simmer for 15-20 minutes or until rice is tender. Stir in spinach. Cook 5 minutes longer or until spinach is wilted.

west african beef stew

PREP: 30 min. • **COOK:** 55 min. • **YIELD:** 6 servings.

My husband and I run a dorm for missionaries' children who live and work with us in Yamoussoukro while their parents work in the interior. This traditional African dish is easy to Americanize and tastes wonderful.

rhonda hunter // ivory coast, west africa

- **1-1/2 pounds beef top sirloin steak, cut into 1-inch cubes**
- **2 medium onions, sliced**
- **2 teaspoons canola oil**
- **1 garlic clove, minced**
- **1 cup water**
- **4 teaspoons beef bouillon granules**
- **4 cups shredded cabbage**
- **2 medium green peppers, julienned**
- **1 medium zucchini, cut into 1/4-inch slices**
- **3 tablespoons creamy peanut butter**
- **Cayenne pepper**
- **Hot cooked rice, optional**

In a Dutch oven, brown steak and onions in oil. Add garlic; cook 1 minute longer. Add water and bouillon; bring to a boil. Reduce heat; cover and simmer for 40-45 minutes or until meat is tender.

Stir in the cabbage, green peppers and zucchini. Bring to a boil. Reduce heat; cover and simmer for 8-10 minutes or until vegetables are tender.

Just before serving, stir in the peanut butter and sprinkle with cayenne. Serve with rice if desired.

ground beef biscuit stew

PREP: 10 min. • **BAKE:** 30 min. • **YIELD:** 6 servings.

I've been making this recipe ever since I married more than 25 years ago. For a different taste, I sometimes add a little chili powder to the meat mixture and top the stew with a prepared cornbread mix. darlene brenden // salem, oregon

- **1 pound ground beef**
- **1 medium onion, chopped**
- **1 can (14-1/2 ounces) stewed tomatoes, cut up**
- **1 package (10 ounces) frozen mixed vegetables**
- **1 can (8 ounces) tomato sauce**

BISCUITS:

- **1 cup all-purpose flour**
- **1-1/2 teaspoons baking powder**
- **2 tablespoons shortening**
- **2/3 cup milk**
- **1 teaspoon prepared mustard**
- **1/2 cup shredded cheddar cheese, *divided***

In a large skillet, cook beef and onion over medium heat until meat is no longer pink; drain. Stir in the tomatoes, mixed vegetables and tomato sauce.

Transfer to a greased 11-in. x 7-in. baking dish. Cover and bake at 400° for 15 minutes.

Meanwhile, for biscuits, in a small bowl, combine flour and baking powder. Cut in shortening until mixture resembles coarse crumbs. Stir in milk and mustard until mixture forms a soft dough. Add 6 tablespoons cheese.

Drop by tablespoonfuls onto stew. Bake for 15-20 minutes or until golden brown; sprinkle with remaining cheese.

bavarian stew

PREP: 15 min. • **COOK:** 1-3/4 hours • **YIELD:** 2 servings.

Guests and family alike are delighted when I serve this. I don't remember where the recipe came from, but it has been a family favorite for many years. It's excellent German fare, similar to sauerbraten, but you don't have to marinate the beef for days. The meat is very flavorful and tender.

barbara pizzi // sycamore, illinois

- **3/4 pound beef stew meat, cut into 3/4-inch cubes**
- **1 tablespoon canola oil**
- **1-1/4 cups beef broth**
- **1/3 cup thinly sliced onion**
- **1 bay leaf**
- **1/2 teaspoon caraway seeds**
- **1/8 teaspoon pepper**
- **1/4 to 1/3 cup white vinegar**
- **1/2 teaspoon sugar**
- **1/4 medium head red cabbage, cut into 2 wedges**
- **1/4 to 1/3 cup crushed gingersnap cookies (about 8 cookies)**

In a large saucepan, cook beef in oil until browned; drain. Stir in the broth, onion, bay leaf, caraway seeds and pepper. Bring to a boil. Reduce heat; cover and simmer for 1-1/4 hours or until meat is almost tender.

Combine vinegar and sugar; stir into beef mixture. Place cabbage on top of meat mixture. Bring to a boil. Reduce heat; cover and simmer for 18-22 minutes or until meat and cabbage are tender.

Remove beef and cabbage; keep warm. Discard bay leaf. Stir gingersnaps into cooking liquid; cook and stir until thickened. Stir in beef. Serve with cabbage.

okra and butter bean stew

PREP: 25 min. • **COOK:** 45 min. • **YIELD:** 12 servings (1 cup each).

Adapted from my mom's down-home Louisiana recipe, this stew turns okra haters into okra lovers—guaranteed! kaya mack // wichita falls, texas

- **7 bacon strips, chopped**
- **1 pound smoked sausage, halved and thinly sliced**
- **1 large onion, chopped**
- **2 small green peppers, chopped**
- **3 cups water**
- **2 cans (16 ounces *each*) butter beans, rinsed and drained**
- **1 can (14-1/2 ounces) diced tomatoes, undrained**
- **1 can (12 ounces) tomato paste**
- **1 teaspoon pepper**
- **1/4 teaspoon salt**
- **1 package (16 ounces) frozen sliced okra**

Hot cooked rice, optional

In a Dutch oven, cook bacon and sausage over medium heat until bacon is crisp. Using a slotted spoon, remove to paper towels; drain, reserving 2 tablespoons drippings.

Cook onion and green peppers in the drippings until tender. Stir in the water, beans, tomatoes, tomato paste, pepper and salt. Bring to a boil. Reduce the heat; simmer, uncovered, for 10 minutes. Add bacon and sausage; cook 10 minutes longer.

Stir in okra. Cover and cook for 8-10 minutes or until okra is tender. Serve with rice if desired.

vegetable pork stew

PREP: 20 min. • **COOK:** 7 hours
YIELD: 6 servings (2 quarts).

Packed with tender pork, veggies and savory flavor, this nutritious soup fills the house with a wonderful aroma as it cooks. deb hall // huntington, indiana

- **1 pork tenderloin (1 pound), cut into 1-inch pieces**
- **1 teaspoon garlic powder**
- **2 teaspoons canola oil**
- **1 can (28 ounces) diced tomatoes**
- **4 medium carrots, cut into 1/2-inch pieces**
- **2 medium potatoes, cubed**
- **1 can (12 ounces) light *or* nonalcoholic beer**
- **1/4 cup quick-cooking tapioca**
- **2 bay leaves**
- **1 tablespoon Worcestershire sauce**
- **1 tablespoon honey**
- **1 teaspoon dried thyme**
- **1/4 teaspoon salt**
- **1/4 teaspoon pepper**
- **1/8 teaspoon ground nutmeg**

Sprinkle pork with garlic powder. In a large skillet, brown pork in oil; drain.

Transfer to a 4-qt. slow cooker. Add the remaining ingredients. Cover and cook on low for 7-8 hours or until meat is tender. Discard bay leaves.

THICK & CHUNKY BEEF CHILI, PG. 360

chilis

CHUNKY CHIPOTLE PORK CHILI, PG. 334

CREAMY WHITE CHILI, PG. 351

ROOTIN'-TOOTIN' CINCINNATI CHILI, PG. 340

great northern bean chili

PREP: 20 min. • **COOK:** 4 hours
YIELD: 8 servings.

Seven ingredients make this mild version of a Southwestern chicken chili. I like to add a dash of hot sauce and some sour cream on top with tortilla chips on the side. It's a great alternative to traditional chili.

mamesmom
taste of home online community

- **2 pounds boneless skinless chicken breasts, cut into 1-inch cubes**
- **1 tablespoon canola oil**
- **1 jar (48 ounces) great northern beans, rinsed and drained**
- **1 jar (16 ounces) salsa**
- **1 can (14-1/2 ounces) chicken broth**
- **1 teaspoon ground cumin, optional**
- **2 cups (8 ounces) shredded Monterey Jack cheese**

In a large skillet, brown chicken in oil; drain. In a 4- or 5-qt. slow cooker, combine beans, salsa, broth, cumin if desired and chicken. Cover and cook on low for 4-6 hours or until chicken is tender. Serve with cheese.

chunky chipotle pork chili

PREP: 15 min. • **COOK:** 20 min. • **YIELD:** 4 servings.

Perfect for using leftover pork roast, this tasty, easy recipe can be made ahead and reheated. It's even better the second day.

peter halferty // corpus christi, texas

- **1 medium green pepper, chopped**
- **1 small onion, chopped**
- **1 chipotle pepper in adobo sauce, finely chopped**
- **1 tablespoon canola oil**
- **3 garlic cloves, minced**
- **1 can (16 ounces) red beans, rinsed and drained**
- **1 cup beef broth**
- **1/2 cup salsa**
- **2 teaspoons ground cumin**
- **2 teaspoons chili powder**
- **2 cups cubed cooked pork**
- **1/4 cup sour cream**

In a large saucepan, saute the green pepper, onion and chipotle pepper in oil until tender. Add garlic; cook 1 minute longer.

Add the beans, broth, salsa, cumin and chili powder. Bring to a boil. Reduce heat; simmer, uncovered, for 10 minutes or until thickened. Add pork; heat through. Serve with sour cream.

white bean chicken chili

PREP: 35 min. • **COOK:** 3 hours • **YIELD:** 6 servings.

My sister shared this chili recipe with me. I usually double it, add an extra can of beans and serve with cheddar biscuits or warmed tortillas. The jalapeno adds just enough heat to notice but not too much for my children.

kristine bowles // rio rancho, new mexico

- **3/4 pound boneless skinless chicken breasts, cubed**
- **1/2 teaspoon salt**
- **1/4 teaspoon pepper**
- **1 medium onion, chopped**
- **1 jalapeno pepper, seeded and chopped**
- **2 teaspoons dried oregano**
- **1 teaspoon ground cumin**
- **2 tablespoons olive oil**
- **4 garlic cloves, minced**
- **2 cans (15 ounces *each*) white kidney *or* cannellini beans, rinsed and drained, *divided***
- **3 cups chicken broth, *divided***
- **1-1/2 cups (6 ounces) shredded cheddar cheese**
- **Sour cream and minced fresh cilantro, optional**

Sprinkle chicken with salt and pepper. In a large skillet over medium heat, cook the chicken, onion, jalapeno, oregano and cumin in oil for 3-4 minutes or until chicken is browned and vegetables are crisp-tender. Add garlic; cook 1 minute longer.

Transfer to a 3-qt. slow cooker. In a small bowl, mash 1 cup of beans; add 1/2 cup broth and stir until blended. Add to the slow cooker with the remaining beans and broth. Cover and cook on low for 3 to 3-1/2 hours or until heated through.

Stir before serving. Sprinkle with cheese. Garnish with sour cream and cilantro if desired.

CHICKEN CORN CHILI: Add 2 cups thawed frozen corn and 1/2 teaspoon ground coriander to the slow cooker along with the broth. Proceed as directed.

EDITOR'S NOTE: We recommend wearing disposable gloves when cutting hot peppers. Avoid touching your face.

colorado lamb chili

PREP: 20 min. • **COOK:** 1-1/2 hours • **YIELD:** 6 servings (2-1/4 quarts).

This hearty and spicy combination of lamb, black beans, peppers, tomatoes and seasonings is wonderful with fresh rolls and my favorite green salad. It's a deliciously different version of chili. karen gorman // gunnison, colorado

- **1 pound lamb stew meat, cut into 1-inch pieces**
- **2 tablespoons canola oil, *divided***
- **1 large onion, chopped**
- **1 large sweet yellow pepper, chopped**
- **4 garlic cloves, minced**
- **1 can (30 ounces) black beans, rinsed and drained**
- **1 can (28 ounces) diced tomatoes, undrained**
- **1 can (14-1/2 ounces) reduced-sodium beef broth**
- **1 tablespoon dried oregano**
- **1 tablespoon chili powder**
- **1 tablespoon brown sugar**
- **2 teaspoons Worcestershire sauce**
- **1 teaspoon ground cumin**
- **1/2 teaspoon fennel seed, crushed**
- **Sliced green onions, chopped tomatoes and corn chips, optional**

In a Dutch oven, brown lamb in 1 tablespoon oil. Remove and set aside.

In the same pan, saute onion and pepper in remaining oil until tender. Add garlic; saute 2 minutes longer. Add the beans, tomatoes, broth, oregano, chili powder, brown sugar, Worcestershire sauce, cumin and fennel. Return lamb to the pan.

Bring to a boil. Reduce heat; cover and simmer for 1-1/4 to 1-1/2 hours or until lamb is tender. Garnish each serving with green onions, tomatoes and corn chips if desired.

CONSIDER GRAIN-FED LAMB

Do you avoid lamb because you think it has a strong flavor? Then try grain-fed lamb, which has a milder flavor than grass-fed lamb. Domestic lamb is usually grain-fed. Also look for lamb rather than mutton, which has a stronger flavor. Lamb meat is pale pink and mutton is light to dark red.

super-duper chili

PREP: 20 min. • **COOK:** 35 min.
YIELD: 14 servings (3-1/2 quarts).

No one ever guesses the "secret ingredient" in this recipe that I created. A can of mushroom soup is what makes the chili so thick and creamy. Take this spicy concoction to a fall potluck or church dinner, and watch folks dig right in!

elizabeth mays // nunnelly, tennessee

- **1 pound bulk pork sausage**
- **1 pound ground beef**
- **2 cans (16 ounces *each*) hot chili beans, undrained**
- **1 jar (16 ounces) salsa**
- **1 can (16 ounces) kidney beans, rinsed and drained**
- **1 can (15 ounces) pinto beans, rinsed and drained**
- **1 can (14-1/2 ounces) diced tomatoes, undrained**
- **1 can (10-3/4 ounces) condensed cream of mushroom soup, undiluted**
- **1 can (8 ounces) tomato sauce**
- **8 ounces process cheese (Velveeta), cubed**
- **1-1/2 teaspoons chili powder**
- **1/2 teaspoon cayenne pepper**

In a Dutch oven or large soup kettle, cook the sausage and beef over medium heat until no longer pink; drain. Stir in the remaining ingredients. Bring to a boil. Reduce heat; cover and simmer for 30 minutes or until heated through.

zippy beef chili

PREP: 30 min. • **COOK:** 6 hours • **YIELD:** 12 servings.

This zesty chili is not only chock-full of ground beef, but it's also loaded with veggies. I put everything in the slow cooker, let it cook and then come home to a delicious, ready-to-eat meal.

bonnie chocallo // wyoming, pennsylvania

- **2 pounds lean ground beef (90% lean)**
- **1 can (16 ounces) kidney beans, rinsed and drained**
- **2 cans (14-1/2 ounces *each*) diced tomatoes**
- **1 can (11-1/2 ounces) pork and beans**
- **2 large onions, chopped**
- **2 medium carrots, shredded**
- **1 medium sweet red pepper, chopped**
- **1 medium green pepper, chopped**
- **2 celery ribs, chopped**
- **1 cup water**
- **1/2 cup ketchup**
- **1 can (6 ounces) tomato paste**
- **2 jalapeno peppers, seeded and chopped**
- **3 tablespoons brown sugar**
- **4 garlic cloves, minced**
- **1 tablespoon dried oregano**
- **1 tablespoon chili powder**
- **1 teaspoon salt**
- **1 teaspoon crushed red pepper flakes**
- **1 teaspoon pepper**

In a large skillet, cook beef over medium heat until no longer pink; drain.

Transfer to a 5-qt. slow cooker. Add the remaining ingredients. Cover and cook on low for 6-8 hours or until heated through.

EDITOR'S NOTE: We recommend wearing disposable gloves when cutting hot peppers. Avoid touching your face.

kids' favorite chili

PREP/TOTAL TIME: 25 min. • **YIELD:** 4 servings.

This sweet and easy chili is sure to warm the whole family up on those chilly fall and winter nights. The recipe has been in my family for three generations. terri keeney // greeley, colorado

- **1 pound ground turkey**
- **1/2 cup chopped onion**
- **1 can (15-3/4 ounces) pork and beans**
- **1 can (14-1/2 ounces) diced tomatoes, undrained**
- **1 can (10-3/4 ounces) condensed tomato soup, undiluted**
- **1 tablespoon brown sugar**
- **1 tablespoon chili powder**

In a large saucepan, cook turkey and onion over medium heat until meat is no longer pink; drain. Stir in the remaining ingredients. Bring to a boil. Reduce heat; cover and simmer for 15-20 minutes or until heated through.

rootin'-tootin' cincinnati chili

PREP: 25 min. • **COOK:** 30 min. • **YIELD:** 4 servings.

Yes, there's root beer in this spicy chili, and it adds a nice touch of sweetness. Serve over spaghetti and let everyone add their own favorite toppings. holly gomez // seabrook, new hampshire

- **1 pound ground beef**
- **1 small onion, chopped**
- **1 small green pepper, chopped**
- **1 garlic clove, minced**
- **1 can (14-1/2 ounces) fire-roasted diced tomatoes, undrained**
- **1 cup root beer**
- **2 tablespoons chili powder**
- **2 tablespoons tomato paste**
- **2 tablespoons minced chipotle peppers in adobo sauce**
- **1 tablespoon ground cumin**
- **1 beef bouillon cube**

Hot cooked spaghetti

Optional toppings: crushed tortilla chips, chopped green onions and shredded cheddar and Parmesan cheeses

In a large saucepan, cook the beef, onion and green pepper over medium heat until meat is no longer pink. Add garlic; cook 1 minute longer. Drain. Add the tomatoes, root beer, chili powder, tomato paste, chipotle peppers, cumin and bouillon. Bring to a boil.

Reduce heat; cover and simmer for 20-30 minutes to allow flavors to blend. Serve with spaghetti. Garnish with chips, green onions and cheeses if desired.

TOMATO PASTE SAVER

Here's a tip that's handy when making recipes that call for a few tablespoons of tomato paste. When I purchase a large can of tomato paste, I line a baking sheet with waxed paper. I drop the paste by tablespoonfuls onto the paper and place the baking sheet in the freezer. When frozen, the tomato paste "drops" easily peel off the paper and can be stored in a resealable bag or freezer container. janine d. // baton rouge, louisiana

roasted vegetable chili

PREP: 35 min. • **COOK:** 30 min. • **YIELD:** 13 servings (5 quarts).

I suggest serving this delicious and satisfying recipe with corn chips, cheese, sour cream and a small salad. To save time, purchase vegetables that have already been diced. hannah barringer // loudon, tennessee

- **1 medium butternut squash, peeled and cut into 1-inch pieces**
- **3 large carrots, sliced**
- **2 medium zucchini, cut into 1-inch pieces**
- **2 tablespoons olive oil, *divided***
- **1-1/2 teaspoons ground cumin**
- **2 medium green peppers, diced**
- **1 large onion, chopped**
- **3 cans (14-1/2 ounces *each*) reduced-sodium chicken broth**
- **3 cans (14-1/2 ounces *each*) diced tomatoes, undrained**
- **2 cans (15 ounces *each*) white kidney *or* cannellini beans, rinsed and drained**
- **1 cup water**
- **1 cup salsa**
- **3 teaspoons chili powder**
- **6 garlic cloves, minced**

Place the squash, carrots and zucchini in a 15-in. x 10-in. x 1-in. baking pan. Combine 1 tablespoon oil and cumin; drizzle over vegetables and toss to coat. Bake, uncovered, at 450° for 25-30 minutes or until tender, stirring once.

Meanwhile, in a stockpot, saute the green peppers and onion in the remaining oil for 3-4 minutes or until tender. Stir in the broth, tomatoes, beans, water, salsa, chili powder and garlic. Bring to a boil. Reduce heat; simmer, uncovered, for 10 minutes.

Stir in the roasted vegetables. Return to a boil. Reduce heat; simmer, uncovered, for 5-10 minutes or until heated through.

30-minute chili

PREP/TOTAL TIME: 30 min.
YIELD: 6-8 servings (about 2 quarts).

On a brisk, windy day, I don't think anything is more appealing than a steaming bowl of this zesty chili. I always make enough so that everyone can have seconds.
susan strout // cheney, washington

- **2 pounds ground beef**
- **2 cups chopped onion**
- **2 cans (16 ounces *each*) chili beans, undrained**
- **2 cans (10-3/4 ounces *each*) condensed tomato soup, undiluted**
- **4 teaspoons chili powder**
- **2 teaspoons paprika**
- **1 teaspoon pepper**
- **1 teaspoon salt**
- **1/4 teaspoon garlic powder**
- **Chopped green pepper**
- **Shredded cheddar cheese**

In a large saucepan, cook beef and onion over medium heat until meat is no longer pink; drain. Add the beans, soup and seasonings; bring to a boil. Reduce heat; cover and simmer for 15 minutes or until thick and bubbly. Garnish with green pepper and cheese.

spicy fajita chili

PREP: 15 min. • **COOK:** 30 min. • **YIELD:** 8 servings (2 quarts).

You'll want to serve this flavorful chili with rolls or corn bread to soak up every delicious drop. Like more heat? Just use spicier versions of V8 juice and chili beans. cathy bell // joplin, missouri

- **1-1/2 pounds ground pork**
- **1 medium onion, chopped**
- **1 medium green pepper, chopped**
- **1 medium sweet red pepper, chopped**
- **1 garlic clove, minced**
- **2 cans (11-1/2 ounces *each*) V8 juice**
- **1 can (16 ounces) chili beans, undrained**
- **1 can (10 ounces) diced tomatoes and green chilies**
- **2 tablespoons chili powder**
- **1 teaspoon seasoned salt**
- **1/2 teaspoon seasoned pepper**
- **Shredded cheddar cheese**

In a Dutch oven, cook the pork, onion and peppers over medium heat until meat is no longer pink. Add garlic; cook 1 minute longer. Drain.

Stir in the V8 juice, beans, tomatoes, chili powder, seasoned salt and seasoned pepper. Bring to a boil. Reduce the heat; simmer, uncovered, for 20 minutes or until slightly thickened. Serve with cheese.

CHILI FROM TACO LEFTOVERS

When I have leftover fixings from tacos, I use them as a starter for spicy chili. In a pot, I combine the seasoned meat, salsa, refried beans, chopped onions and tomatoes. I add a can of chili beans and a bit of seasoning if needed. I cook the mixture until it's thick then serve it with broken taco shells (or tortilla chips) and shredded cheese.

catherine h., evansville, indiana

california pepper chili

PREP: 10 min. • **COOK:** 80 min.
YIELD: 10 servings (2-1/2 quarts).

In my opinion, this is the world's best chili! It features three meats in a peppery, eye-opening broth.

robyn thompson // los angeles, california

- 1/2 pound bacon, diced
- 2-1/2 pounds beef stew meat, cut into 3/4-inch cubes
- 1-1/2 pounds pork stew meat, cut into 3/4-inch cubes
- 2 medium onions, chopped
- 6 to 8 garlic cloves, minced
- 1 to 2 tablespoons chopped seeded fresh serrano chili peppers
- 1 to 2 tablespoons chopped seeded fresh poblano chili peppers
- 1 to 2 tablespoons chopped seeded fresh jalapeno peppers
- 2 to 3 teaspoons cayenne pepper
- 1-1/2 teaspoons dried oregano
- 1 teaspoon salt
- 1 teaspoon ground cumin
- 1 can (15 ounces) tomato puree
- 1 can (14-1/2 ounces) beef broth
- 7 plum tomatoes, chopped
- Shredded cheddar cheese, optional

In a Dutch oven, cook bacon over medium heat until crisp. Using a slotted spoon, remove bacon to paper towels; drain, reserving 3 tablespoons drippings.

In the drippings, cook the beef, pork and onions in batches until meat is no longer pink; drain. Add garlic, peppers and seasonings; cook and stir for 1-2 minutes.

Stir in the tomato puree, broth and tomatoes. Bring to a boil. Reduce heat; cover and simmer for 1 to 1-1/2 hours or until meat is tender. Garnish with reserved bacon and cheese if desired.

EDITOR'S NOTE: We recommend wearing disposable gloves when cutting hot peppers. Avoid touching your face.

three-meat chili

PREP: 30 min. • **COOK:** 70 min.
YIELD: 12 servings (3 quarts).

A combination of pork tenderloin, ground turkey and ground beef make this chili unique. Instead of pinto beans, you can use kidney beans, white beans or black beans.

jan pinard // sabattus, maine

1-1/2 pounds pork tenderloin, cubed
1 large onion, chopped
1 medium green pepper, chopped
3 tablespoons olive oil
1 pound ground turkey
1 pound ground beef
2 cans (15 ounces *each*) pinto beans, rinsed and drained
2 cans (14-1/2 ounces *each*) diced tomatoes, undrained
1 can (28 ounces) baked beans
3 garlic cloves, minced
1/4 cup chili powder
1 tablespoon all-purpose flour
2 to 3 teaspoons ground cumin
1 teaspoon salt
1/2 teaspoon crushed red pepper flakes
1/4 teaspoon pepper

In a Dutch oven or soup kettle, cook the pork, onion and green pepper in oil over medium heat until meat is no longer pink.

Meanwhile, in a large skillet, cook turkey and beef over medium heat until no longer pink; drain. Drain pork mixture; add turkey and beef.

Stir in the remaining ingredients. Bring to a boil. Reduce heat; cover and simmer for 1 hour or until flavors are blended.

italian chili

PREP: 20 min. • **COOK:** 6-1/2 hours • **YIELD:** 6 servings.

By adding Italian seasoning and fresh veggies, we gave an Italian spin to a traditional Southwestern-style chili and created this slow-simmered hearty dish. This is a fun and tasty new twist for chili. It appeals to a broad range of palates.
taste of home test kitchen

1 pound ground beef
1/2 pound bulk Italian sausage
1 can (28 ounces) diced tomatoes
1 can (8 ounces) tomato sauce
1 cup chopped onion
1 cup chopped sweet red pepper
1 cup water
1/2 cup chopped celery
1/4 cup beef broth

1 tablespoon chili powder
1 tablespoon Italian seasoning
1 teaspoon sugar
1 teaspoon minced garlic
1/2 teaspoon salt
1 can (16 ounces) kidney beans, rinsed and drained
1 cup sliced fresh mushrooms
1 cup diced zucchini
3 tablespoons minced fresh parsley
Shredded part-skim mozzarella cheese, optional

In a large skillet, cook beef and sausage over medium heat until no longer pink. Meanwhile, in a 3-qt. slow cooker, combine the tomatoes, tomato sauce, onion, red pepper, water, celery, broth, chili powder, Italian seasoning, sugar, garlic and salt.

Drain beef mixture; add to the slow cooker. Cover and cook on low for 6 hours or until vegetables are tender.

Add the beans, mushrooms, zucchini and parsley. Cover and cook on high for 30 minutes or until vegetables are tender. Sprinkle with cheese if desired.

baked chili

PREP: 20 min. • **BAKE:** 15 min. • **YIELD:** 8 servings.

This main dish is wonderful the first day and also makes outstanding leftovers. As a student living on my own, I love savory one-pot suppers like this that provide several days of tasty meals. michelle gal // toronto, ontario

- **1 pound ground beef**
- **1 large onion, chopped**
- **1 large green pepper, chopped**
- **1 can (16 ounces) kidney beans, rinsed and drained**
- **1 can (15-1/4 ounces) whole kernel corn, drained**
- **1 can (15 ounces) tomato sauce**
- **1 can (14-1/2 ounces) diced tomatoes, undrained**
- **1 can (4 ounces) chopped green chilies**
- **2 teaspoons chili powder**
- **1 teaspoon salt**
- **1 teaspoon ground cumin**
- **1/2 teaspoon sugar**
- **1/2 teaspoon garlic powder**

CORN BREAD BISCUITS:

- **1 cup all-purpose flour**
- **1 cup cornmeal**
- **2 teaspoons baking powder**
- **1/8 teaspoon salt**
- **1 egg**
- **1/2 cup milk**
- **1/2 cup sour cream**

In a Dutch oven or soup kettle, cook beef, onion and green pepper over medium heat until meat is no longer pink; drain. Add the remaining ingredients; bring to a boil, stirring occasionally. Reduce heat; cover and simmer for 10 minutes.

Meanwhile, combine flour, cornmeal, baking powder and salt in a bowl. Beat egg, milk and sour cream until smooth; stir into dry ingredients just until moistened.

Transfer chili to an ungreased 13-in. x 9-in. baking dish. Drop batter by heaping teaspoonfuls onto hot chili. Bake, uncovered, at 400° for 15-17 minutes or until biscuits are lightly browned.

white turkey chili

PREP/TOTAL TIME: 30 min. • **YIELD:** 5 servings.

I combined white corn, great northern beans and leftover turkey to prepare this steaming chili. I appreciate how fast it is to make and that my husband and our four children like it. I often bake a pan of corn bread to go with it.

lauri pobanz // lincoln, nebraska

- **1/3 cup chopped onion**
- **1 celery rib, chopped**
- **1-1/2 teaspoons canola oil**
- **1-3/4 cups chicken *or* turkey broth**
- **2 cups cubed cooked turkey**
- **1 can (15-1/2 ounces) great northern beans, rinsed and drained**
- **1 can (11 ounces) white *or* shoepeg corn, drained**
- **2 tablespoons chopped green chilies**
- **1 teaspoon ground cumin**
- **1/2 teaspoon salt**

Shredded Monterey Jack cheese

In a large saucepan, saute onion and celery in oil until tender. Stir in the broth, turkey, beans, corn, chilies, cumin and salt. Bring to a boil. Reduce heat,; cover and simmer for 15-20 minutes. Garnish with cheese.

roundup chili

PREP: 35 min. • **COOK:** 6 hours • **YIELD:** 12 servings (3 quarts).

Two types of meat make this not-too-spicy chili a hearty meal. Because it's made in the slow cooker, it's a great choice for casual gatherings.

linda stemen // monroeville, indiana

- **2 pounds lean ground beef (90% lean)**
- **1 beef flank steak (1-1/2 pounds), cubed**
- **1 medium onion, chopped**
- **1 celery rib, chopped**
- **1 can (29 ounces) tomato sauce**
- **2 cans (14-1/2 ounces *each*) diced tomatoes, undrained**
- **1 can (16 ounces) kidney beans, rinsed and drained**
- **1 can (15 ounces) pinto beans, rinsed and drained**
- **1 can (4 ounces) chopped green chilies**
- **2 to 3 tablespoons chili powder**
- **3 teaspoons ground cumin**
- **2 teaspoons salt**
- **2 teaspoons pepper**
- **1/2 teaspoon ground mustard**
- **1/2 teaspoon paprika**
- **1/2 teaspoon cayenne pepper**
- **1/4 teaspoon garlic powder**
- **Hot pepper sauce, shredded cheddar cheese and additional chopped onion, optional**

In a large skillet, cook the ground beef, flank steak, onion and celery over medium heat until meat is no longer pink; drain.

Transfer to a 6-qt. slow cooker. Stir in the tomato sauce, tomatoes, beans, chilies and seasonings. Cover and cook on low for 6-8 hours until steak is tender.

Serve with the hot pepper sauce, cheese and onion if desired.

three-bean taco chili

PREP/TOTAL TIME: 30 min.
YIELD: 9 servings.

This chili is nourishing and filling, and it tastes like it simmered all day long. Leftover chili freezes well for a later time, so why not double the recipe?

wanda lee // hemet, california

- **2 pounds ground beef**
- **2 cups water**
- **1 can (16 ounces) refried beans**
- **1 can (16 ounces) kidney beans, rinsed and drained**
- **1 can (16 ounces) chili beans, undrained**
- **1 can (15-1/4 ounces) whole kernel corn, drained**
- **1 can (14-1/2 ounces) stewed tomatoes**
- **1 can (8 ounces) tomato sauce**
- **1 cup chunky salsa**
- **1 envelope taco seasoning**
- **1 can (2-1/4 ounces) sliced ripe olives, drained**
- **1 cup (4 ounces) shredded cheddar cheese**

In a Dutch oven, cook beef over medium heat until no longer pink; drain. Stir in the water, beans, corn, tomatoes, tomato sauce, salsa, taco seasoning and olives.

Bring to a boil. Reduce heat; simmer, uncovered, for 10 minutes. Garnish with the cheese.

bean & bulgur chili

PREP: 25 min. • **COOK:** 40 min. • **YIELD:** 10 servings (3-1/2 quarts).

Come in from the cold to a steaming bowl of this zesty three-bean chili. The bulgur adds great texture and heartiness, so you won't miss the meat. tari ambler // shorewood, illinois

- 2 large onions, chopped
- 2 celery ribs, chopped
- 1 large green pepper, chopped
- 4 teaspoons olive oil
- 4 garlic cloves, minced
- 1 large carrot, shredded
- 2 tablespoons chili powder
- 1 teaspoon dried oregano
- 1/2 teaspoon coarsely ground pepper
- 1/2 teaspoon ground cumin
- 1/8 teaspoon ground cinnamon
- 1/8 teaspoon ground allspice
- 2 cans (14-1/2 ounces *each*) no-salt-added diced tomatoes, undrained
- 1 can (14-1/2 ounces) fire-roasted diced tomatoes, undrained
- 1 can (16 ounces) kidney beans, rinsed and drained
- 1 can (15 ounces) pinto beans, rinsed and drained
- 1 can (15 ounces) black beans, rinsed and drained
- 1 can (14 ounces) vegetable broth
- 1/3 cup tomato paste
- 1 cup bulgur
- Reduced-fat sour cream, optional

In a Dutch oven over medium heat, cook the onions, celery and green pepper in oil until tender. Add garlic; cook 1 minute longer. Stir in carrot and seasonings; cook and stir 1 minute longer.

Stir in the tomatoes, beans, broth and tomato paste. Bring to a boil. Reduce heat; cover and simmer for 30 minutes.

Meanwhile, cook bulgur according to package directions. Stir into chili; heat through. Garnish each serving with sour cream if desired.

GET TO KNOW BULGUR

Look for bulgur in the cereal, rice or organic food aisle of your grocery store. It also makes a great replacement for some of the meat in your favorite casserole recipes.

fruit 'n' nut chili

PREP: 10 min. • **COOK:** 45 min.
YIELD: 7 servings.

Apples, slivered almonds and cocoa add a fun, unexpected taste to chili.
taste of home test kitchen

- **1-1/2 pounds ground beef**
- **1 cup chopped onion**
- **1 cup chopped green pepper**
- **1 teaspoon minced garlic**
- **1 can (28 ounces) crushed tomatoes**
- **2 cups water**
- **2 cups chopped peeled apples**
- **1 can (16 ounces) chili beans, undrained**
- **1 can (6 ounces) tomato paste**
- **1/3 cup slivered almonds**
- **2 tablespoons baking cocoa**
- **2 tablespoons chili powder**
- **1 teaspoon salt**
- **1 teaspoon ground cinnamon**
- **1 teaspoon pepper**
- **Sour cream, optional**

In a Dutch oven, cook beef, onion and green pepper over medium heat until meat is no longer pink. Add garlic; cook 1 minute longer. Drain. Stir in tomatoes, water, apples, beans, tomato paste, almonds, cocoa and seasonings.

Bring to a boil. Reduce heat; cover and simmer for 30 minutes or until heated through. Garnish with the sour cream if desired.

slow-cooked white chili

PREP: 25 min. • **COOK:** 5 hours • **YIELD:** 8 servings (2 quarts).

Try this satisfying slow-simmered chili which features chicken, two kinds of beans and crunchy corn. It's quick, easy and tastes great. It's a family favorite that we enjoy with a pan of golden corn bread. lori weber // wentzville, missouri

- **3/4 pound boneless skinless chicken breasts, cubed**
- **1 medium onion, chopped**
- **1 tablespoon canola oil**
- **1 garlic clove, minced**
- **1-1/2 cups water**
- **1 can (15 ounces) white kidney *or* cannellini beans, rinsed and drained**
- **1 can (15 ounces) garbanzo beans *or* chickpeas, rinsed and drained**
- **1 can (11 ounces) whole kernel white corn, drained *or* 1-1/4 cups frozen shoepeg corn**
- **1 can (4 ounces) chopped green chilies**
- **1 to 2 teaspoons chicken bouillon granules**
- **1 teaspoon ground cumin**

In a large skillet, saute chicken and onion in oil until onion is tender. Add garlic; cook 1 minute longer. Transfer to a 3-qt. slow cooker. Stir in the remaining ingredients. Cover and cook on low for 5-6 hours or until chicken is no longer pink.

creamy white chili

PREP: 10 min. • **COOK:** 40 min. • **YIELD:** 7 servings.

I got this wonderful recipe from my sister-in-law, who made a big batch and served a crowd one night. It was a hit. Plus, it's easy and quick, which is helpful since I'm a college student. In all my years of 4-H cooking, I've never had another dish get so many compliments. laura brewer // lafayette, indiana

- **1 pound boneless skinless chicken breasts, cut into 1/2-inch cubes**
- **1 medium onion, chopped**
- **1-1/2 teaspoons garlic powder**
- **1 tablespoon canola oil**
- **2 cans (15-1/2 ounces *each*) great northern beans, rinsed and drained**
- **1 can (14-1/2 ounces) chicken broth**
- **2 cans (4 ounces *each*) chopped green chilies**
- **1 teaspoon salt**
- **1 teaspoon ground cumin**
- **1 teaspoon dried oregano**
- **1/2 teaspoon pepper**
- **1/4 teaspoon cayenne pepper**
- **1 cup (8 ounces) sour cream**
- **1/2 cup heavy whipping cream**

In a large saucepan, saute the chicken, onion and garlic powder in oil until chicken is no longer pink. Add the beans, broth, chilies and seasonings. Bring to a boil. Reduce heat; simmer, uncovered, for 30 minutes.

Remove from the heat; stir in sour cream and cream.

turkey chili with penne

PREP: 25 min. • **COOK:** 1 hour • **YIELD:** 12 servings.

You can easily turn this chili into a vegetarian dish by leaving out the meat or replacing it with soy crumbles. A topping of goat cheese makes this full-flavored chili stand out from others. patricia burk // north canton, ohio

- **1-1/2 pounds extra-lean ground turkey**
- **1 teaspoon olive oil**
- **3 celery ribs, chopped**
- **3 large carrots, sliced**
- **1 medium onion, chopped**
- **1 poblano pepper, seeded and finely chopped**
- **1/2 cup marsala wine *or* reduced-sodium chicken broth**
- **1 can (28 ounces) diced tomatoes, undrained**
- **2 cans (one 15 ounces, one 8 ounces) tomato sauce**
- **1 can (4 ounces) chopped green chilies**
- **1 tablespoon chili powder**
- **1 tablespoon honey**
- **3-1/2 cups uncooked whole wheat penne pasta**
- **2 cans (15 ounces *each*) black beans, rinsed and drained**
- **8 ounces fresh goat cheese, cut into 12 slices**

In a Dutch oven, cook turkey in oil over medium heat until no longer pink. Stir in the celery, carrots, onion, pepper and wine; cook until vegetables are tender.

Stir in the tomatoes, tomato sauce, chilies, chili powder and honey. Bring to a boil. Reduce heat; simmer, uncovered, for 1 hour or until thickened.

Meanwhile, cook the pasta according to package directions. Stir beans into chili; heat through. Drain pasta; spoon 1/2 cup into each serving bowl. Spoon chili over pasta; top with cheese.

TRY GOAT CHEESE

If you're not so familiar with goat cheese, it's a soft cheese made from the milk of goats. It spreads easily and has a distinctively tangy flavor. Goat cheese is often found in Middle Eastern or Mediterranean cuisines. Common varieties include chevre, a very soft cheese, or feta, a semi-soft cheese.

spicy pork chili

PREP: 10 min. • **COOK:** 6 hours • **YIELD:** 6 servings.

Tender pork adds extra heartiness to this slow-cooked chili. You can use pork tenderloin, boneless pork roast or boneless pork chops for the pork called for in the recipe. taste of home test kitchen

- **2 pounds boneless pork, cut into 1/2-inch cubes**
- **1 tablespoon canola oil**
- **1 can (28 ounces) crushed tomatoes**
- **2 cups frozen corn**
- **1 can (15 ounces) black beans, rinsed and drained**
- **1 cup chopped onion**
- **1 cup beef broth**
- **1 can (4 ounces) chopped green chilies**
- **1 tablespoon chili powder**
- **1 teaspoon minced garlic**
- **1/2 teaspoon salt**
- **1/2 teaspoon cayenne pepper**
- **1/2 teaspoon pepper**
- **1/4 cup minced fresh cilantro**
- **Shredded cheddar cheese, optional**

In a large skillet, cook pork in oil over medium-high heat for 5-6 minutes or until browned. Transfer pork and drippings to a 5-qt. slow cooker. Stir in the tomatoes, corn, beans, onion, broth, chilies, chili powder, garlic, salt, cayenne and pepper.

Cover and cook on low for 6-7 hours or until pork is tender. Stir in cilantro. Serve with cheese if desired.

STORING LEFTOVER CILANTRO

To keep cilantro fresh, place the bunch, stem side down, in a glass with an inch or so of water. Cover with a plastic bag, secure with a rubber band and store in the refrigerator. The cilantro should stay fresh for up to 1 week if you change the water every other day. To freeze, wash and drain whole sprigs, then pat dry with paper towels. Place a few sprigs at a time into small plastic freezer bags and freeze.

one-pot chili

PREP: 25 min. • **COOK:** 20 min. • **YIELD:** 6 servings (2 quarts).

This hearty entree is low in fat and high in flavor. I love that you can cook the dried pasta right in the chili. One less pot to wash! This also reheats perfectly in the microwave. dawn forsberg // saint joseph, missouri

- **1 pound lean ground turkey**
- **1 small onion, chopped**
- **1/4 cup chopped green pepper**
- **1 teaspoon olive oil**
- **2 cups water**
- **1 can (15 ounces) pinto beans, rinsed and drained**
- **1 can (14-1/2 ounces) reduced-sodium beef broth**
- **1 can (14-1/2 ounces) diced tomatoes with mild green chilies, undrained**
- **1 can (8 ounces) no-salt-added tomato sauce**
- **2 teaspoons chili powder**
- **1 teaspoon ground cumin**
- **1/2 teaspoon dried oregano**
- **2 cups uncooked multigrain penne pasta**
- **1/4 cup reduced-fat sour cream**
- **1/4 cup minced fresh cilantro**

In a large saucepan coated with cooking spray, cook the turkey, onion and pepper in oil over medium heat until meat is no longer pink; drain.

Stir in the water, beans, broth, tomatoes, tomato sauce, chili powder, cumin and oregano. Bring to a boil. Add pasta; cook for 15-20 minutes or until tender, stirring occasionally. Serve with sour cream; sprinkle with cilantro.

barley chicken chili

PREP/TOTAL TIME: 25 min.
YIELD: 9 servings (about 2 quarts).

Barley and chicken make this hearty chili unique.

kayleen grew // essexville, michigan

- **1 cup chopped onion**
- **1/2 cup chopped green pepper**
- **1 teaspoon olive oil**
- **2-1/4 cups water**
- **1 can (15 ounces) tomato sauce**
- **1 can (14-1/2 ounces) reduced-sodium chicken broth**
- **1 can (10 ounces) diced tomatoes and green chilies, undrained**
- **1 cup quick-cooking barley**
- **1 tablespoon chili powder**
- **1/2 teaspoon ground cumin**
- **1/4 teaspoon garlic powder**
- **3 cups cubed cooked chicken breast**

In a large saucepan, saute onion and green pepper in oil until tender. Add the water, tomato sauce, broth, tomatoes, barley and seasonings; bring to a boil.

Reduce heat. Cover; simmer 10 minutes. Add chicken. Cover; simmer 5 minutes longer or until barley is tender.

spicy chili

PREP: 15 min. • **COOK:** 45 min.
YIELD: 12 servings (3 quarts).

This recipe is the culmination of several years' worth of experimenting to get just the right flavor. For those who like their chili very hot, the secret is to add more jalapenos. The most I ever used in a recipe was five, and was it ever spicy!

liesha hoek // somerset, new jersey

- **1-1/2 pounds ground beef**
- **1-1/2 pounds bulk Italian sausage**
- **3 cans (14-1/2 ounces *each*) stewed tomatoes**
- **2 cans (16 ounces *each*) kidney beans, rinsed and drained**
- **1 cup chopped onion**
- **1 large green pepper, chopped**
- **1 can (6 ounces) tomato paste**
- **2 jalapeno peppers, finely chopped**
- **2 tablespoons chili powder**
- **2 tablespoons white vinegar**
- **1 tablespoon spicy brown mustard**
- **1 tablespoon dried oregano**
- **2 garlic cloves, minced**
- **1-1/2 teaspoons ground cumin**
- **1-1/2 teaspoons hot pepper sauce**
- **1 teaspoon salt**
- **1 teaspoon paprika**

In a Dutch oven, cook the beef and sausage over medium heat until no longer pink; drain. Add the remaining ingredients; bring to a boil. Reduce heat; simmer, uncovered, for 30 minutes, stirring frequently.

EDITOR'S NOTE: Sprinkle individual servings of Spicy Chili with shredded cheddar cheese and chopped onion if you like. Plus, a dollop of sour cream can cut some of the spiciness. We recommend wearing disposable gloves when cutting hot peppers. Avoid touching your face.

round steak chili

PREP: 15 min. • **COOK:** 3-1/4 hours
YIELD: 6-8 servings.

The addition of round steak gives this chili recipe a nice change of pace. Everyone in my family just loves it!

linda goshorn // bedford, virginia

- **1 pound beef top round steak**
- **1 large onion, chopped**
- **2 garlic cloves, minced**
- **1 to 2 tablespoons canola oil**
- **1 can (46 ounces) V8 juice**
- **1 can (28 ounces) crushed tomatoes**
- **2 cups sliced celery**
- **1 can (16 ounces) crushed tomatoes**
- **2 cups sliced celery**
- **1 can (16 ounces) kidney beans, rinsed and drained**
- **1 medium green pepper, chopped**
- **1 bay leaf**
- **2 tablespoons chili powder**
- **1-1/2 teaspoons salt**
- **1 teaspoon dried oregano**
- **1 teaspoon brown sugar**
- **1/2 teaspoon *each* celery seed, paprika and ground mustard and cumin**
- **1/4 teaspoon cayenne pepper**
- **1/4 teaspoon dried basil**

Cut meat into 1/2-in. cubes. In a Dutch oven or large kettle , brown meat, onion and garlic in oil. Add remaining ingredients; bring to a boil. Reduce heat; simmer, uncovered, for 3 hours. Discard bay leaf before serving.

colony mountain chili

PREP: 25 min. • **COOK:** 6 hours • **YIELD:** 10 servings.

My husband created this chili for a local cooking contest, and it won the People's Choice award. It's loaded with beef, Italian sausage, tomatoes and beans and seasoned with chili powder, cumin and red pepper flakes for zip.

marjorie o'dell // bow, washington

1 pound beef top sirloin steak, cut into 3/4-inch cubes
4 Italian sausage links, casings removed and cut into 3/4-inch slices
2 tablespoons olive oil, *divided*
1 medium onion, chopped
2 green onions, thinly sliced
3 garlic cloves, minced
2 teaspoons beef bouillon granules
1 cup boiling water
1 can (6 ounces) tomato paste
3 tablespoons chili powder
2 tablespoons brown sugar
2 tablespoons Worcestershire sauce
2 teaspoons ground cumin
1 to 2 teaspoons crushed red pepper flakes
1 teaspoon salt
1/2 teaspoon pepper
3 cans (14-1/2 ounces *each*) stewed tomatoes, cut up
2 cans (15 ounces *each*) pinto beans, rinsed and drained
Shredded cheddar cheese

In a large skillet, brown the beef and sausage in 1 tablespoon oil; drain. Transfer meat to a 5-qt. slow cooker. In the same skillet, saute onion and green onions in remaining oil until tender. Add garlic; cook 1 minute longer. Transfer to slow cooker.

In a small bowl, dissolve bouillon in water. Stir in the tomato paste, chili powder, brown sugar, Worcestershire sauce and seasonings until blended; add to slow cooker. Stir in tomatoes and beans. Cover and cook on high for 6-8 hours or until the meat is tender. Serve with cheese if desired.

corny chili

PREP: 20 min. • **COOK:** 3 hours
YIELD: 4-6 servings.

This Southwestern chili full of corn is so delicious and fuss-free, I love to share the recipe. Busy moms really appreciate its simplicity.

marlene olson // hoople, north dakota

1 pound ground beef
1 small onion, chopped
1 can (16 ounces) kidney beans, rinsed and drained
2 cans (14-1/2 ounces *each*) diced tomatoes, undrained
1 can (11 ounces) whole kernel corn, drained
3/4 cup picante sauce
1 tablespoon chili powder
1/4 to 1/2 teaspoon garlic powder
Corn chips, sour cream and shredded cheddar cheese, optional

In a large skillet, cook beef and onion over medium heat until meat is no longer pink; drain.

Transfer to a 3-qt. slow cooker. Stir in the beans, tomatoes, corn, picante sauce, chili powder and garlic powder. Cover and cook on low for 3-4 hours or until heated through. Serve with the corn chips, sour cream and cheese if desired.

jumpin' espresso bean chili

PREP: 15 min. • **COOK:** 45 min. • **YIELD:** 7 servings.

I love experimenting with chili. What a hearty dish! This meatless version I created is low-fat and flavorful. Everyone tries to guess the secret ingredient—and no one ever thinks it's coffee. jessie apfel // berkeley, california

- **3 medium onions, chopped**
- **2 tablespoons olive oil**
- **2 tablespoons brown sugar**
- **2 tablespoons chili powder**
- **2 tablespoons ground cumin**
- **1 tablespoon instant coffee granules**
- **1 tablespoon baking cocoa**
- **3/4 teaspoon salt**
- **2 cans (14-1/2 ounces *each*) no-salt-added diced tomatoes**
- **1 can (15 ounces) black beans, rinsed and drained**
- **1 can (15 ounces) kidney beans, rinsed and drained**
- **1 can (15 ounces) garbanzo beans *or* chickpeas, rinsed and drained**
- **Sour cream, thinly sliced green onions, shredded cheddar cheese and pickled jalapeno slices, optional**

In a Dutch oven, saute the onions in oil until tender. Add the brown sugar, chili powder, cumin, coffee granules, cocoa and salt; cook and stir for 1 minute.

Stir in tomatoes and beans. Bring to a boil. Reduce heat; cover and simmer for 30 minutes or until heated through. Serve with sour cream, onions, cheese and jalapeno slices if desired.

lime navy bean chili

PREP: 15 min. + soaking
COOK: 5 hours • **YIELD:** 6 servings.

A lip-smacking hint of lime flavor makes this low-fat chili a filling family favorite. And relying on my slow cooker adds ease to my day.

connie thomas // jensen, utah

- **1-1/4 cups dried navy beans**
- **3 cups water**
- **2 bone-in chicken breast halves (7 ounces *each*), skin removed**
- **1 cup frozen corn**
- **1 medium onion, chopped**
- **1 can (4 ounces) chopped green chilies**
- **4 garlic cloves, minced**
- **1 tablespoon chicken bouillon granules**
- **1 teaspoon ground cumin**
- **1/2 teaspoon chili powder**
- **2 tablespoons lime juice**

Sort beans and rinse with cold water. Place beans in a large saucepan; add water to cover by 2 in. Bring to a boil; boil for 2 minutes. Remove from the heat; cover and let soak for 1 to 4 hours or until beans are softened. Drain and rinse beans, discarding liquid.

In a 3-qt. slow cooker, combine the beans, water, chicken, corn, onion, chilies, garlic, bouillon, cumin and chili powder. Cover and cook on low for 5-6 hours or until a meat thermometer reads 170° and beans are tender.

Remove chicken breasts; set aside until cool enough to handle. Remove meat from bones; discard bones and cut into bite-size pieces. Return chicken to pan. Stir in lime juice just before serving.

thick & chunky beef chili

PREP: 30 min. • **COOK:** 3-1/4 hours • **YIELD:** 4 quarts.

Hearty, flavorful ingredients and a thick, rich sauce make this a satisfying chili that's sure to win compliments on your cooking. It's a great way to serve a crowd during the big game or to warm up on a chilly evening.

taste of home test kitchen

- **12 ounces center-cut bacon, diced**
- **2 pounds beef stew meat, cut into 1/4-inch cubes**
- **2 medium onions, chopped**
- **4 garlic cloves, minced**
- **3 cans (14-1/2 ounces *each*) no-salt-added diced tomatoes, undrained**
- **1 cup barbecue sauce**
- **1 cup chili sauce**
- **1/2 cup honey**
- **4 teaspoons reduced-sodium beef bouillon granules**
- **1 bay leaf**
- **1 tablespoon chili powder**
- **1 tablespoon baking cocoa**
- **1 tablespoon Worcestershire sauce**
- **1 tablespoon Dijon mustard**
- **1-1/2 teaspoons ground cumin**
- **1/4 teaspoon cayenne powder, optional**
- **3 cans (16 ounces *each*) kidney beans, rinsed and drained**

Shredded reduced-fat cheddar cheese, optional

In a large Dutch oven, cook bacon until crisp; remove to paper towels to drain. Reserve 3 tablespoons drippings.

Brown beef in drippings. Add onion; cook until onions are tender. Add garlic; cook 1 minute longer. Return bacon to pan. Stir in the next 12 ingredients.

Bring to a boil. Reduce heat; cover and simmer until meat is tender, about 3 hours.

Add beans and heat through. Discard bay leaf. Garnish with cheese if desired.

flavorful southwestern chili

PREP/TOTAL TIME: 30 min.
YIELD: 10 servings (2-1/2 quarts).

This great recipe comes from my grandmother. It is full of flavor, freezes beautifully and makes a complete, last-minute meal. I top it with grated cheddar cheese and chopped black olives and serve tortilla chips on the side. If I'm feeding a crowd, I increase the pinto beans to four cans to make the meat go farther. jenny greear // huntington, west virginia

- **2 pounds lean ground beef (90% lean)**
- **1-1/2 cups chopped onions**
- **2 cans (14-1/2 ounces *each*) diced tomatoes, undrained**
- **1 can (15 ounces) pinto beans, rinsed and drained**
- **1 can (15 ounces) tomato sauce**
- **1 package (10 ounces) frozen corn, thawed**
- **1 cup salsa**
- **3/4 cup water**
- **1 can (4 ounces) chopped green chilies**
- **1 teaspoon ground cumin**
- **1/2 teaspoon garlic powder**

In a Dutch oven, cook beef and onions over medium heat until meat is no longer pink; drain. Stir in the remaining ingredients. Bring to a boil. Reduce heat; simmer, uncovered, for 15 minutes.

Serve desired amount. Cool the remaining chili; transfer to freezer containers. May be frozen for up to 3 months.

TO USE FROZEN CHILI: Thaw chili in the refrigerator. Place in a saucepan; heat through.

wild west chili

PREP: 20 min. • **COOK:** 70 min. • **YIELD:** 6 servings.

My sister-in-law, who has cooked for many years at the family ranch, shared this chunky chili recipe with me. I make it often during the winter—it sure can warm you up after being outside doing chores! frances hanson // mills, wyoming

- **2 bacon strips, diced**
- **1 pound ground beef *or* venison**
- **2 teaspoons chili powder**
- **1-1/2 teaspoons salt**
- **1/4 teaspoon garlic salt**
- **1/4 teaspoon dried oregano**
- **1/8 teaspoon cayenne pepper**
- **3 to 5 drops hot pepper sauce**
- **1 can (14-1/2 ounces) diced tomatoes, undrained**
- **1 cup *each* finely chopped celery, onion and carrots**
- **1/2 cup finely chopped green pepper**
- **1 can (16 ounces) chili beans, undrained**

In a large saucepan over medium heat, brown bacon and the beef or venison; drain. Add the chili powder, salt, garlic salt, oregano, cayenne and pepper sauce. Cook and stir for 5 minutes. Stir in tomatoes, celery, onion, carrots and green pepper; bring to a boil. Reduce heat; cover and simmer for 40 minutes. Stir in the beans; cook 30 minutes longer.

chili verde

PREP/TOTAL TIME: 20 min.
YIELD: 8 servings.

Leftover pork adds heartiness to this zippy chili. It's great on a cool night with a stack of tortillas. I've taken it to many gatherings, and it's always gone when the party's over.
jo oliverius // alpine, california

- **2 cups cubed cooked pork (about 1 pound)**
- **1 can (16 ounces) kidney beans, rinsed and drained**
- **1 can (15 ounces) pinto beans, rinsed and drained**
- **1 can (15 ounces) chili with beans, undrained**
- **1 can (14-1/2 ounces) stewed tomatoes**
- **1-1/2 to 2 cups green salsa**
- **1 large onion, chopped**
- **2 cans (4 ounces *each*) chopped green chilies**
- **2 garlic cloves, minced**
- **1 tablespoon minced fresh cilantro**
- **2 teaspoons ground cumin**

In a large saucepan, combine all the ingredients. Bring to a boil. Reduce the heat; simmer, uncovered, for 10 minutes or until heated through.

ham and bean chili

PREP: 20 min. • **COOK:** 15 min. • **YIELD:** 10 servings (about 2-1/2 quarts).

Leftover ham gets an unusual treatment in this creative chili blend that features three kinds of convenient canned beans. I sometimes serve it in bowls over rice or corn bread and garnish it with cheese. carol forcum // marion, illinois

- **2 cups cubed fully cooked ham**
- **1 medium onion, chopped**
- **1 medium green pepper, chopped**
- **1 garlic clove, minced**
- **1 tablespoon olive oil**
- **1 can (28 ounces) diced tomatoes, undrained**
- **1 can (16 ounces) kidney beans, rinsed and drained**
- **1 can (15 ounces) black beans, rinsed and drained**
- **1 can (15 ounces) pinto beans, rinsed and drained**
- **1 jar (8 ounces) picante sauce**
- **1 can (8 ounces) tomato sauce**
- **1/2 cup water, optional**
- **1 can (2-1/4 ounces) sliced ripe olives, drained**
- **1 teaspoon beef bouillon granules**
- **1 teaspoon dried thyme**
- **1 teaspoon salt**
- **1/4 teaspoon pepper**
- **Shredded cheddar cheese**

In a large saucepan, cook the ham, onion, green pepper and garlic in oil until tender. Stir in tomatoes, beans, picante sauce, tomato sauce and water if desired. Bring to a boil. Stir in the olives, bouillon, thyme, salt and pepper. Reduce heat, simmer, uncovered, for 15-20 minutes. Garnish with cheese.

sweet surprise chili

PREP: 30 min. • **COOK:** 2 hours
YIELD: 8 servings (2-3/4 quarts).

I've won three chili cook-offs with this recipe. Everyone loves it, and they're always amazed when I reveal the secret ingredient!
brooke pekkala // duluth, minnesota

3 pounds beef top sirloin steak, cubed
1 tablespoon canola oil
1/2 pound bulk Italian sausage
1 large onion, chopped
5 garlic cloves, minced
2 cups water
1 can (16 ounces) chili beans, undrained
1 can (15 ounces) tomato sauce
1 can (14-1/2 ounces) beef broth
1 package (12 ounces) pitted dried plums, chopped
3 teaspoons chili powder
2 teaspoons ground cumin
1 teaspoon dried oregano
1 teaspoon paprika
3/4 teaspoon salt
Dash cayenne pepper

In a Dutch oven, brown beef in oil in batches. Remove and keep warm. Add sausage and onion to the pan; cook and stir over medium heat until meat is no longer pink. Add garlic; cook 1 minute longer.

Return beef to the pan; stir in the remaining ingredients. Bring to a boil. Reduce heat; cover and simmer for 1-3/4 to 2 hours or until beef is tender.

bold bean and pork chili

PREP: 10 min. • **COOK:** 1-1/2 hours • **YIELD:** 15 servings.

This tempting chili is big on flavor and easy to prepare. Sometimes, on a Sunday, I'll get a good start on it—up to when it's time to add the beans. The next day, I'll take it out of the fridge and finish it off in just a few minutes.
natercia yailaian // somerville, massachusetts

1 boneless pork shoulder butt roast (4 to 5 pounds)
3 tablespoons olive oil
2 large onions, chopped
8 garlic cloves, minced
4 cans (14-1/2 ounces *each*) chicken broth
1 can (28 ounces) crushed tomatoes
1/2 to 2/3 cup chili powder
3 tablespoons dried oregano
2 to 3 tablespoons ground cumin
4-1/2 teaspoons salt
2 teaspoons cayenne pepper
4 cans (15 ounces *each*) black beans, rinsed and drained
Minced fresh cilantro, optional

In a Dutch oven or soup kettle, saute pork in oil until no longer pink; drain. Add onions; cook and stir for 3 minutes. Add garlic; cook 2 minutes longer. Stir in broth, tomatoes and seasonings. Bring to a boil. Reduce the heat; simmer, uncovered, for 1 hour, stirring several times.

Skim fat; stir in beans. Simmer 15-30 minutes longer or until chili reaches desired thickness. Garnish with cilantro if desired.

tex-mex chili

PREP: 20 min. • **COOK:** 6 hours • **YIELD:** 12 servings (1-1/3 cups each).

Hearty and spicy, this is a man's chili for sure! You can also simmer on the stove—the longer, the better!

eric hayes // antioch, california

- **3 pounds beef stew meat**
- **1 tablespoon canola oil**
- **3 garlic cloves, minced**
- **3 cans (16 ounces *each*) kidney beans, rinsed and drained**
- **3 cans (15 ounces *each*) tomato sauce**
- **1 can (14-1/2 ounces) diced tomatoes, undrained**
- **1 cup water**
- **1 can (6 ounces) tomato paste**
- **3/4 cup salsa verde**
- **1 envelope chili seasoning**
- **2 teaspoons dried minced onion**
- **1 teaspoon chili powder**
- **1/2 teaspoon crushed red pepper flakes**
- **1/2 teaspoon ground cumin**
- **1/2 teaspoon cayenne pepper**
- **Shredded cheddar cheese and minced fresh cilantro**

In a large skillet, brown beef in oil in batches. Add garlic to the pan; cook and stir for 1 minute longer. Transfer to a 6-qt. slow cooker.

Stir in the remaining ingredients. Cover and cook on low for 6-8 hours or until meat is tender. Garnish each serving with cheese and cilantro.

LEFTOVER CHILI MAKES A NEW MEAL

When I don't have enough leftover chili for a second meal, I get creative. I bake each family member a big potato, which I split and put in a soup bowl. I heat up the chili and spoon it over the potatoes, then top each with some shredded cheddar cheese. It's a quick and filling new meal. judy b. // goshen, indiana

chili con carne

PREP/TOTAL TIME: 20 min. • **YIELD:** 2 servings.

You'll only need one skillet and 20 minutes to whip up this hearty, slightly spicy Chili Con Carne.

marline emmal // vancouver, british columbia

- **1/2 pound lean ground beef (90% lean)**
- **1-1/2 cups reduced-sodium tomato juice**
- **3/4 cup kidney beans, rinsed and drained**
- **2 tablespoons chopped onion**
- **1 teaspoon chili powder**
- **1/4 teaspoon ground cumin**
- **1/4 teaspoon minced garlic**
- **2 to 3 drops hot pepper sauce**
- **Thinly sliced green onion, optional**

In a large saucepan, cook beef over medium heat until no longer pink; drain. Stir in the remaining ingredients except green onions. Bring to a boil. Reduce heat; simmer, uncovered, for 10 minutes or until slightly thickened, stirring occasionally. Garnish with green onion if desired.

THICKER CHILI TRICK

When I want to thicken up a pot of chili, I mix in a can of refried beans. No one seems to notice my "secret", but they sure enjoy the extra hearty chili.

kara k. // kalamazoo, michigan

family-pleasing turkey chili

PREP: 25 min. • **COOK:** 4 hours • **YIELD:** 6 servings (2-1/4 quarts).

My children really love this recipe, and it's become one of their favorite comfort foods. It's relatively inexpensive, and leftovers are wonderful!

sheila christensen // san marcos, california

- **1 pound lean ground turkey**
- **1 medium green pepper, finely chopped**
- **1 small red onion, finely chopped**
- **2 garlic cloves, minced**
- **1 can (28 ounces) diced tomatoes, undrained**
- **1 can (16 ounces) kidney beans, rinsed and drained**
- **1 can (15 ounces) black beans, rinsed and drained**
- **1 can (14-1/2 ounces) reduced-sodium chicken broth**
- **1-3/4 cups frozen corn, thawed**
- **1 can (6 ounces) tomato paste**
- **1 tablespoon chili powder**
- **1/2 teaspoon pepper**
- **1/4 teaspoon ground cumin**
- **1/4 teaspoon garlic powder**

Optional toppings: reduced-fat sour cream and minced fresh cilantro

In a large nonstick skillet, cook the turkey, green pepper and onion over medium heat until meat is no longer pink. Add garlic; cook 1 minute longer. Drain.

Transfer to a 4-qt. slow cooker. Stir in the tomatoes, kidney beans, black beans, broth, corn, tomato paste, chili powder, pepper, cumin and garlic powder.

Cover and cook on low for 4-5 hours or until heated through. Serve with optional toppings if desired.

zippy sausage chili

PREP: 10 min. • **COOK:** 55 min.
YIELD: 8-10 servings.

Our family loves Mexican food, but I wasn't happy with any of the chili recipes I came across. So I decided to make up my own. It's a winner with everyone who tries it.

laura squire // montrose, pennsylvania

- **1-1/2 pounds bulk pork sausage**
- **1 medium carrot, chopped**
- **1/2 cup chopped green pepper**
- **1 celery rib, chopped**
- **1 can (28 ounces) stewed tomatoes**
- **1 can (16 ounces) kidney beans, rinsed and drained**
- **1 can (16 ounces) chili beans, undrained**
- **1 can (15 ounces) pinto beans, rinsed and drained**
- **1 can (5-1/2 ounces) V8 juice**
- **3 tablespoons dried minced onion**
- **1 teaspoon garlic powder**
- **1 teaspoon pepper**
- **1/4 teaspoon salt**

In a large saucepan or Dutch oven, cook the sausage, carrot, green pepper and celery over medium heat until meat is no longer pink; drain. Stir in all the remaining ingredients.

Bring to a boil. Reduce the heat; cover and simmer for 45 minutes or until heated through.

general recipe index

BROCCOLI

CABBAGE & SAUERKRAUT

CARROTS

CAULIFLOWER

CHEESE

CHICKEN

GROUND BEEF

HAM & BACON

SLOW COOKER RECIPES

SPINACH & KALE

SQUASH & ZUCCHINI

STRAWBERRIES

SWEET POTATOES

TOMATOES

TURKEY & TURKEY SAUSAGE

VEGETABLES (ALSO SEE SPECIFIC KINDS)

alphabetical index

T

U

V

W

Z